Proverbs 31 Devotionals

365 Daily Devotions For God's Daughters

Presented By:

CHRISTIAN APP EMPIRE

For Information:
E-mail: Support@ChristianAppEmpire.com
Website: http://www.Proverbs31Way.com

Special Thank You
Maxine P. Thompson, Steffanie Howard, Nicole "CreativeWrites",
and Sambrosia Curtis

Content Editors
Tricia Hayner and Sambrosia Curtis

Cover Design
Janusvielle A Zate

Layout Design
Rochelle Mensidor

Dedication

To my amazing wife and Queen Amanda and our 3 little Queens to be. God was gracious when He sent you to me, to lead me to Him. Thank you Lord, for the opportunity to share your precious and holy word with your people.

January

Noble Character

"A wife of noble character who can find?
She is worth far more than rubies."
(Proverbs 31:10)

When most girls are young, they spend a lot of time daydreaming about the type of guy that they will marry one day. They envision the way he'll look, dress, talk, and they even begin making early preparations for their wedding day.

As we get older, we discover that the list of wishes we created for our future spouse were probably too superficial for a lasting marriage, and we begin to look for other qualities like his relationship with God and others and the type of character that he has.

Though men may not necessarily think about marriage until much later in life, one of the key components they look for in a spouse is a woman of noble character. Your character says a lot about you and your morality.

A man can view your worth as more valuable than rubies when you have noble character, because someone of noble character is someone that can be trusted. He can trust you with his personal goals, dreams, and desires. He can trust you with his past, present, and future, and he can trust you to commit to keeping the wedding vows you made with him.

Women often spend time looking to find men that fit their list of qualifications, but it is just as important that you exhibit the qualities that you expect to see in your husband.

Prayer

Dear Father, thank you for building me up spiritually to the point of being a woman of noble character. Help me to honor my husband by my actions in Jesus' name. Amen.
Further Studies: *2 Peter 1:5-7*

The Reward of Obedience

*"Honor your father and your mother, as the LORD your God has
commanded you, so that you may live long and that it may go well
with you in the land the LORD your God is giving you."*
(Deuteronomy 5:16)

When some of you read this verse, you probably automatically dismiss it as nothing more than a memory verse for children. After all, it is used a lot in Sunday school, and that's usually where we are first introduced to it. But the fact of the matter is: as long as you are a child to someone, this verse applies to you.

Obeying your parents when you were a child probably seemed like one of the hardest things to do, but sometimes, giving them honor and respect once you've become an adult can be even harder. Why? Because once you grow up, you get "too grown" to be told what to do anymore.

Well, honoring your parents means that you need to patiently listen when they give you advice, even if it doesn't gel with your own perspective. It means that you privately and publicly show them respect and speak well of them. It means that you live a lifestyle that shows them how all of the work they poured into you paid off.

Some of you may have parents that are not believers, so giving them honor in this way is difficult. But this command is not based on the behavior of your parents. It's a command to you to mind your own behavior. Be the kind of child that you want your children to be, starting today.

Prayer

*Dear Father, thank you for my parents. Help me to honor
you as I honor them in Jesus' name I pray. Amen.*
Further Studies: *James 1:22–25*

A Choice to Make

"[It is] better to dwell in the wilderness, than with a contentious and angry woman."
(Proverbs 21:19, KJV)

A contentious woman is quarrelsome, argumentative and controversial. Married or not, being a contentious woman destroys relationships. For marriage relationships in particular, if a man constantly had to come home to a wife that always wanted to argue with him, it would be no wonder that he would choose to set up camp in the wilderness than stick around her!

In order to be a contentious woman, there is one specific quality you must have: pride. Pride refuses to back down – whether you're wrong or right about an issue – pride refuses to let things go, and pride will get you into a hole that you will undoubtedly have a hard time digging yourself out of.

Whenever you find yourself getting angry or in the midst of an argument that is beginning to get heated, you have a choice to make. Will you deal with your pride accordingly or will you allow it to deal with you and destroy your relationships?

If you want to be the kind of woman your husband is happy to come home to, make a choice to lay down your pride and your need to be right, at the feet of Jesus. Humble yourself before Him and before your husband, and allow the Lord to deal with who is right and who is wrong. He's a much better judge than you or I could ever be anyway.

Prayer

Father, I thank you because you have given me the gift of self-control. I choose to be loving and gentle and live in peace with everyone in my world in Jesus' name. Amen.
Further Studies: *Ephesians 4:1-3*

Words

"May the words of my mouth and the meditations of my heart be
pleasing in your sight, O Lord, my Rock and my Redeemer."
(Psalm 19:14)

There are some people that do not know the importance of words, and that is the very reason they speak before thinking. If you know that your words have the power to kill and give life, then it would do you well to think carefully before uttering any word (Proverbs 18:21).

David prayed, *"Set a watch, O LORD, before my mouth; keep the door of my lips"* (Psalm 141:3). He knew the importance of words, so he prayed to God to help him watch his tongue. Some people are miserable and frustrated today because of words spoken to them by their parents, spouses, bosses, or teachers.

As a Christian woman, you must be very careful with your words. You can destroy your children or your marriage with words. If you talk your children down, they will never rise above that which you have said to them. In the same way, you can talk life out of your husband and make him miserable.

Learn to speak comforting and healing words today. The words that are acceptable to God are healing and life giving. If you want your words to be pleasing to God, then meditate on His Word and speak only His word.

Prayer

Dear Father, I thank you because I have the ability to speak healing
and creative words that give life, in Jesus' name. Amen.
Further Studies: *Proverbs 12:18, 15:1, 8:21, 21:23*

Love is

"Love is patient, love is kind, and is not jealous; love does not brag and is not arrogant, does not act unbecomingly; it does not seek its own, is not provoked, does not take into account a wrong suffered, does not rejoice in unrighteousness, but rejoices with the truth; bears all things, believes all things, hopes all things, endures all things."
(1 Corinthians 13:4-7)

When the Bible talks about love, reference is actually being made to God because He is not just the source of Love, but He is Love Himself. *"Dear friends, let us love one another, for love comes from God. Everyone who loves has been born of God and knows God. Whoever does not love does not know God, because God is love"* (1 John 4:7-8).

Paul reveals to us the characteristics of God; the very nature and life of God that is expressed through us. Love is the nature of God that we received at the new birth. It is a nature as well as a spiritual gift. Love is the greatest spiritual gift.

Love is. It's an action word, actively doing, seeking to fulfill the interest of others, it's not centered on self, but is centered on others. Think of the love of a parent for a child. Regardless of how the child behaves, love covers and conquers it all.

If you are planning to live in eternity with God, you must learn to live like Him on earth by giving vent to His nature and character in you. All the attributes of love listed in our opening scriptures are in your spirit, let them out today by living the life that God expects you to live. Let love flow out of you. Exude the love, character, and nature of God in your spirit today to bless your world.

Prayer

Dear Lord, thank you for putting your nature of love into my spirit. I live today conscious of my love nature because as you are so am I in this world, in Jesus' name. Amen.
Further Studies: *Mark 12:30-31*

Corruption

"Do not be misled: 'Bad company corrupts good character.'"
(1 Corinthians 15:33)

D o you remember the mischief you got yourself in when you were growing up? How many times did that happen because you were following your friends or hanging with the wrong crowd? This is the classic case of bad company corrupting good character. It always leads to corruption.

It is very likely that your parents warned you to stay away from certain types of peers, as they could foresee the trouble you would get into, but if you're like the majority of kids, you probably didn't pay them any mind.

As adults, we must choose wisely who we interact with and deliberately keep away from corruption at all cost. No matter how good you are, you can easily be corrupted just by listening to the wrong things, watching the wrong movies, hanging out with the wrong crowd, and so on.

Some families have been destroyed and separated because inappropriate friends shared inappropriate counsel. We can easily be corrupted by the misaligned intention of friends, so we must be diligent in checking the morality of our friends against the Word of God. It is the only way to let your light shine without having someone coming along and snuffing it out.

Prayer

Dear Father, thank you for helping me to stay away from the wrong people. Thank you, Lord, in Jesus' name. Amen.
Further Studies: *Proverb 13:30, Psalm 1:1-4*

Living Sacrifice

"Therefore, I urge you, brothers and sisters, in view of God's mercy, to offer your bodies as a living sacrifice, holy and pleasing to God—this is your true and proper worship."
(Romans 12:1)

In the days of traditional sacrifice, an animal or bird (most often a lamb), without spot or blemish, was the only acceptable sacrifice to bring the Lord. Fast forward to today; your life is the ultimate sacrifice to give to God. In the above scripture, the Apostle Paul implores the Romans to live each day in a sacrificial way in order to please God.

To sacrifice something is to lay down an object that is valuable to you as a way to esteem someone else or to offer thanks. When we accepted Christ as our savior, we forfeited the claim the father of this world, Satan, had on our lives and became joint heirs with Christ. If that isn't enough reason to offer the one thing that is most valuable to us—our lives—to Him, then I don't know what is!

The process of making a sacrifice looks like choosing the narrow path of righteousness even when you want to traverse the road everyone else is on. It looks like choosing the good part and spending time with God in the secret place even though you have a million things on your plate and what seems like no free time. It's giving whatever is in your hands, be it time, money, affection, etc., to God.

We are to live our lives as those who belong to God. Our lives are not our own. Jesus laid down His life for us, though we did not deserve it, so the least we can do it lay down ours for Him, too.

Prayer

Dear Father, thank you for teaching me to live in such a way that is pleasing to you. Lord, help to live my life to be pleasing to you in Jesus' name. Amen.
Further Studies: *Colossians 1:10, 1Corinthians 6:15-20*

Be Humble

*"Humble yourselves, therefore, under God's mighty
hand, that he may lift you up in due time."*
(1 Peter 5:6)

There are many times in our lives when we would just like a little praise and admiration from others. Whether it's because of the way we parent our children or the way we perform a task or even for the good things we do for others, it feels good to have people acknowledge that you have done something special.

There is actually nothing wrong with that feeling at all. In fact, the Bible tells us that God loves to rejoice over us and lift us up for His name's sake. The problem occurs when we seek to find our praise in the mouths of men instead of God.

Jesus tells us in Matthew 6:1-21 that when we do things for the sake of the praise of others, their praise is our reward. We receive nothing from our Father in heaven. When you look at the scope of what you receive from men and what you receive from God, is the number of "likes" you receive for your good deed really worth it?

God gives grace to those who are humble, and He resists the proud. Continue to fulfill your obligations, take care of your family, and do kind things for others, even if you are not recognized for it. Remember that God sees what is done in secret and will reward your for your kindness and faithfulness. Though it may be hard to perform a "thankless" task, remain humble as you wait for the day that God will give you grace and lift you up.

Prayer

Dear Father, I choose to be humble and to seek your approval instead of others'. I thank you for giving me grace and promotion in all that I do in Jesus' name. Amen.
Further Studies: *James 4:6-7*

Charity

"Above all, love each other deeply, because love covers over a multitude of sins."
(1 Peter 4:8)

When we really love someone, we tend to find it easy to excuse some of the negative things they do. Think of a mother whose teenage son is facing juvenile detention for something bad he's done. Though the mother knows what he did was wrong, she will never stop worrying about her son or wanting to care for and protect him. Her love reaches beyond his faults.

Christ's love looks beyond our faults, too. As multitudinous as our sins may be, for the sake of love, He never lets go of us, and He pursues us day in and day out. Even when we deliberately try to run away from Him, He still goes after us. How deep the love of Jesus is!

This same love has not only been extended towards us, but it has been placed in us so that we can have compassion and mercy on those who need love the most. Therefore, we must remember the depth of love that we have access to, even in those moments when people are hurting us most. The same love the Father has extended to us, we extend to others.

When you let the love of Christ flow through you, you will find that it becomes easy for you to love others, overlook their errors, and even help to shield them from the destructive consequences of their actions. Scripture tells us that it's God's kindness that leads us to repentance. As you love someone regardless of their faults, you might be surprised to discover what your kindness will lead them to do. Let God's nature of love flow through you today.

Prayer

*Dear Father, I thank you for making me the expression of your love.
I will let you love flow through me in Jesus' name. Amen.*
Further Studies: *1 Corinthians 14:4-8, 1 John 4:17*

Born Again

*"Jesus declared, "I tell you the truth, no one can see the
kingdom of God unless he is born again.""*
(John 3:3)

This is one of the concepts of the New Testament that has caused several disputes in the body of Christ because of false doctrines and false teachings. If you want to be a daughter of God, you must be born again. This is what happens when you confess Jesus as your Lord and personal savior:

*"If you declare with your mouth, 'Jesus is Lord,' and believe in
your heart that God raised him from the dead, you will be saved.
For it is with your heart that you believe and are justified, and it
is with your mouth that you profess your faith and are saved"*
(Romans 10:9-10).

Our first birth came through our mother's womb. Being born again comes through the Holy Spirit: acceptance of Christ as Lord and Savior. The moment you confess the lordship of Jesus, according to Romans 10:9-10, the Holy Spirit of God baptizes you into the body of Christ, and you miraculously become a child of God from that moment.

When you are born again, God becomes your heavenly Father, and you become a new member of His family, which is the body of Christ. Your brothers and sisters are like-minded believers. Together, you learn to trust in Jesus Christ and depend upon the Holy Spirit to live this new life. You are an heir of God with privileges such as being able to see the Kingdom of God. Welcome!

Prayer

*Father, thank you for the miracle of the new birth. I am a member of the family
of God now. I have the life of Christ. Thank you, Lord, in Jesus' name. Amen.*
Further Studies: *1 Corinthians 12:13*

Bearing with One Another

"Be completely humble and gentle; be patient, bearing with one another in love.
Make every effort to keep the unity of the Spirit through the bond of peace."
(Ephesians 4:2-3)

I f you let this Scripture be your guide, you can have peace in your marriage and in every other sphere of your life. The one condition this scripture outlines though, much to the chagrin of many, is that the responsibility of ensuring a peaceful co-existence with others lies on our shoulders as believers.

As Christians, we should live by a totally different standard than the rest of the world. We must be humble, gentle, and patient with the understanding that as we embody these characteristics, we greatly influence the response of those around us.

There may be times that we have to dismiss debates or refuse to give attention to an issue in order to maintain peace and unity, and that can be hard to do, but we are ambassadors of peace for the kingdom of God, so there is an expectation that we should show the world what being a child of God looks like.

Oh, it is so easy to become intolerant with someone who is going through a situation that you've already conquered, but for unity to reign, we must be humble, gentle, and patient in love, so that peace may abound. It is always useful to remember where we have journeyed from, how long it took us, and what we learned along the way. This attitude will help us to become gentle with them in the same way the Lord has been gentle with us.

Prayer

Dear Father, thank you for making me an agent of peace. I will allow your
peace that fills my heart to fill my world in Jesus' name. Amen.
Further Studies: *James 1:19*

With All

*"Love the LORD your God with all your heart and with
all your soul and with all your strength."*
(Deuteronomy 6:5)

Loving God goes beyond making a proclamation. Your love for Him has to be expressed by your actions. That is why Jesus said, *"If you love me, keep my commandments. He who has my commandments and keeps them, it is he who loves me. And he who loves me will be loved by my Father, and I will love him and manifest myself to him"* (John 14:15, 21).

Loving God with all your heart means to love Him with the depth of your being. Loving Him with your soul means your thoughts and emotions are involved, and loving Him with all your might refers to your abilities, your power, and your creative ideas.

The kind of love that is described here is complete and absolute. It encompasses every aspect of who we are and goes much deeper than the superficial love we may extend to others. This kind of love will propel you to keep God's commandments. This kind of love will ensure that you hold onto His hand even when times get tough.

God created you, planned your life, has been with you, stood up for you, fought for you, died for you, opened doors for you, provided for you, healed you from sickness, and protected you. He's done it ALL for you. When you reflect on all that He's done, you should naturally want to respond by loving Him with your all your heart, soul, and strength.

Prayer

*Dear Father, I will love you with all my being as a token of my
appreciation for all that you have done for me and my family. Thank
you Lord for loving us so much, in Jesus' name. Amen.*
Further Studies: *Matthew 22:36-40*

Your Soul

"What good will it be for someone to gain the whole world, yet forfeit their soul? Or what can anyone give in exchange for their soul?"
(Matthew 16:26)

This is one of the most important truths in the New Testament that must never be toyed with. In this Scripture, the Lord Jesus is talking about the value of a soul.

What is your soul worth?
Can its worth be measured materially?
What would you exchange for your soul?

These are valuable, thought provoking questions that only YOU can answer.

Your soul is the spiritual part of you, your emotions and intellect, the part of you that will last for eternity. I can assure you that NOTHING is more precious than your soul, which is the sum total of who you are.

Any item is as valuable as the price on it or the price paid for it. Jesus said the whole world is not valuable enough for you to give up your soul. The soul is an eternal being, whereas this world will fade away. Your soul is your unique identity, which is not perishable.

Your soul will live forever, either in hell or in heaven, and only God can keep it safe or redeem it out of the rebellion of the garden of Eden, so submit your soul to God today.

Prayer

Dear Father, I thank you for my soul. I submit it to your authority today. Lord Jesus, you are Lord over my soul from this day forth in Jesus' name. Amen.
Further Studies: *Jeremiah 29:13*

Who is Your Master?

"No one can serve two masters. Either you will hate the one and love the other, or you will be devoted to the one and despise the other. You cannot serve both God and money."
(Matthew 6:24)

Serving the Master goes beyond words. Our Christian service is demonstrated by our actions and our manner of life. In our opening scripture, Jesus said that it is impossible to serve two masters. This means that if you are a Christian, then live like one, because you can't be a Christian and live like an unbeliever.

> *"Do you not know that when you continually offer yourselves to someone to do his will, you are the slaves of the one whom you obey, either [slaves] of sin, which leads to death, or of obedience, which leads to righteousness (right standing with God)?"*
> Romans 6:16 (Amp)

Some people are actually slaves to money. They would rather go after money instead of going to church or giving of their possessions to serve others, specifically the poor, and by so doing, money has become their master.

The dividing factor is your heart posture; where your loyalties lie and what your motives are and who your master really is. God often likes to test our faithfulness with small amounts before He trusts us with bigger amounts. If you're faithful with little, He will grant you more. What He first needs to see is a heart that is devoted to Him regardless of the amount. What's the condition of your heart today?

Prayer

Dear Father, you are my Lord and Master. I commit to being a cheerful giver and refuse to hold on too tightly to the fleeting wealth of this world in Jesus' name. Amen.
Further Studies: Luke 16:10

Good Counsel

"The godly offer good counsel; they teach right from wrong."
(Psalm 37:30)

This is one of the reasons we're taught to keep good company and have the right friends around us. There is a saying, "Show me your friends, and I will tell you who you are." This is because your friends have a great influence on you.

It is only a godly people that can give you a godly counsel. Listening to the wrong people has cost some people their marriage, their job and even their family. It is only good Christians that can stand and boldly tell you what is right from wrong.

King David gives a characteristic of a godly person. Godly people, on a whole, speak positively and offer insight and intellect; they speak the truth and can guide you rightly with the word of God. Our speech and instructions are important as children of light and as salt of the earth. If we don't give good counsel and teach what is right, who will?

It is our responsibility to represent Christ in all that we do, as more people are influenced by our actions than we realize. If you are the only Bible that those in your sphere of influence will ever read, what will they read from your actions and lifestyle?

We are the ones who bring life and hope into situations everywhere we go. It's much more than we know and it's much bigger than we are. We must open our mouths to give good counsel and teach right from wrong to a dying desperate world.

Prayer

Dear Father, I thank you because your word is continually in my heart and in my mouth to teach and instruct others in the name of Jesus. Amen.
Further Studies: *Titus 2:3-5*

No Disgrace

"When pride comes, then comes disgrace, but with humility comes wisdom."
(Proverbs 11:2)

Marsha was the secretary of her church's women's ministry and had maintained that position for many years. One day it came to the attention of someone in the ministry that Marsha had been misappropriating their funds. Even though this was the truth, Marsha refused to admit that she had done anything wrong. The women's ministry had no choice but to strip her of her title.

This is a classic case of pride followed by disgrace. Had Marsha humbled herself and simply admitted her wrongdoing, no disgrace would have befallen her. A wise woman will receive instruction and correct her ways, but pride will not allow an arrogant woman to listen to correction. Don't be a Marsha.

Sometimes it can be really hard for women to admit that they are wrong about something, especially if it means that their husbands are right. Even if we know they're right, we may still try to justify our opinion and try to explain away the fact that he is right. Exhibiting such behavior does nothing but make our husbands lose respect for us. However, when we humble ourselves and admit that we are wrong, we learn; we show that we are teachable; we grow.

Listen to what people have to say about your character and attitude, and allow God to grow you through this experience.

Prayer

Dear Father, thank you for teaching me to be humble. All that I have is yours, and I bow myself to your word, your will and your ways in Jesus' name. Amen.
Further Studies: *1 Peter 5:5, James 4:6*

Healing

"Reckless words pierce like a sword, but the tongue of the wise brings healing."
(Proverbs 12:18, NKJ)

Some peoples' lives and families have been torn apart because of harsh, negative, or idle words. Words can be considered the most dangerous weapons on earth, and guess what? Women are generally very skilled at knowing how to wield their words as a weapon. That can make us very powerful, but it also puts a great weight of responsibility on our shoulders.

When we get overcome by emotion and allow that emotion to influence our speech, we can say a lot of things that we know we shouldn't. Maybe you know very well the feeling of dread that comes after you've spit some harsh words at someone out of frustration. It's not a feeling that anyone enjoys at all.

Your words can pierce and destroy others, including yourself, or your words can encourage and give life, even to those who have nothing more to live for. Learn to speak life-giving words. The tongue of the wise can mend broken hearts and strengthen legs that have become weary on the journey, but there is no honor in being bitter and sharp tongued. Our words should bring healing at all times.

We must endeavor to use our tongue to edify and bring healing instead of tearing down and destroying lives.

Prayer

*Dear Father, thank you for giving me a wholesome tongue. I speak
healing, health, life, prosperity, peace and stability to my family,
my marriage and my business in Jesus' name. Amen.*
Further Studies: *Proverbs 18:21*

Take Heed

""Be careful, or your hearts will be weighed down with carousing, drunkenness and the anxieties of life, and that day will close on you suddenly like a trap."
(Luke 21:34)

The parable of the wise and foolish virgins in Matthew 25 is very instructive. It gives us an idea of how to prepare for the coming of Jesus. The virgins were all going to meet the bridegroom. Some of them were so concerned about other things that they neglected to purchase extra oil for the lamp.

In the same way, we can forget to keep the oil of intimacy in our relationship with Jesus, when we allow our hearts to become weighed down by the cares of this world. That includes the things we enjoy doing that distract us from our relationship with God, and even allowing worry to overtake our faith.

We know from the Scriptures that Jesus will return like a thief in the night. No one knows the day or the hour. Because of that truth, those who are not watching and waiting and living their lives unto His glory will find themselves missing out in the end.

The end is near; things are winding down, so be careful that your hearts do not get overloaded with consuming too much, with drunkenness, or with the cares of this life, so that you miss the day when Christ returns.

Prayer

Father, please help me keep my heart focused on you and not on the cares of this life. I put my trust in you, taking heed and leaning upon your everlasting arms in Jesus' name. Amen.
Further Studies: *Micah 7:7*

An Overcomer

"Who is it that overcomes the world? Only the one who
believes that Jesus is the Son of God."
(1 John 5:5)

At the end of this life, there will be winners and there will be losers. Those who spent their lives chasing after Christ will find themselves on the winning side, whereas those who lived only for themselves will fall short.

If anyone is to be an overcomer in this world, they must not live by the standards and systems of the world, but they must have a mind that is renewed by the Holy Spirit that gives them insight as to how to transcend the ways of the world.

As Christians, we actually operate by a different sets of rules than everyone else in this world. Jesus said in His prayers to the father, *"They are not of the world, even as I am not of the world"* (John 17:16). When Jesus spoke about the WORLD, He was referring to the systems, principles, and domain of the devil.

John tells us that the only way to live above the system of this world is to believe that Jesus is the Christ. As Christians, we always have the advantage and are always on the winning team, because we dare to believe the impossible, the invisible, and the word of God. Maintain your faith and your confession. That is our victory.

Prayer

Dear Father, I thank you for making me an overcomer. I have overcome this world and its crippling systems of unbelief in the name of Jesus Christ. Amen.
Further Studies: *John 17:14-16, 1John 4:4*

The Spirit of the Lord

"The Spirit of the LORD will rest on him-- the Spirit of wisdom and of understanding, the Spirit of counsel and of might, the Spirit of the knowledge and fear of the LORD."
(Isaiah 11:2)

Have you ever entered a place, maybe an office or a mall, and people approach you simply to ask if you are a Christian? It's a really great indicator that the Spirit of the LORD is visibly resting on you whenever that happens.

Sometimes people notice because of the way your countenance appears, but for most people, they know it by your behavior, the things you say, and how you respond to adversity. They can see that the wisdom you utilize is not the wisdom of this world.

God has blessed us with His presence so much so that when we show up, people just notice something about us. The Spirit of the Lord is an asset for our lives as believers; it is a vital necessity for survival, allowing us to partake of wisdom, understanding, counsel, might, knowledge, and the fear of the Lord.

We who are born again have the same Spirit that Christ has. Encourage the ministry of the Holy Spirit of God in your life by continual fellowship and study of the word. Allow the Spirit of the Lord to rest upon you as He did on the Messiah and empower you throughout life's journey.

Prayer

Dear Father, I thank you for the ministry of the Holy Spirit in my life. Only the counsel of the Lord will prevail in the name of the Lord Jesus. Amen.
Further Studies: *Ephesians 3:19*

Money

"For the love of money is a root of all kinds of evil. Some people, eager for money, have wandered from the faith and pierced themselves with many griefs."
(1 Timothy 6:10)

I have heard Christians make statements like, "Money is the root of evil," but according to the Apostle Paul, it is the *love of money* that is the root of all evil. When we set our affections on those green bits of paper instead of on Christ, that is what is considered the root of evil.

Money is very important. In fact, God stewards it to us for the advancement of His kingdom. We cannot send missionaries to reach the world with the gospel or build meeting places for believers, or do any form of outreach without money. It is an essential component of ministry.

But there are those who are so crazy about money that they will do anything to get it. These are those who the Bible is referring to in our opening scripture. These are those who will compromise their faith for the sake of money.

Money in and of itself is not evil; the excessive love of it, what drives you to acquire it is. Evil acts such as deception, theft, betrayal, murder, lying, blackmail, overwork, neglect (of self & others), and sexual immorality may result from the love of money.

The remedy for this evil is balance. Money should serve you, you should not serve money.

Prayer

Dear Father, thank you for making me a king. I will work to steward over all things including money and other resources in the name of Jesus Christ. Amen.
Further Studies: Matthew 6:24

Secret Place

"Whoever dwells in the shelter of the Most High will rest in the shadow of the Almighty."
(Psalm 91:1)

The secret place can be found in the presence of God, and dwelling there provides a refuge from difficulties. The shadow of being under His wings gives protection from the scorching sun. It's a quiet, safe resting place.

Where is the presence of God and how do we dwell there today? The presence of God is where God's government is operational, that place where His word has been given in the first place, that place where Jesus is Lord and King.

The Lord Jesus was asked if it was possible for us to continually enjoy His presence on earth. He gave the answer and also told us how to maintain our stay in His presence.

> *"Judas (not Iscariot) said to Him, 'Lord, what then has happened that You are going to disclose Yourself to us and not to the world?' Jesus answered and said to him, 'If anyone loves Me, he will keep My word; and My Father will love him, and We will come to him and make Our abode with him.'"*
> John 14:22-23

You can dwell continually in the presence of the Most High by living in accordance with His word. Understand that God is our father and we were born into His very presence when we were born again. All we need to do now is to continue in His love and in His word. God doesn't make His abode in us again because we have already become His abode in the new birth. Our responsibility now is to stay there.

Prayer

Dear Father, I thank you for making me your dwelling place, your abode. Lord, I live in your presence and I choose to remain in your presence forever in Jesus' name. Amen
Further Studies: *Hebrews 10:35-38*

With All Your Heart

"Give me understanding and I will obey your instructions;
I will put them into practice with all my heart."
(Psalm 119:34, NLT)

In our opening verse, the psalmist prays for something important. Understanding comes from studying the word of God, and when we study and meditate on His word, we receive the ability to obey. The understanding that we need to obey God's instructions is of a spiritual nature; our carnal minds will not grasp God's laws.

"Keep this Book of the Law always on your lips; meditate on
it day and night, so that you may be careful to do everything
written in it. Then you will be prosperous and successful."
Joshua 1:8

As you study and meditate on the word of God, He will give you understanding to know what to do and how to go about your life.

Once we have gotten this divine understanding, our hearts can do the will of God, as long as they are set on obeying his instructions. When we understand something, it results in acceptance of that thing because our minds can rationalize it. Understanding "why" leads us to be obedient, and it becomes easier to execute with all our heart.

Therefore, we must understand that we need to obey and follow God with all of our heart.

Prayer

Dear Father, I thank you for granting me the understanding of your word today. I receive knowledge of your will and ways as I meditate on your word in Jesus' name. Amen.
Further Studies: *Ephesians 1:17-19*

Walk Worthy

"We pleaded with you, encouraged you, and urged you to live your lives in a way that God would consider worthy. For he called you to share in his Kingdom and glory."
(1 Thessalonians 2:12, NLT)

As Christians we must understand that we are to live our lives to please our Master. *"You were bought at a price. Therefore honor God with your bodies"* (1 Corinthians 6:20). This is what we would call "walking worthy of the Lord."

You cannot just live your life to please yourself. Your life is a gift of trust, and you are accountable unto God. This is why the Spirit of God prayed this prayer for all Christians through the Apostle Paul.

Because God has called us into His Kingdom and glory, our response of gratitude should be to walk worthy before Him. What an awesome privilege He has bestowed upon us, a position that we could not work hard enough to gain.

Loving and serving others, being patient, obedient, content, joyful, helpful, and determined, encouraging others, giving time, talent and resources, and feeding the hungry are examples of walking worthy. Imitating His works of holiness, kindness, righteousness, and unconditional love is our main focus and assignment here.

We show our gratitude by walking worthy as we imitate Him, testifying to His goodness to us in Christ.

Prayer

Dear Father, thank you for helping me live a life acceptable to you in Jesus' name. Amen.
Further Studies: *Colossians 1:10*

The Mind of Christ

"In your relationships with one another, have the same mindset as Christ Jesus."
(Philippians 2:5)

To fully understand and appreciate our opening scripture, you must first have a very good understanding of the four Gospels, because within their pages, we see the way Jesus lived His life while He was on this earth. We see the mind of Christ, including His disposition and His responses to many different types of people.

The mind of Christ is the character of Christ. There was a famous slogan that went around Christian circles many years ago called "What Would Jesus Do? (WWJD)" Anytime someone was about to engage in an activity of questionable nature, they would ask themselves that question as a way to remind themselves of Christ and how He would respond.

Life could be so easy to coast through if we didn't have to deal with challenging relationships with people. Sometimes people do things that can infuriate you to the point of no return, and yet we never saw Jesus fly off the handle at anyone.

A woman of God must humble herself as she imitates Christ's character. She must train her mind in the Word of God in order to cultivate the mind of Christ. Emotions will run high and tensions may strain your relationships, but that's no excuse. If Jesus came to earth and treated others with kindness and compassion, so can you.

Prayer

Dear Lord, thank you for the privilege of living on earth with the mind of the heavenly. I choose to live for you and live to represent and reflect your kingdom in Jesus' name. Amen.
Further Studies: *1 Corinthians 15:49*

Do not Presume

"Where there is strife, there is pride, but wisdom is found in those who take advice."
(Proverbs 13:10)

Have you ever been in a meeting where a group of people had to make a decision and there were one or two people who would continually butt heads? No matter what the topic was, they could never agree on an answer. That is what is known as strife, and according to this scripture, the culprit behind strife is pride.

Pride can blind us to the truth and ruin relationships with others, because all we can see is what we want to see. As believers, we are to have a spirit of unity and agreement with one another. Achieving that is impossible when pride is in the picture.

This is where wisdom comes in. Wisdom is taking the advice of others, even if you think that you're right. Wisdom is listening without interrupting so as not to offend others. Wisdom is showing value in the wisdom God has given others, and knowing that you don't have all of the answers.

Sometimes people may give you bad advice, but to railroad them or ignore them altogether is not extending the grace that God extends to us each and every day, when we propose ideas that totally go against His will.

We must be mindful of how patient the Lord is with us as we deal with others.

Prayer

*Dear Lord, I open my heart to your wisdom and counsel. I refuse
to act base on sentiments, anger, presumption and fear. I choose
to be guided by your wisdom in Jesus' name. Amen.*
Further Studies: *Proverbs 29:11*

Pure Heart

*"The goal of this command is love, which comes from a pure
heart and a good conscience and a sincere faith."*
(1 Timothy 1:5)

All through the Bible, we are instructed to love. The Old Testament instructs us to love God, and the New Testament instructs us to love God and our neighbors. Oftentimes we look at the way we live our lives and interact with others and strive to love to the best of our abilities.

But what does that really mean?
How do we love?
What needs to happen in order for us to love the way that God wants us to?

As the scripture says, love is the overflow of a pure heart, a good conscience, and a sincere faith. Let's take a closer look at each of these...

A pure heart is a heart that has desires that are clean and is fixed solely on the pure desires of God. A good conscience is a mind that allows your intentions to be clear of sin. A sincere faith is one that is built on nothing less than wanting to live your life to honor God in everything that you do.

Essentially, this means to let your heart be founded on God and God alone. Love God with your whole heart and do His Word as He instructed, and as you pursue Him, He will teach you how to love others in the same way that He loves you.

Prayer

*Dear Father, thank you for teaching me to love you with a perfect heart. I am
committed to living for you till my King returns in Jesus' name. Amen.*
Further Studies: *Matthew 5:8*

Hold your Tongue

"Sin is not ended by multiplying words, but the prudent hold their tongues."
(Proverbs 10:19)

A friend once told me that as a teacher she would often hear some of the most imaginative stories from her students, as they explained the various reasons why they weren't able to complete their homework. Sometimes, once a kid get started telling stories, they just don't know when to stop.

The same actually happens to us as adults. If we feel like we're being misunderstood or we need to justify something, we can also ramble on and on, multiplying words. The problem is that the more we talk, the more susceptible we are to saying something false or harsh, or even just to explain away something wrong that we have done. That's one of the pitfalls of the tongue. It's hard to tame.

Jesus demonstrated the incredible ability to hold His tongue when He was being persecuted before His crucifixion. People were lying and speaking all kinds of evil about Him, and yet He made no remark. He could have responded to Pilate, when asked if He truly was the Son of God, and gone on and on about who He really was. Though He had every right to do that, all His words would have done is demonstrate pride, and that's not the nature of God.

We need to follow suit in our own personal lives. There may be times when it's well within reason to rebut something someone else has said, or to defend ourselves, but a wise and humble person will weigh their words carefully and let their words be few.

Prayer

Dear Father, I thank you for teaching me to control my life
by controlling my tongue in Jesus' name. Amen.
Further Studies: *James 3:1-6*

Where is your Treasure?

"For where your treasure is, there your heart will be also."
(Matthew 6:21)

Abby looked at the things around her. They were many, and they were extremely beautiful. She had married a wealthy man, so she lacked nothing. Even so, her brush with death several years ago changed her focus dramatically, so that she now sees these possessions with little value.

Yes, she is grateful, but she is more grateful to be alive. Her heart is set on the one who saved her and delivered her from death. That is where her treasure is, not in the things around her.

We can be enticed to become lovers of the things of this world, so we must keep our hearts focused on Christ, the giver of all things. If you set your heart on your riches, certificates and professional goals, what will happen when they are no longer relevant?

Everything we have today will eventually come to an end. Only those things that we have stored in heaven will remain forever. If all your hope is on earth at the moment, it's time now to start laying up treasures in heaven.

Prayer

Dear Father, I thank you for teaching me to store up treasures in heaven, treasures that are indestructible. Lord, my heart and my life are founded on your Word that will never pass away in Jesus' name. Amen.
Further Studies: *Matthew 6:19-20, 1 John 2:15-17, 2 Peter 3:2*

More than Silver and Gold

"How much better to get wisdom than gold, to get insight rather than silver!"
(Proverbs 16:16)

Wisdom is better than Gold, Solomon declared. Here are some interesting facts about gold and silver.

Gold:

- ♪ Seen as a symbol of wealth.
- ♪ Popular choice for achievement medals, statues and trophies.
- ♪ Most popular precious metal for investment.

Silver:

- ♪ In approximately fourteen languages the words for money and silver are the same.
- ♪ It is exceptionally shiny and the most reflective element.
- ♪ A precious metal used to make jewelry, utensils and coins.

Regardless of these facts, wisdom and understanding are worth more than silver and gold.

King Solomon was the wisest and richest man on earth before Jesus came. He had both gold and silver in abundance. His wisdom and words are credible, so believe what he says, and get wisdom and choose understanding over these precious metals.

Prayer

Dear Father, I thank you for teaching me about the most important thing life. Your word is my wisdom and I prefer your word to gold and silver because they are life and health to me in Jesus' name. Amen.
Further Studies: *Proverbs 8*

Good or Bad?

"For we must all appear before the judgment seat of Christ, so that each of us may receive what is due us for the things done while in the body, whether good or bad."
(2 Corinthians 5:10)

The entirety of the human race, including nonbelievers and believers alike, will stand before the judgment seat of Christ where our "works" in the flesh will be judged. One question will be asked:

Have we done good or bad "works" in the flesh?

Our deeds, words, actions, and perceptions are considered works of the flesh. Good works result when we obey God's law, and bad works result when we are disobedient to His law. It's not about salvation and eternal life in this instance for the believer, but a reward for doing what is good. For us, good works take precedence.

"Do not be deceived, God is not mocked; for whatever a man sows, this he will also reap. For the one who sows to his own flesh will from the flesh reap corruption, but the one who sows to the Spirit will from the Spirit reap eternal life. Let us not lose heart in doing good, for in due time we will reap if we do not grow weary. So then, while we have opportunity, let us do good to all people, and especially to those who are of the household of the faith."
Galatians 6:7-10

Prayer

Dear Father, I thank you for helping me to lay up treasures in heaven. I know that there is great reward for living according to your word and I choose to live my life by your revealed principles in Jesus' name. Amen.
Further Studies: *Philippians 6:7-8*

February

Bears Good Things

"Her husband has full confidence in her and lacks nothing of value.
She brings him good, not harm, all the days of her life."
(Proverbs 31:11-12)

The value that you bring to your marriage is priceless. It's not just about the things that you do for your husband, but it's about who you are that makes him feel secure and confident in your love.

When you recited your marriage vows to your husband, you undoubtedly promised to love and honor him. As you continue through life together, your actions each day affirm that initial covenant or disprove it, and you can believe that your husband is paying attention.

He knows you better than anyone else. He knows your character, how loyal you are, how kind and virtuous you are, and anything else there is to know about you. He also knows that whenever trouble comes, he can count on you to be a strong support not only for him but for others, and you really can't put a price on that.

Prayer

Dear Father, thank you for teaching me how to be the kind of wife that my husband can depend on. Help me to continue honoring you in that way in Jesus' name. Amen.
Further Studies: *Ephesians 5:22-33*

Fruit of the Spirit

"But the fruit of the Spirit is love, joy, peace, patience, kindness, goodness, faithfulness, gentleness, self-control."
(Galatians 5:22-23a, NASB)

The works of the flesh are the characteristics that you exhibited before you were born again. It was normal and natural for you to manifest the works of the flesh. In the same way, it is natural for you to exhibit the fruit of the Spirit after you are born again. The fruit of the spirit is the reality of Christ dwelling inside of you.

Like an orange with segments, so is the fruit of the Spirit. Each segment of the piece of fruit is one aspect of the nature of the Holy Spirit working in and through you. Oftentimes we read this scripture as "fruits of the spirit", and we believe that we can hone in on one particular aspect and make ourselves love better or be more kind, but each and every characteristic of the spirit listed above should be a natural overflow of a life saturated in the Spirit of God.

Even so, just having the nature of Christ in you does not mean you will automatically be able to live the fruit of the Spirit out. It takes some effort, but thankfully, we have help. *"But you have received the Holy Spirit, and he lives within you, so you don't need anyone to teach you what is true. For the Spirit teaches you everything you need to know, and what he teaches is true--it is not a lie. So just as he has taught you, remain in fellowship with Christ"* (1 John 2:27). The Holy Spirit of God will teach you and help you to live the life of the new creation.

Prayer

Dear Father, thank you for your life and nature in me. I am a new creation, and I live as such in the name of Jesus. Amen.
Further Studies: *1 Corinthians 15:49*

Togetherness

"And let us consider how we may spur one another on toward love and good deeds.
Let us not give up meeting together, as some are in the habit of doing, but let us
encourage one another--and all the more as you see the Day approaching."
(Hebrews 10:24-25)

I f you have ever belonged to a club or a fraternity, you probably know that as a member, you are obligated to attend group meetings. Organizations such as these take membership responsibilities very seriously. Every member should be an active participant.

As Christians, we are not under such laws, when it comes to attending church, but we should view our involvement with our local church with just as much seriousness as any other organization would. Our opening scripture encourages us to motivate one another to love and to do good deeds, but how can we do this without a common meeting place? We must gather together in order to properly support one another.

Fellowship with one another is a vital part of the Christian brotherhood. None of us can withstand the pressures of life by ourselves, but when we join with others, we can soar to new heights and achieve many goals.

Each time we attend church services, we get to praise God together, pray together, listen to God's word, share testimonies with one another, and have the privilege of worshipping God through giving our offering. It is in these moments of unity between believers that the Lord really moves. Try it and see for yourself.

Prayer

Dear Lord, I desire and long for your house. Thank you for the privilege
of fellowshipping with other believers in Jesus' name. Amen.
Further Studies: Psalm 122:1

Speech

"For it is with your heart that you believe and are justified, and it is
with your mouth that you profess your faith and are saved."
(Romans 10:10)

Have you ever had someone tell you that they love you, but you just knew that if their heart had two lips, it would be telling you a different story? Anyone can say one thing with their mouth but feel something completely different in their heart. That is why God requires that there be total unity between our mouth and our hearts when it comes to salvation.

As the Bible tells us, out of the heart the mouth speaks (Luke 6:45), so it stands to reason that before we can confess anything with our mouth, there must be some kind of transformation on the heart level. We must have had an encounter with God that thoroughly convinced our hearts to believe that He is real and that He loves us.

Once you believe in your heart that Jesus is the Son of God, you are made right with God, and your heart, which was once wicked through and through, begins to pump the purifying blood of Jesus and becomes clean.

When your heart is so filled with faith in Christ, you can't help but keep it from spilling out of your mouth. That is the profession of our faith. When we speak anything, the matter is established; therefore, when we declare our faith, the work of salvation is complete. This same principle applies to our daily lives in Christ as well. Check the connection between your lips and your heart today and make sure they're still in sync.

Prayer

Dear Father, I want the words of my mouth and the mediations
of my heart to be pleasing to you in Jesus' name. Amen.
Further Studies: *Psalm 89:1-18*

Agreement

"Do two walk together unless they have agreed to do so?"
(Amos 3:3)

If two cows are yoked together to plow a farm, at first they may fight against each other to go their separate ways, but they will quickly discover that the yoke constrains them. Whether they like it or not, they have to keep traveling the same path; together.

Unlike cows, we have no yoke to constrain us when it comes to relationships. If there is a serious enough disagreement, we can choose to drop relationships and go our separate ways. In some cases that's good and in others it's bad.

Think of your relationship with your parents, spouse, boss, friends, or anyone else. Unless you have a common goal in view, you cannot walk together. It's impossible. Think of how many relationships have been broken up because of disagreements that turned into bitterness that led to separation.

This aspect of agreement is something that we cannot take lightly, because it is what determines the success of any relationship. Sometimes you have to agree with your husband for the sake of peace even when you do not believe in what he wants to do, and sometimes you have to agree to disagree with people.

Regardless, walking in agreement with others is really a matter of humility. You have to value the opinion of the other person as much as you value your own and be willing to trust in God's sovereignty to ensure the path you both walk is the one He wants you on.

Prayer

Dear Father, help me to humble myself and walk in
agreement with others in Jesus' name. Amen.
Further Studies: *Matthew 18:19*

Melody

*"And be not drunk with wine, wherein is excess; but be filled with
the Spirit; Speaking to yourselves in psalms and hymns and spiritual
songs, singing and making melody in your heart to the Lord."*
(Ephesians 5:18-19, NASB)

If you or anyone you know has ever been drunk on alcohol, you know the way alcohol can greatly influence a person's behavior. Some people become loud and belligerent, others become very talkative, and one person may become very happy, whereas another person may become very sad. Alcohol affects people in different ways, but generally speaking, these are some of the noticeable symptoms of drunkenness.

This scripture compares the Holy Spirit to alcohol in the sense that when we are filled with the Spirit, there are certain types of "symptoms" or *fruit* – to put it more biblically – that should be evident in our lives.

Just as you can see a person staggering down the street, smell the alcohol in their skin or hear them slurring their words and know that that person is drunk, so should the world be able to see your lifestyle and know that you have the Holy Spirit living inside of you.

Some of the fruit of being filled with the Spirit looks like speaking and singing Scripture from your heart to the Lord. When the Holy Spirit of the living God fills our beings, we can't help but to have songs of praise bubble up from our lips. Let your temple be filled with the right kind of Spirit today, and enjoy the fruits!

Prayer

*Dear Lord, I thank you for the privileges of having your
Spirit dwell in me in Jesus' name. Amen.*
Further Studies: *Acts 2:1-4, Acts 4:31*

Love = Obedience

"If you love me, keep my commands."
(John 14:15)

Do you have children who profess to love you but never obey your instructions? It can be a little hard to "feel the love" when that happens. Some people are used to saying "I love you," but don't realize that those words must be accompanied by action in order to be genuine.

Love is not selfish. God so loved the world that He *gave*. If you love God, you must also give. You must give up your lifestyle, ideas and principles of life to take up His. The Bible contains the Word of God, and if we claim to love Him, then we must keep His word.

Our love for God is linked directly to our obedience to Him. Obedience can be difficult at times, but becomes easier to accomplish when we focus on His love and His plans for us. Our love for God is shown primarily by obeying His word. When we focus on His love, mercy, and grace that He extends to us, it propels us to respond to what He asks.

Because you love someone, you do what they ask of you, not always immediately and with a good attitude, but you do. So too, if we love God, that love equals our obedience to Him. The more you obey God, the easier it becomes for you to obey him.

Give yourself completely to the love of Christ, and you will find that obeying Him is as simple as breathing in oxygen. If you allow your love for Christ to fill your heart, it will propel you to love Him more and do His word.

Prayer

Dear Father, thank you for loving me and giving me the ability to love you by keeping your commandments. It gets better every day in Jesus' name. Amen.
Further Studies: *2 Corinthians 5:14-15*

Nothing Separates

"For I am convinced that neither death nor life, neither angels nor demons, neither the present nor the future, nor any powers, neither height nor depth, nor anything else in all creation, will be able to separate us from the love of God that is in Christ Jesus our Lord."
(Romans 8:38-39)

We live in desperate times. Jesus talked about these days, and Paul also made reference to some of the terrible things that will happen to the children of God. But like the apostles and other disciples who died for the gospel, you must make up your mind that nothing can separate you from your love of Christ.

"...in the last days it is going to be very difficult to be a Christian. For people will love only themselves and their money; they will be proud and boastful, sneering at God, disobedient to their parents, ungrateful to them, and thoroughly bad. They will be hardheaded and never give in to others; they will be constant liars and troublemakers and will think nothing of immorality. They will be rough and cruel, and sneer at those who try to be good. They will betray their friends; they will be hotheaded, puffed up with pride, and prefer good times to worshiping God. They will go to church, yes, but they won't really believe anything they hear. Don't be taken in by people like that."
2 Timothy 3:1-5 (TLB)

All of these things are already happening, and it is becoming more and more difficult to find sincere and genuine Christians. Do not allow the temptation to be worldly or the persecution of being a Christian to separate you from our Father. Remain persuaded; keep fanning the flame, because the Master is here.

Prayer

Dear Lord, my love for you is so strong. I keep my gaze on you and refuse to be distracted by worldliness or persecution. Nothing can separate me from you in Jesus' name. Amen.
Further Studies: *Matthew 25*

Love not the World

*"Do not love the world or anything in the world. If anyone
loves the world, love for the Father is not in them."*
(1 John 2:15)

Several major bills that have been passed into law during this generation directly contradict the word of God. There are even many people that continually work very hard to discredit the very existence of our God.

There are several types of vices and immoralities condoned, all in the name of progressive civilization and freedom, but in reality are bondage to sin and the devil. These are tricks of the devil and his servants to lure you into darkness and rebellion against your heavenly Father.

The world offers the good, the bad, and the indifferent. The preferences we develop and the choices we make mirror where our heart lies: for God or for the world. Achievements and temptations assail us in our daily lives and it is in the active pursuit of balance that we will be victorious in overcoming the world and demonstrating our love for God.

If we want to be known as Christian women who love not the world but who love the Father, we must deliberately pursue righteousness and holiness in this ungodly world. You will be tempted to choose evil over good, but you must make deliberate effort to maintain your Christianity in the face of staggering opposition.

Prayer

*Dear Father, thank you for teaching me how to live in the end times. I pray that by
the help of the Holy Spirit, I will maintain my Christian fervor in Jesus' name. Amen.*
Further Studies: *Matthew 24:11-13*

Love of Neighbor

"For the entire law is fulfilled in keeping this one
command: "Love your neighbor as yourself."
(Galatians 5:14)

This is a repeat of the Old Testament passage, Leviticus 19:18, imploring love of neighbor. The definition for love of self is the instinct by which one's actions are directed to the promotion of one's welfare or well-being, especially an excessive regard for one's advantage.

Love of neighbor means respecting their boundary, blessing them, being a good listener, not stealing from them, holding no grudge against them, not being deceptive in dealing with them, and treating them how you want to be treated.

Just as we love and would work to achieve goals for ourselves, we are hereby asked to do the same thing for our neighbor. There is nothing wrong with loving yourself, because you should love yourself. You are God's creation, and as such, must appreciate His work in creating you.

What the Bible is teaching us here is to also give the same preference to our neighbors that we would give to ourselves. Sometimes you have to give up your own pleasure and comfort for others to be happy. Never fail to show kindness to those around you, because in so doing, some have entertained angels (Hebrews 13:2).

The law is summed up in this single commandment of love for our neighbors. Allow the love of God to flow through you today to your world.

Prayer

Dear Father, I thank you for this beautiful life you have given
me. I thank you for my neighbors, and I choose to love them as
I love myself. Thank you, Lord, in Jesus' name. Amen.
Further Studies: *Matthew 25:31-46, Matthew 10:42*

Be Wise

"The wise woman builds her house, but with her own hands the foolish one tears hers down."
(Proverbs 14:1)

A woman's role, regardless of the capacity she fills, carries an onus of influence. She must be very careful then to build up and not tear down. It is all too easy to be swayed by emotions that ebb and flow and to say things in the heat of your anger that you may wish you had never said. In a matter of seconds, you could be the bearer of that gust of winds that knocks your home down.

You must be very careful therefore, to take your role as a builder seriously.

View each exchange you have with your children as an opportunity to lay a foundation that will be set within their hearts forever. Children are very much like wet cement in the sense that impressions you leave on them early on, will likely become pivotal to who they become when they get older.

Take each opportunity with your husband to speak kind and loving words and to refrain from speaking negatively to or about him. Challenge yourself to only speak things that would be edifying to his identity or his spirit, and seek to honor and respect him as much as you can.

This is your purpose, this is your calling; fulfill it today.

Prayer

Dear Father, thank you for making me a builder. I choose to be a builder in my family and in every aspect of my life in Jesus' name. Amen.
Further Studies: *2 Corinthians 3:18*

Your Song

*"And Mary said: My soul glorifies the Lord and my spirit rejoices in
God my Savior, for he has been mindful of the humble state of his
servant. From now on all generations will call me blessed..."*
(Luke 1:46-48)

There is something beautiful about responding to God in praise. Mary had been chosen to be Jesus' mother, and her response to that revelation is what is widely known as *Mary's Song of Praise*. Can you imagine how she felt?

Though there were plenty of other women God could have chosen, He chose a seemingly insignificant twelve year old. Logically speaking, Mary might not have been the best choice to parent the Son of God, but when you look at the way Mary responded to the news, you begin to see why God chose her.

She responded in praise and acknowledged that the tremendous gift she had been given had nothing to do with her own merit, but because God was gracious towards her. We should respond to God's involvement in our lives in the same way.

*"Be filled with the Spirit, speaking to one another in psalms
and hymns and spiritual songs, singing and making melody
in your heart to the Lord, giving thanks always for all things
to God the Father in the name of our Lord Jesus Christ."*
Eph. 5:18b-20, NASB

Choose to fill your heart with the word of God today. Let your mouth be filled with praises unto God, continually making melody openly and in your heart to God for all his goodness and wondrous works. Praise God!

Prayer

*Heavenly Father, your praise is continually in my mouth
and in my heart for all that you have done and all that
you will do. Thank you, Lord in Jesus' name. Amen.*
Further Studies: *Exodus 15:1-22*

Safe Heart

"Above all else, guard your heart, for everything you do flows from it."
(Proverbs 4:23)

The heart is the central organ of the human body. Without a properly functioning heart, the rest of the body cannot survive, because the heart is responsible for pumping blood to the other organs of the body. In the physical sense, it is essential to life.

The same could be said of the spiritual heart, which is the type of heart referred to in this passage: the very core of your being, the seat of your emotions and desires. Your heart in this sense also affects the rest of your body as it can determine the course of action your life will take.

The type of information you allow to penetrate your mind will determine your thoughts, your thoughts will determine your actions, and your actions will determine your life. That is why Proverbs 23:7 says, *"For as a man thinks in his heart, so is he."*

Just as you have a responsibility to keep your physical heart healthy, you are also cautioned to keep your spiritual heart healthy. Keep it in good condition by forgiving quickly, loving unconditionally, serving others, thinking positive thoughts, and expecting good things from God. Protect your heart and you will protect your life.

Prayer

Dear Father, I thank you for this unique counsel to protect my heart. Teach me to diligently guide my heart so that I can live a good life in Jesus' name. Amen.
Further Studies: *Proverbs 4:20-22*

All Times

"A friend loves at all times, and a brother is born for adversity."
(Proverbs 17:17)

There is no one better to fill your life with than friends and family. Family members are the ones that God has put directly in our lives. God created a special bond between family that is not easily broken. Whether we like it or not, we're stuck with them.

On the other hand, we choose our friends. God may put people in our path to encourage and edify us, but it is our choice who we want to spend our time with. When we make wise choices in friendships, we've got a relationship that will often stand the test of time.

This proverb notes the admirable qualities of both friends and brothers. The tricky thing about friends is that when you go through hard times, that person can leave you and find new friends. You're replaceable. But a true friend will love you at all times, regardless of if you're having a bad day and said something you shouldn't, or if you're going through something and want to be left alone.

It's a different situation in the case of family members though. You are irreplaceable to them because you are their blood. When you go through difficult times, in most cases they will rally beside you and support you as you go through it. The bonds of family have helped many a women survive the obstacles life has thrown at them.

Embrace and enjoy the benefits of friendship and family. You need them to get through life, and they need you to do the same.

Prayer

Dear Father, thank you for my friends and family members. Lord, teach me to love them unconditionally just as you have loved me, in Jesus' name. Amen.
Further Studies: *John 15:13*

Edification

"Let us therefore make every effort to do what leads to peace and to mutual edification."
(Romans 14:19)

Sharon and Betty have been friends for many years. They do not always agree on everything, but at least when they disagree, they aim to strike a balance by taking some time to cool down and pray together in order to make peaceful resolutions.

Does this sound like any of your relationships with your friends? For most of us, when we have disagreements, the first thing we want to do is slander, gossip, backbite, and react in anger. It's human nature.

That's why Paul says we have to make *every effort* to do the right thing; to achieve peace and mutual edification. The word effort connotes a sort of force. When those feelings begin to rise up within us, we have to force them back down and put off the old nature, which is rotten through and through, so that we can put on the nature of Christ; the nature of a peacemaker.

The enemy loves division, and he especially loves to see division between the members of the church, but as Paul tells us numerous times in his epistles, one of our utmost goals as believers should be to edify one another in love. Each and every day of our lives we are to draw from the strength of the Lord in those areas where we are weak, so that by the words of our mouth we can help strengthen the church.

Prayer

Dear Lord, I deliberately seek peace and the wellbeing of everyone in my world today as your world has instructed me to in Jesus' name. Amen.
Further Studies: *Matthew 5:9*

Together

"Therefore encourage one another and build each other up, just as in fact you are doing."
(1 Thessalonians 5:11)

L ife is easier to live when you are not living it alone. Two are always better than one. Just ask God. Those were His own words after observing Adam in the Garden of Eden all by his lonesome.

For us women, it is helpful to have at least one good girlfriend with whom we can be honest. Your husband may be your best friend and you may be able to tell him anything that you feel and think, but chances are that his approach to your emotional unloading will be to try and fix the problem.

Not only do women typically like to just talk about what's going on in their life, but we like to hear from our friends their similar stories and tidbits of advice and wisdom that they have gleaned from their own personal experiences.

When a missionary friend of mine moved to her new home in a country that she was unfamiliar with, she discovered firsthand how important it was for her to get connected with other missionaries and locals, because the stress of adjusting was just too much for her to handle on her own.

We need each other. That's why God created us to be a body of many parts that can't function otherwise. When life hurts, comfort one another, when life is tough, edify each other. Together does it.

Prayer

Dear Father, I thank you for placing people in my life that I can confide in and support as they support me. Bless our friendship in Jesus' name. Amen.
Further Studies: *Proverbs 27:17*

Perfect Unity

"And over all these virtues put on love, which binds them all together in perfect unity."
(Colossians 3:14)

As believers, we are called to demonstrate the fruit of the Spirit, but love is the binding agent, the glue that holds all of these Christian virtues together in perfect unity. Nothing else will.

In a cake, flour, sugar, baking powder, and spices are held together by the eggs, which is the binding agent. So too, chastity, temperance, charity, diligence, patience, kindness, humility are held together by love.

Think about it: if love, in the most basic sense, is a deep regard for the life of someone, it takes love to be kind to someone (even if they're not being kind to you). It takes love to be patient with people, and it takes love to be gentle. Before you can exercise any other virtue, you must first exercise love.

At the heart of every message Jesus spoke on earth was love. At the heart of every decision God made concerning the human race was love. At the heart of every decision we make, every interaction we have, every thought we think, and every word we speak should be love.

Instead of trying to force yourself to become more patient or more kind or more gentle, why not focus on learning to love, and the power of love will perfect the rest.

Prayer

Dear Father, I ask that you would teach me how to love as you do in Jesus' name. Amen.
Further Studies: *Hosea 11:4*

Filled

"Blessed are those who hunger and thirst for righteousness, for they will be filled."
(Matthew 5:6)

There are several beautiful graces in store for us as the children of God; the only way to receive them is by seeking them passionately. In our opening scripture, the Lord Jesus said that those who hunger and thirst after righteousness shall be filled. This means that when you crave the ability to live right, you will begin to see God's reign established in your life.

Have you seen how a hungry man devours food that is set before him? He's not timid, and ravenously he fills his stomach to his content and with great haste. David understood this hunger. He knew exactly how to seek God and how to function in the will of God for his life.

"As a deer pants for flowing streams, so pants my soul
for you, O God. My soul thirsts for God, for the living God.
When shall I come and appear before God?"
Psalm 42:1

Maybe you've studied the Bible, read it cover to cover and even attended Bible school. You have a goal in mind: you want all of God; you hunger and thirst for righteousness. But when you're overwhelmed with all of your responsibilities, how do you fit into all those roles and fulfill all those obligations? You find time for the things that matter, for the things that are of eternal value.

Do not be dismayed, you will be filled.

Prayer

Dear Lord, I thank you because my heart is set on you. I long
for your righteous government and peace every day and thank
you for filling me up in the name of Jesus. Amen.
Further Studies: Psalm 107:9

Things Above

"Set your minds on things above, not on earthly things."
(Colossians 3:2)

Paul urges the Colossians to live holy with eternity in view. We cannot afford to live as though life on earth is all there is. We are pilgrims on earth; we represent a greater kingdom and must live our lives by the principles of our kingdom if we have hopes to return home someday.

"But our citizenship is in heaven, and from it we await a Savior, the Lord
Jesus Christ, who will transform our lowly body to be like his glorious body,
by the power that enables him even to subject all things to himself."
Philippians 3:20-21 (ESV)

We must train our minds to think of heavenly things. It is easy and effortless to set our minds on the things that we can see and understand, rather than on things we can neither see nor understand.

"While we look not at the things which are seen, but at the
things which are not seen: for the things which are seen are
temporal; but the things which are not seen are eternal."
2 Corinthians 4:18

The Apostle Paul reminds us that it is to our benefit not to dwell on earthly things that are temporal, but on things above that are eternal. This is also helpful to get us through the pitfalls of life, cushioning the effects, making them bearable. When the dust is settled, and the race is over, when the curtain is drawn, only eternity will matter.

Prayer

Dear Father, I thank you for the hope I have in Christ Jesus. I live as a citizen of heaven here on earth, and I choose to live my life in hope of eternal glory in Jesus' name. Amen.
Further Studies: *Matthew 25:1-13*

Beware

"Then he said to them, 'Watch out! Be on your guard against all kinds of greed; life does not consist in an abundance of possessions.'"
(Luke 12:15)

Jennifer, a middle aged woman, looked out the window of her limousine. She was very wealthy. Whatever she desired, she bought; money was not an issue. She had worked hard to amass her wealth; however, she was not happy. She was lonely.

Living an enjoyable life here on earth is not wrong. In fact, we ought to live well, own the best houses, send our children to the best schools, work in the best offices and enjoy all the pleasures on earth, simply because *"the earth is the LORD's, and everything in it, the world, and all who live in it"* (Psalm 24:1).

But in the midst of all that, you must understand that life is beyond riches and fame. All you see is not all there is. Life is spiritual, and the spiritual controls the physical. There has never been a time on earth where a man's wealth was able to save him from eternal death. Our faith ought to be solely on God and not on the physical and material things that lose value with time.

Wealth and riches that are not founded on God will fail. Prosperity without salvation only leads to sorrow. God can give you all that you require in life, but you must trust in Him and not in material things.

Prayer

Dear Father, thank you for teaching me to set my priorities right. You are the giver of wealth, and my trust is in you in Jesus' name. Amen.
Further Studies: *Matthew 6:19-20*

Among the Wise

"Whoever heeds life-giving correction will be at home among the wise."
(Proverbs 15:31)

t is always easy to correct a child who listens to instruction. There are some people who will easily take rebuke if they are wrong, but there are some that will refuse to listen to you, even if they are headed for destruction.

Proverbs 15:13 tells us that a woman who listens and takes corrections will live among people who are wise. What makes one wise is his or her willingness to be corrected. If you are the type of person who receives instruction and brings it before the Lord instead of before your emotions, people will seek to guide you until you become knowledgeable and start minimizing your errors.

Gena doesn't say much these days, but she is a keen listener. She prefers to learn from the mistakes that other people have made rather than to learn by making them herself. She takes criticisms in stride. Many people think she is very wise because of the decisions she makes and by how she lives her life on a day to day basis.

She has learned that changes come by deliberate actions, and that one must deal with the advice given and not the feeling. Dwelling among the wise requires practice and diligence, dismissing feelings of hurt and shame, working at the advice that will change life, and implementing it.

Prayer

Dear Father, I value your wisdom that comes from above and acknowledge that sometimes I can gain wisdom from listening to instruction. Help me to humble myself so that I can hear what you desire to speak to me through others in Jesus' name. Amen.
Further Studies: *Proverbs 9:9*

Wisdom & Justice

"The mouth of the righteous utters wisdom, and his tongue speaks justice."
(Psalm 37:30)

If there was a king who was known to be wise, insightful, and always concerned about the wellbeing of his people, if he was respectful, genuine and just on everyone's behalf, and if he were to make a decree that the people didn't understand, his subjects would still be at peace, because they could rest in the assurance that whatever decision he made is in their best interest.

Likewise, we too should utter wisdom and speak justice to edify and build up those that we come in contact with. Wisdom and justice flow from a righteous woman such as you, and the world takes notice.

In your family, you have a priestly ministry as a wife and mother. If you store up God's word in your heart and meditate daily on His counsel, wisdom and sound judgment will naturally flow out of your mouth.

"For the lips of a priest ought to preserve knowledge,
because he is the messenger of the LORD Almighty
and people seek instruction from his mouth."
Malachi 2:7

People will seek to hear the truth from you when they need someone to tell it, and other women will seek your counsel on how to live their lives, because you have made God's word the standard for yours.

Prayer

Dear Father, I thank you for giving me wisdom. My mouth speaks your wisdom and sound judgment because my heart is stayed on your word in Jesus' name. Amen.
Further Studies: *Malachi 2:4-7*

From Above

"But the wisdom that comes from heaven is first of all pure; then peace-loving, considerate, submissive, full of mercy and good fruit, impartial and sincere."
(James 3:17)

Here, the Apostle James is giving a revelation of two types of wisdom and stating which is more profitable. The wisdom from above is that which is available to all Christians, and the wisdom of this world is based on the principles of this world.

Let's take a closer look at the apostle's comparison of the two types of wisdom:

"Who among you is wise and understanding? Let him show by his good behavior his deeds in the gentleness of wisdom. But if you have bitter jealousy and selfish ambition in your heart, do not be arrogant and so lie against the truth. This wisdom is not that which comes down from above, but is earthly, natural, Demonic. For where jealousy and selfish ambition exist, there is disorder and every evil thing. But the wisdom from above is first pure, then peaceable, gentle, reasonable, full of mercy and good fruits, unwavering, without hypocrisy."
James 3:13-17, NASB

The wisdom of this world will result in bitterness, strife and envy, because it is based on the flesh, which is rotten through and through. So how can one get the wisdom of God? God will give you wisdom and sound judgment, if you ask Him.

Prayer

Dear Father, I thank you for your wisdom that supersedes all the knowledge of man. Father, I ask that you grant me the wisdom that is from above in the name of Jesus. Amen.
Further Studies: James 1:5

First fruits

"Honor the LORD with your wealth, with the first fruits of all your crops."
(Proverbs 3:9)

Whether you are a believer with a lot of money or only a little, we are all called to honor God with our wealth. Rich and poor alike, we are all members of God's kingdom, and subject to the same principles.

Though the New Testament perspective of giving differs from the Old Testament perspective, the basic truth remains: give God your best. We see this demonstrated in the woman who gave her last two mites as well as in the description of the way the early church members supported one another financially.

In the Old Testament, first fruit was a term for the first harvest, or profit, received by the people. This could even include their firstborn. Giving of the first fruit was a way of symbolically dedicating everything back to God.

Of course a covenant is made by two parties coming to agreement on the terms, so God also has a role to play. When we honor Him with our wealth, He commits to provide for every need that we may have.

One pastor has shared his perspective on giving as such. "All that I have belongs to the Lord, so I freely dedicate it back to Him. He is the one who allows me to take a portion of my income to provide for my needs." What an awesome perspective to have when it comes to giving! Let it challenge you today as you consider your own wealth.

Prayer

Dear Father, I choose to honor you with my wealth today
by obeying your word in Jesus' name. Amen.
Further Studies: *Romans 11:16*

Gain

"For to me to live is Christ, and to die is gain."
(Philippians 1:21)

The Christian life extends far beyond our days on earth. We are here on earth to prepare for eternity. Eternity cannot be measured in terms of days or time. It is both timeless and dateless.

This is the revelation of the Apostle Paul; that is why he was not perturbed in the face of death. He knew that death for the Christian is gain. To die is to gain?

To die is to gain, from the perspective of a life in Christ who gives everlasting life. Both physical death and dying to one's self are gainful, as we decrease and Christ increases. When we are alive, we live for Christ, and when we die we will be in eternity with Him.

The words for today: live every day for Christ, exhibiting Godly qualities, making an impact. When death comes, think of it as a promotion, it is not the end, just the beginning. To die is GAIN!

Death itself will be defeated and we will receive eternal life from Christ who is our life. *"When Christ, who is our life, shall appear, then shall ye also appear with him in glory"* (Colossians 3:4).

Prayer

Father, thank you for I have eternal life in Christ. I am not afraid to lay down my life and worldly pleasures for you because I know that dying for you is great gain in Jesus' name. Amen.
Further Studies: *1 Corinthians 15:46-58*

Fame of the Humble

"Blessed are the meek, for they will inherit the earth."
(Matthew 5:5)

Oftentimes, when we try to imagine what meekness looks like, we envision someone who is shy, timid, and maybe even overly pious. But meekness does not mean that you intentionally portray a poor appearance or that you talk poorly about yourself. Instead, it is a lifestyle of putting others first.

Meekness was one of the ultimate traits of Jesus. Though He had the greatest position of authority, He chose to take on the frail nature of humanity and serve those that were created for His Father's glory. Day after day He demonstrated meekness by gently leading the disciples through seasons of questions, doubts, and discouragement. He even stooped so low as to wash their feet, an act that someone of His stature would never have done.

Society back then, and even today, would say that those in power should demonstrate their authority by lording it over those who are beneath them. There is a general assumption that those in high positions have the right to be harsh and authoritative. But Jesus came into this world to set a new precedent.

He set an example of meekness and then gave a special promise to those that followed suit. The inheritance of those who are meek is the earth. If we spend our lives actively serving others instead of trying to gain power by climbing on or over them and satisfying our own desires for attention or popularity, then we have that promise to claim as our own. That is the fame of the humble.

Prayer

Father, thank you for the example of meekness you gave me through your son, Jesus. Help me to imitate Him so that I can receive the fulfillment of your promise in Jesus' name. Amen.
Further Studies: *Philippians 2:5-11*

Praise, Honor, and Glory

*"So that the proof of your faith, being more precious than gold which
is perishable, even though tested by fire, may be found to result in
praise and glory and honor at the revelation of Jesus Christ."*
(1 Peter 1:7, NASB)

I f you are a believer, it is a given that multiple times throughout your walk with God you have undergone or will undergo some serious trials. That is the stark reality for every believer, since the Bible clearly tells us that every Christian's faith <u>must</u> be tested and tried. Although it may initially sound like one of the more unpleasant aspects of being a Christian, the truth is that the testing of our faith is one of the greatest advantages we have in our relationship with Christ.

Fire is the greatest determinant of how pure our faith is, because as it burns, it purifies. It searches for any impurity and purges it from deep within to bring forth pure gold. Everything we do, everything we say, and everything we are gets categorized into objects that either can or cannot endure the consuming fire of our Father. In order for God to reveal the true nature of our faith, we must go through the purifying fire of testing, and this is one test that we cannot afford to fail.

Being able to continually give praise, honor, and give glory to the Lord will require a great deal of sacrifice on our part, but take heart in the reward that is promised to the faithful. The greatest reward is that one day, when Jesus is revealed to the entire world as the true King, everyone is going to want to be on His side, but the King is only going to call those to stand by His side that stood with Him through thick and thin during their days on their earth. Will you be among that number?

Prayer

*Dear Father, thank you for the tests and trials you send my way and for the way you
challenge me to grow stronger in my faith and my reliance on you in Jesus' name. Amen.*
Further Studies: *1 Corinthians 3:12-13*

Problems with Perfectionism

"Be perfect, therefore, as your heavenly Father is perfect."
(Matthew 5:48)

Perfectionism has been an issue for women since the Garden of Eden. When we think of the word "perfect", we often think of our physical appearance, our accomplishments, or maybe even our performance in something, but when God commands us here in His Word to be perfect, He is speaking of the spiritual nature.

God is the only perfect being. That's why our scripture, and any other scripture that commands us to be holy, points to God as our standard of perfection. We must put on the image of Christ and daily be conformed to His likeness, if we want to be perfect.

When we put on the image and nature of Christ, God sees us through the righteousness of His Son. This certainly is encouraging! Instead of trying to be perfect by following a long list of rules and berating ourselves whenever we think that we don't measure up, all we have to do is rely on the nature of Jesus inside of us.

Through humility, repentance of sin, and a mind saturated in the Word of God, we become less and allow the perfect nature of Christ within us to become great. It's that simple! Trust that Christ in you is truly your hope of glory today and watch His righteousness shine through!

Prayer

Dear Father, I thank you for giving me your righteousness. I do not trust in my perfections or my abilities to do things right but I trust you, the God that justifies the ungodly in Jesus' name. Amen.
Further Studies: *Romans 8:29-30*

Looking for the Way Home

*"Jesus answered, I am the way and the truth and the life. No
one comes to the Father except through me."'*
(John 14:6)

I remember driving with my cousin after she first got her license. We were sleep deprived and only had an outdated road map to guide us, so it was no surprise when we accidently found ourselves one highway exit from Toledo, Ohio, when we were trying to get to Detroit, Michigan!

Sometimes we trust a faulty sense of intuition and an inappropriate guide to get us to heaven too. But Jesus assures us that there is only one way—through faith in Him. It may interest you to know that most of the religions of this world were established to find God, but Jesus remains the only way to God, and there is no other.

Man was created in the image of God. The very life that runs in our veins is the life of God, and our bodies are but dust. At death, the body returns to dust, while the soul and spirit go back home to the owner. In looking for our way home, we must first know where home is.

We belong to God and He is our home. Unless we get to know and acknowledge Him, there is no home for us. Jesus is not one of the ways to God. He is the only way. Affirm your faith in His Word and trust His death on the cross as the only acceptable payment for sin.

Prayer

*Dear Father, I thank you for life and showing me the way to you. I
thank you for revealing yourself to me and now I am sure that I can
return to you to spend eternity with you in Jesus' name. Amen.*
Further Studies: *John 15*

March

Works with Her Hands

*"She selects wool and flax and works with eager hands. She is
like the merchant ships, bringing her food from afar."*
(Proverbs 31:13-14)

There's a song called "Grandma's Hands," in which the singer Bill Withers reminisces about life as child and the way his grandmother used her hands to work hard, care for others, and even praise God.

Your hands and the way that you use them also have a great impact on those around you. The Proverbs 31 woman is described here as having eager hands with which she works.

She is not content to sit back and watch someone else take care of her family, but she is actively involved in making sure that all of their needs are met. Even if the work is tedious and tiresome, she is committed to doing what is necessary.

As a Proverbs 31 mother and wife, commit to using your hands to care for your family as well as to honor God.

Prayer

*Dear Father, thank you for giving me hands with which I can praise you by
working hard. I seek to honor you always with them in Jesus' name. Amen.*
Further Studies: *Colossians 3:23*

New Lifestyle

"Anyone who has been stealing must steal no longer, but must work, doing something useful with their own hands, that they may have something to share with those in need."
(Ephesians 4:28)

When you were a child, were you ever tempted to take something that didn't belong to you? Most of us probably were. Maybe your friend had the latest and greatest toy and you just had to have it, so when they weren't looking... You know how the story goes.

As adults, we may not steal in the same manner (going into someone's house and taking something that doesn't belong to us), but sometimes when we are responsible for funds that have been set aside for church or clubs or events, we may skim off the top or, in other cases, we may borrow from others with no intention of returning what we have borrowed. No matter what we try to tell ourselves, this is stealing.

Not only should we discontinue these methods of stealing because they're against God's law, but we should also stop stealing because God gives to us so that we can give to others. He blesses us so that we can be a blessing to others. When your first objective is to *take* something for yourself, you're breaking the first and greatest commandment to love your neighbor as much as you love yourself.

If you were stealing before now, you can receive forgiveness for your sins. Ask God to help you gain a new perspective. Success is looking out for a human need and meeting it. This is God's calling for our lives.

Prayer

Dear Father, I receive forgiveness for all my sins and the grace to start afresh. Thank you for opening my eyes to see new opportunities in Jesus' name. Amen.
Further Studies: *2 Thessalonians 3:10*

Wise or Foolish?

"Five of them were foolish and five were wise. The foolish ones took their lamps but did not take any oil with them. The wise ones, however, took oil in jars along with their lamps."
(Matthew 25:2-4, NASB)

Alexander Graham Bell quotes, "Before anything else, preparation is the key to success."

If you were taking your family on a vacation, there would be no way that you would leave the house without ensuring that you had first packed diapers, clothing, snacks, and anything else you might imagine you would need while on the trip. To do otherwise would put you in a bad spot later on down the line.

This is a basic principle that we understand within the realm of our daily activities and plans, but how many of us apply this principle to our spiritual lives? We know that spiritual disciplines, such as reading the Bible, praying, and making melody to the Lord are expected of us as believers, but we don't often view those spiritual disciplines as a form of preparation.

As a young Christian, I was taught that prayerful preparation prevents poor performance. Before you get into anything, prepare with prayer. When you pray, you are giving the Holy Spirit the opportunity to guide you. He will ensure that the rest of the details work out.

As a Christian woman, you already have access to the wisdom of God. Take advantage of this wisdom and ask for it, if you haven't done so already, so that you can deal wisely in the affairs of this life and bring glory to God.

Prayer

Dear Father, I choose today to always seek you first in every decision that I make in the name of Jesus. Amen.
Further Studies: *Matthew 25:1-13*

In The Light

*"Anyone who claims to be in the light but hates a
brother or sister is still in the darkness."*
(1 John 2:9)

A life in God means living your life in a spotlight. It can be likened to a declaration of purity and righteousness. Anyone who walks in the light is essentially telling the world that they are following the footsteps of Christ.

*"When Jesus spoke again to the people, he said, 'I am the
light of the world. Whoever follows me will never walk
in darkness, but will have the light of life.'"*
John 8:12

Walking in the light is working in and through the revelation of God's word. As Christians, the word of God lights our path, instructing and commanding us to love. If you work in love, then you are working in the Word of God; if you work in hatred, anger, bitterness and resentment, then you definitely do not know God, and you are still in darkness.

Jesus said, *"If you love me, keep my commands"* (John 14:15). You cannot love Jesus and not live by his word. The only proof that we are Christians is LOVE. *"By this everyone will know that you are my disciples, if you love one another"* (John 13:35).

If you do not obey the Master and walk according to His word (as a child of God would do), there is no eternal hope for you in the world to come. Father God will never manifest himself to you or show up on your behalf, because you do not love Him.

Prayer

*Dear Father, I thank you for teaching me to walk in your light.
Lord, I follow Jesus and I have the light of life. Because I do your
word, there is no darkness in my life in Jesus' name. Amen.*
Further Studies: *John 14:21*

Honest Earnings

"Dishonest money dwindles away, but he who gathers
money little by little makes it grow."
(Proverbs 13:11)

Have you ever wondered why some rich and influential people go bankrupt? Some of them became wealthy through dishonest means, and the Bible tells us that such money will always dwindle away. The little you earn and gather diligently grows as you save it.

If we're all being honest with ourselves, when it comes to gaining wealth, we all want to get rich quickly. Yes, we'll commit our lives to making an honest living by working a job that we may or may not enjoy, but if someone were to offer us an easier way out, 99.9% of us would undoubtedly take it.

The problem with getting money quickly, is that you typically have to cut corners somewhere, whether it's cheating someone, stealing from someone, or even compromising your standards. Quick money generally comes with quick problems.

Quick money also disappears just as quickly as it appears. When you don't have to work for something, you'll have a frivolous perspective about how to spend it. When you work for it, every dollar counts for an hour that you that you were working hard to achieve it.

We all want to provide for our families, and the Bible counsels us on how to do so. If you can be diligent with the little that you have been blessed with, God will reward your faithfulness.

Prayer

Father, I thank you for teaching me to be diligent and for blessing me with all that I have this day. I choose to handle all that you have entrusted to me in the name of Jesus. Amen.
Further Studies: *Proverbs 12:24*

Worry is a Sin

"Can any one of you by worrying add a single hour to your life?"
(Matthew 6:27)

There are several things that we are bound to worry about in this life, but worrying over things that are beyond your control is actually an effort in futility. Margaret Feinberg penned this quote, "Worry is a subtle way of telling God that He's fallen asleep at the wheel and that things aren't under His authority, but ours."

How dare we challenge God's control of the universe! Worry, anxiety, doubt, fear, and disbelief are the direct opposite of what a life in Christ is supposed to look like. Worry is like a rocking chair that keeps us moving but takes us nowhere; Christianity, on the other hand, is all about moving forward in faith.

The recipe for overcoming worry: Learn to trust God and all that He does and allows.

We can't change or control anything, but if we believe that God is faithful, powerful, and sovereign, then there is no reason to worry. We can stand on faith that no matter what comes our way, God is in control.

God cares for us genuinely, and He alone can handle those hard situations that may cause us to worry. Fear is faith in the ability of the enemy, it is the basic reason for worry, so stop trusting the enemy, and start trusting God.

Prayer

Dear Father, I thank you for teaching me to live a good life. I submit all my worries and anxieties to you today and choose to rest because you've got my back in Jesus' name. Amen.
Further Studies: *Philippians 4:6*

Do Good

"Therefore, as we have opportunity, let us do good to all people,
especially to those who belong to the family of believers."
(Galatians 6:10)

Doing charitable works and rendering help to those in need is one of our Christian responsibilities. God has raised you up so that through you others can be raised. God wants to touch the world around you, but He can only do it through you.

The Apostle Paul counsels us to take advantage of every opportunity we have to do good, especially when it comes to helping fellow Christians. Likewise, the Apostle James relates the purest form of religion with helping the poor and needy.

"Religion that God our Father accepts as pure and faultless
is this: to look after orphans and widows in their distress
and to keep oneself from being polluted by the world."
James 1:27

We all know people who are in need; we ourselves are also in need at different times in our lives. Needs are everywhere. Look along the street you live, throughout your community, in the church you attend, at the office where you work, or on your route to work.

There are opportunities everywhere to do good and to be of help to someone else. Remember that each time you give to the poor in obedience to the word of God, you are actually lending to the Lord (Proverbs 19:17), and rest assured that He will pay you back with interest in His own time and way.

Prayer

Dear Father, I thank you for the privilege and opportunity
to help those in need, in Jesus' name. Amen.
Further Studies: *Matthew 25:31-46*

Count the Cost

"Suppose one of you wants to build a tower. Won't you first sit down and estimate the cost to see if you have enough money to complete it?"
(Luke 14:28)

There is a story of a missionary who felt the call to travel to a foreign country and share the Good News of Jesus. The prospect of living a life fulfilling the Great Commission was very exhilarating, until the missionary came face to face with reality.

It didn't take long before he realized that he would have to sell all of his possessions, leave everyone he had ever known and loved, and settle amidst a people who would not be receptive, and maybe even at times volatile, towards the word of God. That missionary had a very long road ahead him.

It is practical to evaluate a situation before attempting to tackle it. Likewise, as followers of Christ, it is practical to count the cost of discipleship. Discipleship requires a commitment to the call, dying to self, and putting Christ first. When weighed on the scale against the reward, which is eternal life in Christ, it is a small price to pay.

Each person must count the cost and answer the call. Following Christ is actually the best life that we will ever have because a relationship with Jesus is worth the cost to follow Him. Our reward will be given to us in a place where no rust and no thief can touch it.

Prayer

Dear Father, I willingly give up everything that I hold dear, because I know that you are all that I will ever need and you are all that I need to be what I will be in Jesus' name. Amen.
Further Studies: *Mark 8:34-38, Matthew 27:27-30*

Abounding Love

*"I pray that your love will overflow more and more, and that you
will keep on growing in knowledge and understanding."*
(Philippians 1:9, NLT)

A common analogy that believers use, when referring to our relationship to the Holy Spirit, is that of a glass being filled with water. We often pray and ask God to fill us up, but what we don't realize is that when we simply seek to be filled, we are only getting enough to satisfy our needs.

In this scripture the Apostle Paul prays instead that we would be filled to overflowing. Why? Because it's from the increase that we are able to give love to others. It is when we are abounding in love that we can serve others.

Logically speaking, if we fill our cup and then pour it out, we leave ourselves at a deficit. This explains why we can sometimes serve others and still find ourselves becoming angry, cranky, or rude. Our cup needs a refill.

Now, when your cup is overflowing and you give to other from the amount that runs over, you are able to stay full while you help other people to get full. That should be our goal!

As the scripture says, the most important thing we can do to increase our love to that point is to increase our knowledge and understanding of God and His love. The more we understand about the way His love works, the greater our capacity will be to receive and give love.

Prayer

*Dear Father, I lift my cup to you to fill it up in overflowing. Thank you for
more of you and more knowledge of your love in Jesus' name. Amen.*
Further Studies: *1 Peter 4:8*

Labor of Love

"God is not unjust; he will not forget your work and the love you have shown him as you have helped his people and continue to help them."
(Hebrews 6:10)

Any action you take to ensure the comfort of others is recorded in your heavenly account. That day you gave your transport or lunch money to that beggar or colleague and inconvenienced yourself for their comfort, God was there, and He saw it all. He knew exactly what the $5 meant to you at that time.

God is always watching. Unrighteousness and forgetfulness are not attributes that can be ascribed to God; He is very faithful to reward you and pay you back in His own good time. Just as He can orchestrate you to be a blessing to someone at the perfect time, so can He orchestrate a blessing to return to you at the perfect time.

Laboring for God and ministry catches His attention and moves His compassion. A labor of love in God's name to the saints could simply be a prayer for a missionary overseas or it could be as technical as becoming a missionary to a foreign country. The fact that you do it, is what matters, and He remembers.

You can pray, you can give for missions abroad, you can help the needy around you, or you can give for a church building project. Just keep your eyes open to see those that need your help, and do something that will count in eternity.

Prayer

Dear Father, thank you for teaching me to be a relevant member of the body of Christ in Jesus' name. Amen.
Further Studies: *Philippians 4:15-19, Matthew 25:31-46*

Prosperity

"But his delight is in the law of the LORD, and in His law he meditates day and night. He will be like a tree firmly planted by streams of water, which yields its fruit in its season and its leaf does not wither; and in whatever he does, he prospers."
(Psalm 1:2-3, NASB)

I n this psalm the Lord reveals to us a very profound revelation. Delighting and meditating on the Word of God is the secret to spiritual prosperity. Spiritual prosperity and success come by the principles revealed in His word, and this is one of such principles.

> *"Keep this Book of the Law always on your lips; meditate on it day and night, so that you may be careful to do everything written in it. Then you will be prosperous and successful."*
> *Joshua 1:8*

You've watched sisters in the women's ministry work diligently at serving and living by the principles of God's word. As you may remember, it was their actions that propelled and influenced you to join the ministry. You too have embraced the same principles and service etiquette which has borne fruit for every person.

Spiritual prosperity is the reward of meditating on God's word. Good success is the result of meditation on the word of God. Do not only practice God's word, but teach others to do the same. By that action you are spreading godly counsel and helping others succeed.

Prayer

Dear Father, I thank you because I know how to succeed and make progress. Your word produces in me the result of what it talks about in Jesus' name. Amen.
Further Studies: *Matthew 7:24-25*

The Greatest of These

"And now these three remain: faith, hope and love. But the greatest of these is love."
(1 Corinthians 13:13)

Paul states here that faith, hope and charity (love) will be with us forever, though eternity. The love expressed in 1 Corinthians 13 is no mediocre kind of love; it is rooted and stems out of God's pure and perfect love.

Have you ever wondered why the Bible tells us that our God is a jealous God, yet we are commanded not to be jealous? Well, it's because God is... well, God. He is not tainted by the stains of sin like we are, so when He is jealous, there are no wicked intentions behind His jealousy.

Likewise, God's love is spiritual, not carnal. That is why we need to rely on the love of God in us to help us love others. We will not be successful at expressing love except through the Spirit of God. Trying to truly love others solely out of our flesh just simply will not work.

God is love, so when we allow His Holy Spirit to come and fill our hearts, we are essentially allowing love to fill our hearts. Therefore, love should be the greatest testimony of Jesus in our lives. As believers, it should flow from the way we walk, the way we talk, and the way we carry ourselves.

What is your life telling others about the love of Christ?

Prayer

Dear Father, thank you for filling me with your love. Help me to pour out your love to everyone that I come in contact with in Jesus' name. Amen.
Further Studies: *1 John 4:19*

Blessed

"Blessed is the one who does not walk in step with the wicked or stand in the way that sinners take or sit in the company of mockers..."
(Psalm 1:1)

Which do you want? Blessing or curse? The first chapter of Psalms goes on to tell us the fate of those who choose unrighteousness over righteousness.

"That person is like a tree planted by streams of water, which yields its fruit in season and whose leaf does not wither—whatever they do prospers. Not so the wicked! They are like chaff that the wind blows away. Therefore the wicked will not stand in the judgment, nor sinners in the assembly of the righteous."
Psalm 1: 3-5

As the verses prior to this one state, to be called blessed, you must avoid that which is evil. Evil works, evil company, evil deeds, and evil speech must all be shunned. Though none of us are completely righteous, God is looking for those who pursue righteous living for the sake of His name. Those are the ones He will lift up.

Yes, we may live in the world, but we are called to live our lives in a totally different manner. Living under the blessings of God demands a different lifestyle. Do not be pressured by the way of the world which wages war against the way of God. Walk the righteous path and be called blessed to the honor and glory of your Father above.

Prayer

Dear Father, walking the path of the righteous isn't always easy. Help me to live worthy of your blessing, that you may call me righteous in the end. In Jesus' name. Amen.
Further Studies: *Psalm 1*

God's Handiwork

"The heavens declare the glory of God; the skies proclaim the work of his hands."
(Psalms 19:1)

When you look up at the sky, it is impossible to believe in the depths of your heart and soul that an earth such as ours, created in such perfect order and with such immense beauty, could have been made without a Supreme Being, a Creator.

Seasons follow the proper order generation after generation, the oceans and the seas maintain their boundaries, and animals thrive within their habitats. This whole marvelous thing can only have been performed by intelligent being; it can only have been done by God.

We have heard of the ozone layer depleting and temperature changes in different climatic conditions. These are all results of man's actions, but we have never seen the earth stop rotating. We have never seen a day without clouds in the sky or clean air to breathe. Everything around us testifies to the greatness of God and His ability to sustain and provide for us.

That is God's handiwork! He created everything everywhere; those that have already been discovered and those yet to be revealed. All things declare God's glory just by existing; flowing, glowing, growing, moving, reproducing, and breathing. The heavens declare the glory of God and the firmament shows His handiwork.

Prayer

Dear Father, thank you for being such an awesome creator. I am awed and humbled by the works of your hands. Thanks for being my father in Jesus' name. Amen.
Further Studies: *Romans 1:20*

Not By Works

"He saved us, not because of righteous things we had done, but because of his mercy.
He saved us through the washing of rebirth and renewal by the Holy Spirit."
(Titus 3:5)

I struggled with sin when I was growing up, because I thought I would only attain righteousness by my works. Each time we would go for confession, the priest told us to say some prayers or do some things as our penance for the sins we committed.

When I started reading the Bible, I discovered that Jesus had died in my place and gave me righteousness, which I couldn't have attained even if I were to die for my own sins. There is nothing like justification by works, and if we cannot be justified by our works then we cannot be righteous by them either.

"For by grace you have been saved through faith; and that not of yourselves,
it is the gift of God; not as a result of works, so that no one may boast."
Ephesians 2:8-9

No matter how good you are, how hard you work, or how "righteous" you are, you must accept Christ as Lord and Savior. It is not by works of righteousness that salvation comes. You are saved according to His mercy, so stop wearing yourself out trying to be righteous, because that's not how you get acceptance from God.

Accepting Him by faith and yielding to the Holy Spirit is how the journey starts; simple and uncomplicated. Rest in the assurance that God's mercy supersedes "works of righteousness."

Prayer

Dear Father, I thank you for giving me the righteousness of Jesus in the place of my sins.
Further Studies: *Romans 4, 2 Corinthians 5:21*

Ask, Seek, Knock

"Ask and it will be given to you; seek and you will find;
knock and the door will be opened to you."
(Matthew 7:7)

One of the fascinating things about the Bible is God's promise to always answer our cries. Each time I think about the vast number of people that depend on our God for survival, I marvel at His greatness and bow to His majesty.

God promises to always answer any day, at any time we call on Him. He even promised to act swiftly when we are in trouble or danger. Knowing that God always answers should give you comfort and peace, even in the midst of turbulence.

God's promise should give you faith and courage to ask, just like a child is relentless and fearless in pursuit of what he or she wants. Children will ask for what they want without processing the claim beforehand. They just ask!

In our opening scripture, Jesus tells us to ask, seek, and knock for the things we desire. It's common sense really, but our adult minds sometimes rationalize everything, and before we know it, we chicken out and keep silent.

Today, we will let common sense prevail; we will ask to get, seek to find, and knock for the door to be opened for us. We should just simply trust God and take Him at His word. If He says we should ask, seek, and knock, let us simply do so with faith knowing that He is faithful to a thousand generations.

Prayer

Dear Father, thank you for your word. I believe your word and act in
accordance, knowing that your word will never fail in Jesus' name. Amen.
Further Studies: *Psalm 50:15*

Diligent

"A sluggard's appetite is never filled, but the desires of the diligent are fully satisfied."
(Proverbs 13:4)

Diligence is steadfast application, assiduousness and industry; the virtue of hard work. It is a heavenly virtue. This is one of the qualities that puts us over in life and guess what; there is great gain when you are diligent.

We all want our children to become all that God has dreamed for them. Well, when God entrusts them into our care, we have the responsibility to train them up in the way they should go. The woman that takes her responsibilities as a mother and a wife seriously will see the fruit of her diligence.

Children have a lot of energy and they require the same from us as parents. It can sometimes be easy to become sluggish with handling them, and to let the television babysit them or to leave them to amuse themselves in a room very far away from us, but that is not what God has called us to do!

Do not go about your business with a slack hand. Wishful thinking and dreaming will not get your desires met. You must be willing to work and keep working to reap the benefits. If you want to see your children grow to honor the Lord, teach them how to honor the Lord through your own lifestyle and the way that you instruct them.

Prayer

*Dear Father, thank you for teaching me what to do as I prepare
my children for the future in Jesus' name. Amen.*
Further Studies: *Proverbs 22:29*

Meaningless

"Whoever loves money never has money enough; whoever loves wealth is never satisfied with his income. This too is meaningless."
(Ecclesiastes 5:10)

These words came from the lips of the richest man who ever lived. You must understand that Solomon was rich beyond our present day evaluation. Here is a glimpse of how rich this man was:

"All King Solomon's cups were gold, and all the utensils for the hall [which he called] the Forest of Lebanon were fine gold. (Nothing was silver, because it wasn't considered valuable in Solomon's time.)"
1 Kings 10:21 (GWT)

Although King Solomon possessed much of the world's wealth in his treasury, in his wisdom he understood that the pursuit of wealth itself was meaningless. In all actuality, you can replace the world wealth in this statement with any earthly possession that may distract us from our relationship with Jesus.

Anything that we love enough to put our time, money, and affection behind becomes a rival to the attention we should be giving God, therefore it is an idol. Money is one of the most common idols for us, which is probably why King Solomon highlighted it in this verse. It is important we search our hearts to see if we have been chasing after meaningless things.

Prayer

Dear Father, my hope is built on nothing else but Jesus' love and righteousness. I dare not trust the sweetest frame but I wholly lean on Jesus name. Glory to God!
Further Studies: *1 Timothy 6:17*

Give Thought

"The wisdom of the prudent is to give thought to their
ways, but the folly of fools is deception."
(Proverbs 14:8)

Wisdom is a gift that God delights in giving to His children who ask for it. This wisdom is a force that pilots your life, guiding you to make the right decisions even with little or no facts to guide you.

When I was 19, I was offered a job managing a friend's company. He wanted me as an employee because he knew that I was a very committed and a sincere Christian. There was a family friend who was really pressing me to take the job.

I remember telling them to give me time to pray about it, because at that time I still wanted to further my education, but was also really in need of money. Still, they kept pressuring me, so I prayed, and God led me to choose my education over the job.

The next few months were very terrible for me. I almost dropped out of school because of financial constraints, but guess what? A few months later, I visited the family that had been pressuring me, and they told me that the business had gone bankrupt. The man that had been employed in my place was in debt, and he had been arrested and charged for bad management.

If I had not allowed God to guide my thoughts and give me wisdom to make that decision, I would have started out my adult life in debt. God is always talking, and if you listen, you will hear Him. Never make any decision without consulting with your heavenly father.

Prayer

Dear Father, thank you for filling my heart with your wisdom
to think right and act right in Jesus' name. Amen.
Further Studies: *Isaiah 30:21*

Not "Whatever Works"

"Simon answered, 'Master, we've worked hard all night and haven't caught anything. But because you say so, I will let down the nets.'"
(Luke 5:5)

Many frustrated mothers have commented that biblical parenting just does not work with their children. Try as they may, they feel like it bears no fruit. Even though they have diligently taught their children biblical principles and involved them in the church, their children still rebel against God and cause the parents such grief and heartache.

Take a moment to reflect on the stories of people in the Bible such as Jonah, who tried to run away from God's calling but eventually returned to Him. Think about Peter and how his denial of Jesus could have been the end, but God redeemed his story and made him into a founding father of the church. Think about your story. Have you always walked with God? Was there ever a point in your life when God had to chase you down?

We all fall short of the glory of God, and like sheep go astray, but if we have a solid foundation in Christ, we always have something to return to. You may not be able to see the initial fruit of your labor in your child's spiritual life, but who plants a seed and then immediately finds a sprout? It takes time for plants to mature and develop, and it will take time for your children to do the same.

Jesus calls us to keep letting down our nets, to keep laboring His way, even if it seems like it does no good. God will bring the fruit; all He asks of us is to obey.

Prayer

Dear Father, thank you for never giving up on me when it takes me a while to learn spiritual lessons in life. Help me to not give up on my children either in Jesus' name. Amen.
Further Studies: *Proverbs 22:6*

Imitators of the Faith

"We do not want you to become lazy, but to imitate those who through faith and patience inherit what has been promised."
(Hebrews 6:12)

When you were growing up, did you have a role model? If she dressed a certain way, did you buy the same clothes? If she displayed unique mannerisms when she spoke, did you channel those traits when you spoke? If she had a deep life in God, did you feel compelled to spend more time with God yourself? One of the natural results of finding someone you look up to, is that you inherently begin to pick up on their behaviors.

There are quite a number of people listed throughout the Bible that have demonstrated what it means to live a life of faith. Their accounts offer much inspiration for our lives. Now, as the great cloud of witnesses surrounding the throne, let them spur you on in your faith.

This verse speaks of the need for Christians to be followers of those with a legacy of faith. So it is beneficial for us to find the most Christ-like people we know and learn from them. Ask them questions about their walk with God or about what is happening in your life. Gain wisdom and understanding from them. Imitate them as they imitate Christ.

For busy wives and mothers, this may seem like a difficult commitment. God is aware of this—that's why He says it will only be done "through faith and patience". It will be a labor of love well worth it, when we become joint-heirs of God's promises.

Prayer

Dear Father, thank You for sending your son to this earth to demonstrate what holiness looks like fleshed out. And thank you for those in my life that give me a great spiritual example to follow in Jesus' name. Amen.
Further Studies: *Hebrews 11*

Loving your Enemies

"But love your enemies, do good to them, and lend to them without expecting to get anything back. Then your reward will be great, and you will be children of the Most High, because he is kind to the ungrateful and wicked".
(Luke 6:35)

When many of us reflect on our days in school, we vividly remember which students were known as the bullies. Maybe you were bullied, maybe you were forced to watch others be bullied, or maybe you were even the bully yourself (I'm sure you've repented and turned over a new leaf). Regardless of which end of the spectrum you were on, we all can agree that bullies were the least-liked people on the playground.

We all have enemies in one sense or another. They vary in severity, but generally speaking, they can make our lives miserable. Their behavior can make it so difficult to persist in kindness, because the minute you decide to do the right thing, the person will do something to hurt you or make you angry all over again.

Yet, Jesus tells us that it's easy to love those that are lovely, but the kind of love He wants us to demonstrate loves even if we're being slapped in the face. That request might seem totally unreasonable, but stop for a second and remember what Jesus endured when He was on this earth.

If you have someone in your life that you're finding very difficult to love, remember Jesus. Remember the sacrifice He made to give you life, even though He knew how many times you would reject His gift. Let the example of Christ spur you on in your own life to love others as Christ has loved you.

Prayer

Dear Father, thank you for loving me even when I was your enemy. Please teach me how to extend the same love to my enemies in Jesus' name. Amen.
Further Studies: *Luke 6:27-36*

Have You?

"I have fought the good fight, I have finished the race, I have kept the faith."
(2 Timothy 4:7)

According to Jesus, not many people will be able to say this in the end. As you know, this Christian walk is not easy. There are lots of ups and downs and twists and turns. It will take a lot of perseverance and stamina in order to answer yes to all of the questions listed above.

As daunting as that may seem, be encouraged. This race is not won by the person who runs the fastest or hardest; all you have to do is endure. Keep going and keep trusting that it's not your strength you have to rely on, but God's. If you can maintain that mindset, you don't have to struggle so much in your own strength. You can just lean back and let the flow of the Holy Spirit carry you to your final destination.

This race is won on a day by day basis. Each day that you wake up, you renew your commitment to Christ and press on. God will show you how to live your life that day in a way that honors Him, all you have to do is follow His leading.

Fight the good fight: rely on the Spirit of God to help you overcome the wiles of the enemy and the temptations of this world.
Finish the race: allow the Lord to gird up your legs so that they don't give out on you as you run with perseverance and determination.
Keep the faith: without faith you have nothing; faith is the means by which you hold onto God's hand. Never lose your faith.

Put up a good fight and keep the faith as you move towards the finish line, and while you're at it hold someone else's hand to help them along the way. Together you'll make it.

Prayer

Dear Father, please strengthen me to complete this journey in Jesus' name. Amen.
Further Studies: *Ecclesiastes 9:11*

Word and Deed

"So whether you eat or drink or whatever you do, do it all for the glory of God."
(1 Corinthians 10:31)

I n this scripture, the Apostle Paul implores the Christians of Corinth to live in such a way that everything they do glorifies God. This is also the admonition of the Spirit to us today.

We are representatives of Christ on earth. Therefore, we must be careful of how we walk and talk, as the only gospel our friends might know is the gospel according to the standard we set by the way we live our lives. Your life is an open book, and whether you realize it or not, people are reading your pages.

> *"In the same way, let your light shine before others, that they may see your good deeds and glorify your Father in heaven."*
> *Matthew 5:16*

As a Christian, you represent Christ, and therefore, your words and deeds should represent His character and nature. To be a Christian literally meant to the early church to be a "mini-Christ." Does that definition describe your current lifestyle?

Our lives and conduct should be such that glorifies God, that brings people close to God, and that will cause the people of this world to believe in the gospel of Jesus Christ. Represent Him well.

Prayer

Dear Father, I thank you for making me a light in this dark world. As I live every day for you, my life is causing others around me to come to Jesus. Thank you, Lord.
Further Studies: *Timothy 3:10-17*

Working For God

"Whatever you do, work at it with all your heart, as working for the Lord, not for men,"
(Colossians 3:23)

The section of Colossians where the apostle Paul gives this counsel is titled: *Character of the Christian Life*. This verse contains an important rule for holy living and an encouragement for us to adopt a shift in perspective.

Let's take working a job that you basically loathe, for example. Now, most of us would feel totally justified to treat customers or co-workers or even employers poorly if they treat us poorly, and maybe we wouldn't put our best effort forward when it comes to doing the job to the best of our abilities, but that's because we're maintaining a horizontal perspective.

We're looking at people, but we should be looking at God. Everything we do, in whatever sphere of influence, is all supposed to be done to the glory of our Father in heaven. The way we live is the way we worship. If you want your lifestyle to count as worship, shift your perspective upwards.

Even if others laugh at you, scorn you, scoff at you, or call you an idiot, you must keep doing the right thing. Show up for work on time after you've been up all night with a sick child, prepare your husband's meals even though he's having an affair, and clock in your normal volunteer hours although you are not recognized for what you do. It hurts sometimes, but keep working for God regardless of what men say or do. He is your rewarder, and like Sarah said, God will cause you to laugh, and all those that laughed at you will laugh with you.

Prayer

*Father, I am a diligent woman and I discharge all my duties knowing
that you always reward a diligent woman in Jesus' name. Amen.*
Further Studies: *Proverbs 22:29*

Co-Workers With Christ

"The one who plants and the one who waters have one purpose, and they will each be rewarded according to their own labor. For we are co-workers in God's service; you are God's field, God's building."
(1 Corinthians 3:8-9)

We have had our children in our home and under our care for at least eighteen years. During those eighteen years we go through many ups and downs with them, spend countless hours in prayer for them, and pour as much truth into their foundation as we possibly can.

Some parents get to sow into their children and see the reward of their child coming to know Christ right away, while others sow and sow into their children but are forced to watch their kids walk down the wrong path. Parents in those situations cannot help but to feel as though they've failed their children somehow.

But I want to share some good news with you. If you are fulfilling your role as one who plants the seed of God's Word into your children, God will reward you accordingly. He may allow you to be part of the harvesting of the seed, or He may send someone else to water the seeds that you planted, but that's His prerogative. He ultimately is your child's savior, not you or anyone else, so He can use whatever or whomever He desires.

If you have children that have yet to know Christ, keep sowing. One day the Lord will bring them into the harvest.

Prayer

Dear Father, show me how I can partner with you to plant and water seeds in my children and in those around me in Jesus' name. Amen.
Further Studies: *John 4:37*

Working for Grace?

"Come to me, all you who are weary and burdened, and I will give you rest."
(Matthew 11:28)

The heart of our Father God is tender, loving and kind. He is gracious to all, especially the weary. Those who come to Him wearied, burdened, and tired of running, He promises to give rest. This promise doesn't exist simply because He is merely capable of giving us rest, but because He *desires* to give us rest.

Imagine you come home to find your child crying over something that happened at school. How would you respond? As much as you hate to see your children suffering emotionally, God cannot bear to see His children suffer. He wants nothing more than to gather us under his wings like a mother hen to protect us from danger.

For women especially, it can be difficult to allow God to take on our burdens. God gave women unique discernment and creativity to deal with problems, but we sometimes put our trust in our own efforts rather than in Christ's authority over all. Regardless of how gifted we may be at solving problems, our own efforts will never produce the rest we desire. Think of all the striving we have to do in order to get rest. It leaves us more tired in the end than we would have been if we had given the problem to the Lord in the beginning.

Have you ever needed something from someone but were afraid to ask them because you felt you might be a burden to them? We never have to feel that way with God. He is ready and willing to deal with our pain, our fears, and our doubts. All that He is waiting for is for you to come to Him. If you are weary and burdened, Christ will give you rest.

Prayer

*Dear Father, I come to you today and cast my cares
upon you. Thank you for caring for me.*
Further Studies: *1 Peter 5:7*

He has the Authority to Forgive

"But I want you to know that the Son of Man has authority on earth to forgive sins."
So he said to the paralyzed man, "I tell you, get up, take your mat and go home."
(Luke 5:24)

One summer Johnny and Sally went to visit their grandmother. She had a pet duck that she loved very much. One day Johnny was playing with his slingshot outside, and he accidentally shot his grandmother's pet duck and killed it. In shock, he hurriedly buried it in the woods.

That evening Sally approached Johnny and demanded that he do her chores. Johnny tried to get out of it, but then Sally blackmailed him. "I saw what you did to Grandma's duck, and I'll tell if you don't do it." Fear crept into Johnny's heart, and he lowered his head and obliged.

For weeks Sally tormented Johnny by forcing him to do her bidding. It didn't take long before Johnny got so frustrated that he felt anything his grandmother would do to punish him would be better than what his sister was doing to him. So one evening he mustered up the courage to tell his grandmother what happened. With tears in her eyes, she listened before reaching out to grab his shoulders. "Johnny," she said. "I saw you shoot the duck. I knew from the beginning. I was wondering how long you were going to let Sally torture you before you came to me."

So often we find ourselves in the same position as Johnny. When we sin, instead of bringing it to the one who is able to forgive us and totally wash us clean of our wrongdoing, we allow the enemy to torment and condemn us. This should not be true of a follower of Christ. Choose this day to confess your sins and allow Jesus to forgive you.

Prayer

Dear Father, I submit to you today and receive your forgiveness in Jesus' name. Amen.
Further Studies: *Luke 7:48*

God Answers

"When I called, you answered me; you greatly emboldened me."
(Psalm 138:3)

Megan had so many questions: "Why did my parents die?" "What is the purpose of my life?" "When will the struggles end?" "Who is responsible for this mess?" "Where will help come from?"

Like Megan we all have questions that we need answers for, and it's only God who will give us answers that will suffice. We can search online or go to our most trusted friends and advisors, but why seek out the middle man when you can just go directly to the source?

The awesome thing about going to God with our questions is that when He answers us, His answers increase our faith, build our trust, and embolden us to continue on our journey. It's similar to the way a child falls and scrapes his knee. When he brings his "boo boo" to his mother to kiss it, her simple kiss is just what the child needs to feel like everything will be okay, and then the next thing you know, he's off and running again!

Wherever you are and whatever situation you find yourself in today, call out to your Father. He'll not only answer you, but His loving response will increase your courageousness, so that you can remain steadfast as you go through the obstacles and turns of life. He'll cause you to triumph.

Call to Him today and every day. He'll answer.

Prayer

Dear Father, you hold every answer to any question I could ask in the palm of your hand. Help me to come to you first whenever I have questions in Jesus' name. Amen.
Further Studies: *James 4:3*

Not Yours to Have

"You shall not steal."
(Exodus 20:15)

Without realizing it, we often look at this commandment as a rule of thumb for children. You may remember that first time you left the store and discovered something in your child's possession that you had not bought. We typically teach the lesson of stealing in that moment, and unless they struggle with it again, we don't revisit it.

But stealing is not just taking something that doesn't belong to you; it is also taking something that wasn't meant for you. This can include another person's attention, a relationship, and we even steal glory from God.

Every single day of our lives, God is working behind the scenes to bring everything together for our good. During those times we often operate in pride, believing that what we've done or what we have is the result of our own strength. It can be so easy to forget that God is in control, as we begin taking the credit for ourselves.

Remember that everything in the earth is the Lord's and the fullness thereof. Everything that occurs is because He allows it or wills it. Nothing happens outside of Him. Even the achievements we make in life are not because of our strengths or talents, they were made possible because the One who gave us the talent and strength in the first place.

Consider areas in your life where you might be gaining things that are not yours to have; reconcile them and resolve to live by this command.

Prayer

Dear Father, forgive me for the areas in my life where I have stolen anything from you or anyone else in life in Jesus' name. Amen.
Further Studies: *Isaiah 42:8*

Fruitful and Multiplying

"But the fruit of the Spirit is love, joy, peace, patience, kindness, goodness, faithfulness, gentleness, self-control; against such things there is no law."
(Galatians 5:22-23)

The Bible tells us that Christians and non-Christians alike will know what kind of person we are by the type of fruit we produce. *"Every good tree bears good fruit, but the bad tree bears bad fruit. A good tree cannot produce bad fruit, nor can a bad tree produce good fruit. Every tree that does not bear good fruit is cut down and thrown into the fire. So then, you will know them by their fruits."* (Matthew 7:17-20)

When the Spirit is truly present in our lives, it should be evident. The most prominent evidence of the Spirit's involvement in your life is through the ninefold fruit of the Spirit.

Love	the act of sacrifice, service, and submission
Joy	peaceful confidence in God, despite trials and difficult circumstances
Peace	commitment to resolutions of conflict, despite differences
Longsuffering	persevering without resentment
Gentleness	communicating with mercy and humility, verbally and non-verbally
Goodness	strong moral character
Faith	hope with assurance
Meekness	humility before God and others
Temperance	restrictions and convictions that are maintained without wavering

Can you recognize God's presence in your life through the fruit of the Spirit?

Prayer

Dear Father, thank you for giving me access to your Spirit and for pruning my heart so that I can produce the fruit of the Spirit in Jesus' name. Amen.
Further Studies: *John 15:1-8*

April

Provides for Her Family

"She gets up while it is still night; she provides food for her family."
(Proverbs 31:15)

A mother's job is one of the hardest jobs on the planet. There are expectations to be dealt with from your spouse, your children, and even from your relatives. One of the biggest expectations is that you are always able set food on the table.

When a guy first starts dating a girl, one of the first things he looks at is how well she can cook. They don't say that the way to a man's heart is through is stomach for nothing!

This can be seen as a duty, especially on the days when you have to get up very early or stay up very late in order to prepare lunches for your kids, or meals for visiting friends and family members, but cooking for your family is truly a labor of love.

View your late night acts of service to your family as an act of service to God, and know how much honor you bring to them both as you make the sacrifice of serving.

Prayer

Dear Father, on those days when I find it hard to serve my family, please give me strength and help me to remember that I'm serving both you and them in Jesus name. Amen.
Further Studies: *Matthew 25:40*

Seek First

"But seek ye first the kingdom of God, and his righteousness;
and all these things shall be added unto you."
(Matthew 6:33, KJV)

"What is the Kingdom of God?" you may ask. The kingdom of God referred to in this scripture is not a **geographical location**, but **a government, a system; a way of life.**

The Kingdom of God is the reign of God, the government of God, a system of life that is centered on God and His principles. Jesus said that if we seek God and His system of life, the daily provisions that we need in this life will be ours now and for all eternity.

I once heard a story of how an elderly woman preached the gospel to a younger woman with this scripture, and the young woman's response was, *"Ma, you have enjoyed your life. You are old now, so you can seek the Kingdom of God because you may be joining him soon, but for me, I am still young. I need to enjoy myself first, pursue my career and do other things. When I am old, I will seek God."*

This young woman was completely ignorant of the truth. If you serve God with your life from a young age, He will give you rest and help you accomplish His great plans for your life. Real success, fame, wealth and life is in Christ—not in the shallow substitutes that our world offers. There is fullness of joy and pleasure for evermore in His presence.

Prayer

Dear Father, I thank you for opening my eyes to see that real life and pleasure is in your kingdom. I set my heart on you today, to seek your kingdom and your reign on earth in Jesus' name. Amen
Further Studies: *Psalm 16:11, Isaiah 48:17*

A Room for You

"In my Father's house are many rooms; if it were not so, I would have told you. I am going there to prepare a place for you."
(John 14:2)

Because of the peculiarity of our ministry as mothers and wives, we find ourselves working, sometimes all day, to keep the family together. Our day can be very hectic and stressful. Some days, we don't get to do anything for ourselves.

Sometimes you may feel like just giving up because of the workload. Some of us even had to give up our dreams of pursuing a career in order to meet our motherly obligations.

I believe that mothers are the greatest people on earth. From conception to maturity, you are there every day taking care of them; feeling their pains and suffering in times of sickness. We do a lot, but thank God there is rest for us in Christ Jesus.

The Lord Jesus comforted His disciples before His crucifixion with this promise of an eternal dwelling place and eternal rest from all the struggles and troubles on earth. What more can one ask for?

A room for you and a room for me, this promise from Jesus is always viable and timely. It brings comfort to us when things are awry, including sickness in the body, loss of a job, or a death in the family. It gives us an eternal perspective, and hope to make it through.

Prayer

Dear Father, I thank you for the rest I will enjoy in eternity. I have hope that someday very soon all these will be over and I will rest in your arms of love in Jesus' name. Amen.
Further Studies: *Philippians 3:20-21*

What Hour?

*"But about that day or hour no one knows, not even the angels
in heaven, nor the Son, but only the Father."*
(Matthew 24:36)

The big question revolving around the second coming of Christ is, "When will Jesus return?" Matthew states that no one knows. Over the years, some people have prophesied the coming of Jesus with specific dates and times, but it is very clear from the words of the Master that no one actually knows the date and time.

Because there is no specific date given for the Master's return, some people have stumbled and even given up hope; some think it is no longer true. Others will tell us that they have heard this same message of Christ's return since they were kids. If you are wise, you will understand that most of the events that will precede the master's arrival are already happening today.

No one knows except the Father, and the exact date should not matter if we are in Christ. Our primary concern should be winning others to Christ so that they too can be ready for Christ's return.

What hour will it be? No need to waste precious time on trying to figure it out. Let us be ready and seek to make others ready; our loved ones, family, friends, neighbors, co-workers. Time is of the essence, so let's get busy winning our sisters and brothers to Christ for His return.

Prayer

Dear Lord, my heart is established on the truth that Jesus is coming very soon. I am ready and waiting for my master, and with haste I propagate the goodness of the kingdom and ready others for His great return. Thank you, Lord, in Jesus' name. Amen.
Further Studies: *Matthew 24:45-51*

Watching

"Look, I come like a thief! Blessed is the one who stays awake and remains clothed, so as not to go naked and be shamefully exposed."
(Revelation 16:15)

The parable of the ten virgins in Matthew 25 is a lesson on how we ought to watch and wait in anticipation of the Master's return. We are not to be carried away by the cares and worries of this life or by the distractions that were orchestrated by the devil to remove us from the faith.

The wise virgins are those, who in the midst of persecutions, trials, and distractions, keep their attention on Jesus. The virgins in this parable had extra oil and were ready to move at any time. The coming of the Lord is at hand, and whether you like it or not, He will come when the Father tells Him to. Our duty is to be ready at all times.

It's very easy to get off track when waiting for someone's return. Let's suppose that there's a woman waiting for her fiancé to return from war. Years have passed without any news about him, so she presumes that he is dead. Hesitantly, she decides to "move on" with her life, gets married to someone else, and starts a family. Imagine what would happen if the man were to suddenly return.

Christ will also return when we least expect Him, so let us be watching, clothed in faith and righteousness, waiting patiently. Let us be diligent and productive as we wait for Christ's return.

Prayer

Dear Father, thank you for the hope of Jesus' return. Thank you for helping me to stay spotless and live a righteous and holy life as I wait in Jesus' name. Amen.
Further Studies: *Matthew 25:5-7*

Take your Place

"People will come from east and west and north and south, and will take their places at the feast in the kingdom of God. Indeed there are those who are last who will be first, and first who will be last."
(Luke 13:29-30)

This is very instructive counsel from the Master about our placement in God's scheme of things. The Kingdom of God is an ever increasing kingdom, and God is always raising people to do His work, so it matters not when you came to know Christ or which nation you came from, but what is important is that you came and took your place.

When the Lord Jesus returns in glory, He will judge the world and Christians alike, but the judgment of Christians is for reward. There is the crown you will receive for being a Christian and there are several crowns you will receive for your relevance in the body of Christ.

Trusting Jesus is the best decision one can make. It is life transforming. This I am sure you can attest to. The benefits are enormous; the joy and peace you now have are worth every ounce of taking the stand for Christ, and the best is yet to come.

Do something today. Do not be a church goer, one that comes to receive after all things have been prepared and arranged by others. Be financially involved today, join the evangelism team, sponsor church projects, be the relevant and vital member that God has created you to be, today.

Prayer

Dear Father, I thank you for making me a vital and relevant member of your body. I take my place today and I am relevant to the kingdom of God today in Jesus' name. Amen.
Further Studies: *Esther 4:14, Daniel 12:2, Proverbs 11:30*

Every Tear

"He will wipe every tear from their eyes. There will be no more death or mourning or crying or pain, for the old order of things has passed away."
(Revelation 21:4)

This promise is one of the reasons you must serve God with your life and teach others to do the same. This world is full of pain, sickness, poverty, want, and wars. Our sadness and pain are the result of the fall of Adam and Eve back in the Garden of Eden. Our sadness and pain are the result of sin.

A life of sin is, as the scripture puts it, the old order of things, but Jesus has promised that He comes to make all things new. Under His government a new order will be established, and it will be a government of peace.

Under His rule, there will be no reason to shed any tears, for the God of peace will govern our hearts with peace beyond all understanding. What's even more, is that this verse speaks of the tender mercy and compassion of our king.

To wipe someone's tears away demonstrates not only a sense of closeness, but a genuine concern for the person's feelings. The verse could have said that we will no longer cry, but we're told that in a very intimate and personal way, God will wipe the tears from our eyes.

God's promise is real and true, and one day we will experience his tender mercies as He wipes EVERY tear from our eyes.

Prayer

Dear Father, my hope is in you and I look forward every day to the coming of Jesus Christ, because I know that you alone can wipe my tears and comfort my heart with your presence in Jesus' name. Amen.
Further Studies: *Romans 5:17*

A Shout

"For the Lord himself will come down from heaven, with a loud command, with the voice of the archangel and with the trumpet call of God, and the dead in Christ will rise first."
(1 Thessalonians 4:16)

There is something spiritual about shouting. I grew up in an orthodox church, where the services were very quiet. The only times we sang were when we were asked to, and most of the songs were hymns. It was a very pious church and the priests or the ordained minister did most of the talking.

When I was 18, I attended a Christian church, and I was not very comfortable at first, because of the shouting and rejoicing, but I couldn't help but notice that these people were so full of life. There was a vibrant joy emanating from their faces.

Over time I learned that they shouted in response to God's Word, and they danced in praise to God. And guess what? When I joined in the rejoicing, my life took a drastic turn. Why? Because I learned that shouting to God helps drown out the sound of my fears and it emboldens me to feel the power of God working in and around me.

The children of Israel brought down the walls of Jericho by a shout, and Jehoshaphat defeated the three kings by shouting and singing praises to God. Here Paul tells us that we can look forward to a shout from heaven when the Lord returns. That shout will wake those that have died in the faith and will rapture those of us alive. Let's anticipate the shout of the Lord.

Prayer

Dear Father, I thank you for giving me victory in Christ Jesus. I proclaim my victory and drive away every adversary with a loud shout in Jesus' name. Amen.
Further Studies: *Psalm 118:15-24 (NASB), Joshua 6:15-20*

The Foolishness of God

"... the foolishness of God is wiser than men, and the
weakness of God is stronger than men."
(1 Corinthians 1:25)

Some people are so wise (in their own eyes) that their wisdom becomes their destruction. Our wisdom can only take us so far; therefore, if you truly want to be wise, you must seek wisdom from the Lord.

King Solomon, the wisest man on earth before Jesus came, received his wisdom from God. He was so wise that he knew something about everything. Hear his counsel:

"Trust in the Lord with all your heart and lean not on your own
understanding; in all your ways submit to him, and he will make your paths
straight. Do not be wise in your own eyes; fear the Lord and shun evil."
Proverbs 3:5-7

What we may perceive as weakness in Him is actually strength; we cannot fathom God, His ways are past finding out. God may not do things your way, but just trust Him, because He is the only wise God. If you do not understand His working, remember that His ways are different from ours, but they are revealed in the Scriptures. Learn to trust His wisdom today.

Prayer

Father in heaven, I thank you that I can trust you to work all things out for
my good, especially those that seem foolish. I praise you that your perceived
weakness is indeed strength, and you are assiduously working on my
behalf and we magnify your holy name in the name of Jesus. Amen.
Further Studies: *1 Timothy 1:17*

Narrow Gate, Narrow Road

"Enter through the narrow gate. For wide is the gate and broad is the road that leads to destruction, and many enter through it. But small is the gate and narrow the road that leads to life, and only a few find it."
(Matthew 7:13-14)

The narrow gate here has to do with the way we live our lives. You cannot live any way you want, because you belong to God. To enter into the narrow gate means that there are things that you have to suffer or deliberately give up to gain the kingdom of God.

No one enjoys suffering, just like no one really enjoys sacrifice, and yet that is exactly what the narrow road has to offer anyone who wants to be a follower of Christ. That also explains why there are not many people who choose to walk the narrow way. It's not easy.

In this day and age, we typically prefer doing things that are easy. I had someone say to me once that they wanted to give up a particular sin they were struggling with, but they wish I knew how hard it was for them to let it go. I had to respond by saying that it's not supposed to be easy!

Giving up those sinful things that are pleasurable to our flesh will always be hard, but it's also going to be worth it. Remember that God is your ultimate source, so stay on track. Look to the hills, and take the narrow gate and road which leads to life.

Prayer

Dear Father, my heart is fixed on you. I will not give up my salvation and Christian testimony for jobs, recognition, promotion or fame. I live every day with heaven on my mind in Jesus' name. Amen.
Further Studies: *Acts 14:22*

Listen and Learn

"Wisdom belongs to the aged, and understanding to the old."
(Job 12:12)

Most societies around the world consider elderly people to be wise because they have seen many days and gained much wisdom over the years. This kind of wisdom comes through experience and a commitment to learn from those experiences.

In the Old Testament we're told the story of Rehoboam. When his father died, leaving the people of Israel under his care, he consulted the elders for advice on what to do. They gave him sound counsel, but he still wasn't convinced, so he went to his friends, and was given terrible advice. Guess whose advice he took.

"But Rehoboam rejected the advice the elders gave him and consulted the young men who had grown up with him and were serving him."
1 Kings 12:8

As a result of this decision, Rehoboam was responsible for the division of the tribes of Israel. All of it could have been prevented, had he listened to the men who had seen a number of kings rise and fall, and who had the wisdom of the Lord.

In our own lives we would do well to attach ourselves to older women in the faith who can give us wise counsel on behalf of the Father. Of course it goes without saying that not all elderly people have godly wisdom to share, but out of respect for them and their experience, we should always seek to listen and learn.

Prayer

Dear Father, I thank you for the older women you have placed in my life and challenge myself to sit at their feet and learn from them in Jesus' name. Amen.
Further Studies: *Job 32:6-9, 1 John 2:27*

When He Appears

"When Christ, who is your life, appears, then you also will appear with him in glory."
(Colossians 3:4)

Christ not only gives us life, but He is our life.

From the Nile Valley in North Africa to Sudan and South Asia's Pakistan, women face death every day because of their faith in Jesus Christ. For most of us, our faith journey is not that extreme, but denying our fleshy desires is vital so that Christ can live in and through us.

Christ died for us, and now His life is manifested in our bodies. He lives through us. So in other words, when He appears at the second coming, we too will appear, being glorified with Him. For Christ to have full reign in our lives, we must submit to Him instead of our own wishes and desires.

> *"Then he called the crowd to him along with his disciples*
> *and said: "Whoever wants to be my disciple must deny*
> *themselves and take up their cross and follow me."*
> *Mark 8:34*

You must understand that life on earth is very short, but it is preparation for eternity. That is why we must live for Christ while we have the time to do so. If we are to reign with Him in glory, then we must live for Him and let Him live through us in this world. He is our life here on earth, and in the world to come.

Prayer

Dear Lord, thank you for giving me your Son. I boldly
live every day for you in Jesus' name. Amen.
Further Studies: *Colossians 3:1-3*

Incomprehensible

"But, as it is written, 'What no eye has seen, nor ear heard, nor the heart of man imagined, what God has prepared for those who love Him.'"
(1 Corinthians 2:9)

Paul's declaration is that it is impossible for men to understand God; He is incomprehensible.

Because of our love for God, we yield to Him and He imparts supernatural wisdom, knowledge, and understanding to us.

Whatever our eyes can see, whatever our ears can hear, and even whatever we can imagine, NONE of these things can compare to what God has in store for us. It is incomprehensible; impossible to understand or comprehend, unintelligible, limitless!

This revelation makes me very happy, and it should make you happy too. Our Daddy loves us and has made extra special provisions for us. This is why we must serve God with our lives, because we know that there is an incomprehensible glory for us in Christ Jesus.

At times we may not have any physical or material things to show for our godliness, but we have hope and we know that our inheritance in the world to come is beyond what we can imagine.

"In my Father's house are many mansions: if it were not so, I would have told you. I go to prepare a place for you. And if I go and prepare a place for you, I will come again, and receive you unto myself; that where I am, there ye may be also"
(John 14:2-3, KJV).

Prayer

Dear Father, I thank you because you love for me is incomprehensible, you grace is beyond what my mind can imagine. Thank you for loving me so much in Jesus' name. Amen.
Further Studies: *Colossians 1:27*

The Lords

"The earth is the LORD'S, and the fullness thereof; the
world, and they that dwell therein."
(Psalm 24:1)

Sometimes when I see people dying in order to amass wealth, I wonder if they know that God owns the whole world. King David recognized this fact and that is why he is referred to as a man after God's own heart. If you know that God owns everything, you will seek to maintain a good relationship with Him.

The earth and everything and everyone in it, belongs to the Lord. From the smallest creature to the largest, the poorest person to the richest, known or unknown, the ugliest landscape to the most beautiful, from the smallest brook to the largest ocean, the best day or the worst day, hidden or seen, it all belongs to Him.

It's not difficult to see that everything points to the Lord; He knows about it all. Let us therefore give Him praise and use what He has made available to us to the glory and honor of the Lord's name.

This knowledge should inspire you to seek Him first and refuse to let anything else bother you. We need to live comfortably and enjoy our stay on earth, but if your only option to have a good life on earth is to give up the giver, it would be wiser for you to give up the gifts and seek the giver.

"But seek ye first the kingdom of God, and his righteousness; and
all these things shall be added unto you." Matthew 6:33

Prayer

Dear Father, you are the giver of life and the world is yours. I thank you for
freely giving me all things you want me to enjoy in Jesus' name. Amen.
Further Studies: *1 Timothy 6:17, 2 Peter 1:3-4*

Fulfill the Law

"Let no debt remain outstanding, except the continuing debt to love
one another, for whoever loves others has fulfilled the law."
(Romans 13:8)

Romans 13 contains a series of instructions to Christians on how we should live and conduct ourselves within our societies. Here the Roman Christians were encouraged to put on Christ, obey authority, and love their neighbor. The Apostle Paul explained the chain of authority in society and that our government institutions are actually ordained by God to represent Him, hence we should obey them and give to every man his due.

"Let everyone be subject to the governing authorities, for there
is no authority except that which God has established. The
authorities that exist have been established by God."
Romans 13:1

Knowing that we have been instructed by God to be subject to civil authority is enough reason for us not to default in our taxes and bills. We must be law abiding citizens so that people can't look at our behavior and blame the whole of Christianity. We must honor the civil authority and show them love, because they represent God.

For Christians, love for others is not optional; it is likened to a debt owed that must be paid, and in doing so, we fulfill the law. Regardless of who the person is, what they have done, what they can or cannot do for us, our only obligation is to love. We will love and thus fulfill the law.

Prayer

Dear Father, thank you for giving us government to structure our societies. I see
them as your representatives, and as such, I obey them in Jesus' name. Amen.
Further Studies: *1 Timothy 2:1-3*

My Shepherd

"The LORD is my shepherd; I shall not want."
(Psalms 23:1)

There's a reason why this is one of the most memorized scriptures of the Bible. It just so happens to be one of the most inspirational verses in the Bible. King David often penned inspirational psalms that were based on his life. In this case, he shares a valuable piece of information using his vocation as a shepherd as a point of comparison.

A shepherd is a person who guides, tends to, feeds, and guards herds of sheep. During the years that David was on the run from King Saul, he saw himself as a sheep in need of a protector. It was then that he got to know God as his shepherd.

Sheep are directionless, weak, dumb, dependent and defenseless. Without the guidance of a shepherd, they are vulnerable and lost. I imagine that this is exactly how David felt while he hid in the Cave of Adullam, hoping beyond all hope for some respite.

In the same way, we are unable to provide for ourselves and are in need of a shepherd, so the Lord—the good shepherd that He is—makes the necessary provisions that we need for every day and every circumstance of our lives, whether we're suffering through the valley or prospering on the mountaintop.

Is the Lord your shepherd? He is willing and capable to keep you, so entrust your life to Him. He will take care of you!

Prayer

Dear Father, thank you for being my shepherd. Because you lead me, Lord, I know my life and future is secure. I am safe on every side and all my needs are met in Jesus' name. Amen.
Further Studies: *1 Peter 5:7, Psalm 91*

Safe & Secure

"I give them eternal life, and they shall never perish;
no one will snatch them out of my hand."
(John 10:28)

One of the many depictions we can find of Jesus in the Bible is as the Good Shepherd. The responsibilities of a shepherd include but are not limited to:

- Protecting
- Feeding & Watering
- Anointing
- Grooming
- Leading
- Delivering lambs
- Comforting & Nurturing

Just as any good shepherd would, Jesus performs each of these tasks because He cares about us; He cares about our wellbeing. Just as any good shepherd would defend his sheep against any predator, Jesus has done and continually does the same.

If anyone were to send a hired hand to look after his sheep, whenever great adversity would come, that person would leave the sheep vulnerable and alone because they have no personal attachment to them. But Jesus is a gentle, kind, and loving shepherd, and we have a great promise that He will never leave us nor forsake us. And that is what makes Him such a Good Shepherd.

Prayer

Dear Father, I thank you for being my shepherd. I am rest assured of my
safety, peace and continue supplies in the name of Jesus. Amen.
Further Studies: *Psalm 23:1-6*

Comfort

"As a mother comforts her child, so I will comfort you;
and you will be comforted over Jerusalem."
(Isaiah 66:13)

Have you ever been bereaved without any idea of how to get through your sorrow? In such times, only the comfort of God can bring you peace. People may come around and try to comfort you; some may even claim to know what you are going through and how you feel, but it is only God that can touch the deepest hurts of your soul.

As a child, you may remember how good it felt to climb up onto your mother's lap where she would rock you or sing a lullaby, especially after an unpleasant ordeal. Or maybe when there was a thunderstorm outside, you would climb into your parents' bed and nestle under your mother's arms—the one place where you could always feel safe.

Really take a moment to reflect on the feeling of comfort, peace, and safety that you felt in those moments and compare that to the way your heavenly Father comforts you. Feel the warmth of His embrace in your heart.

As a believer, this presence is always available to you; not just when you're brokenhearted, but because the Holy Spirit of God lives in us every day. He is our comforter. He will comfort you in all situations. He is a friend that sticks closer than a brother.

If you live your life conscious of the indwelling and ever present Spirit of God, you will never be at a disadvantage, come what may. Embrace His comfort.

Prayer

Dear Father, I thank you for comforting me all day. I receive
your comfort today in Jesus' name. Amen.
Further Studies: *2 Corinthians 1:3-4*

Example to Others

"Be shepherds of God's flock that is under your care, watching over them--not because you must, but because you are willing, as God wants you to be; not pursuing dishonest gain, but eager to serve."
(1 Peter 5:2-3)

Christianity is a life of example. The Lord Jesus came to earth and demonstrated that himself. *"To this you were called, because Christ suffered for you, leaving you an example, that you should follow in his steps"* (1 Peter 2:21). He taught us exactly how to live and how to lead.

This is the same admonition the apostle is passing down to us as leaders in the house of God. As Christians we all lead in one capacity or another. Regardless of whether or not you don a leadership title, there are people looking up to you. You are a role model, a light in the dark for others to see.

For those that have been given official leadership responsibilities in the church, people have been placed under you to be cared for and nurtured. God will hold you responsible for your influence on these people. Did you guide them and point them to Christ?

Sometimes, as leaders, we are given the opportunity of nurturing people who are "RICH," and we may be distracted into doing our work for gain. The Apostle Peter counsels us to be cautious of the role we play as leaders, because God made us overseers to give light, to point men to Christ, and to help raise disciples unto Him and not ourselves.

Prayer

Dear Father, I thank you for charging me with the responsibility of raising up other believers. I choose to be faithful in my ministry as a leader in Jesus' name. Amen.
Further Studies: *Acts 20:28*

Increase in Love

*"May the Lord make your love increase and overflow for each
other and for everyone else, just as ours does for you."*
(1 Thessalonians 3:12)

God does not merely want us to love one another; He actually instructs us in His word to love, and Jesus reiterates that point by saying that love is proof of our discipleship. By our love we show the world that we are sons of God, who is the very personification of love.

The more you love, the more you become like God, and the more you love, the more you become liberal in your giving. Anyone who truly loves someone gives. Mothers give their time to their children, men and women give each other gifts, and the list goes on. When you love, you give.

God will always take care of you as you give, so don't worry that you won't have enough to survive (Luke 6:38). That is a common deterrent from love for most people. They start looking at themselves and what they have or what they will lack if they give to others, but real love doesn't even ask such questions. Real love says, "I will give even if it costs me everything."

After all, that's what Jesus did for us, is it not? He laid down His life for us for the sake of love. The least we can do is put the needs of others before our own. Love for each other should increase and flourish more and more as we walk daily with the Lord.

Prayer

*Dear Father, I choose to increase in my works of love today and be your source of
encouragement, support and supply to those in my world in Jesus' name. Amen.*
Further Studies: *John 13:35*

Be Content

"Then some soldiers asked him, 'And what should we do?' He replied, 'Don't extort money and don't accuse people falsely--be content with your pay.'"
(Luke 3:14)

Contentment is a mental or emotional state of satisfaction drawn from being at ease in one's situation, body and mind. This is something that most of us mothers struggle with; we are hardly contented with what we have.

There is nothing wrong with aiming higher in life, wanting to be more or achieve more. The story of the Israelites taking over the land of Canaan shows us that God wanted them to get all the land and claim what He had promised them, albeit from a position of rest (Joshua 13:1).

But as much as you would like to achieve more or push yourself, your husband, your children, and even your staff members to greater achievement, you must see God as your source and be satisfied with that which He has given you.

Whatever God has blessed you with today, placed in your care, or given you control over, be satisfied with it. I realize that people who are not contented are hardly appreciative. They just keep asking for more and looking for more. But those of us who are appreciative are always blessed because each time we say, "thank you," we are actually stirring the hearts of God and people.

Prayer

Dear Father, thank you for teaching me to be appreciative of all that you have given me. Lord, I am contented and I know that everything I have and enjoy is a good gift that comes from your hand in Jesus' name. Amen.
Further Studies: *Matthew 6:36, 1 Timothy 6:6*

Wardrobe and Heart

"You have heard that it was said, 'Do not commit adultery.' But I tell you that anyone who looks at a woman lustfully has already committed adultery with her in his heart."
(Matthew 5:27-28)

As humans, we understand and communicate with the world and those in it through our senses. This is how God created all of us, but in the case of men, this is especially true. They are highly influenced by their senses.

For that reason, clothing will always be an issue of importance. Men may be moved to lust after our bodies, and we can unwittingly make the challenge harder for them by wearing revealing clothing.

Now, a man's actions cannot be blamed on whether or not we cover up, but it is ourresponsibility to be good stewards towards our brothers in faith, and do what we can to keep from being a source of temptation for them.

Adultery does not occur when the physical relationship begins; it begins much sooner. It begins the moment an individual desires another individual that is not his wife or her husband. Women who want to be desired are not shy about using clothing (or the lack thereof), and fawning mannerisms to get the affections or compliments of men.

As a Christian woman, you must dress decently at all times. Your body is for your husband and not for every man out there, so be sure to be properly dressed.

Prayer

Dear Father, I thank you for the teaching me to dress to please you alone. My dress and my life bring praises to you and I glorify you with my body in the name of Jesus. Amen.
Further Studies: *Matthew 18:6, 1 Peter 3:1-5*

United We Stand

"Every kingdom divided against itself will be ruined, and every city or household divided against itself will not stand."
(Matthew 12:25)

In school – whether primary, secondary, or post-secondary – teachers often put their students into what they call cooperative groups. They typically choose four students that they believe will work well together, or that will at least complement each other's strengths and weaknesses, and place them in a group setting.

Sometimes these groups can turn out for the best, but other times the students may have personal or communicative issues that cause them to erupt into arguments or keep them from working together properly. Such behavior can create a very unproductive setting in the classroom.

Imagine there was an assignment due by the end of class. How far would the group get if they could not cooperate with one another? Just about as far as we would get in the Body of Christ if we did not pursue unity with our brothers and sisters.

Our God is a God of order, and within Him there is no dissension or division. Being part of His kingdom means that the way we engage with one another should be rooted in humility and love. For division to happen in any group setting, someone has to be exhibiting traits of selfishness in one form or another.

If we truly have the Holy Spirit inside of us, this should not be so in the lives of believers.

Prayer

Dear Father, I thank you for my brothers and sisters in Christ and seek to honor you as I honor them in the name of your son. Amen.
Further Studies: *Proverbs 6:22*

The Cure for Worry

"Do not worry about tomorrow, for tomorrow will worry about itself. Each day has enough trouble of its own."
(Matthew 6:34, NASB)

My family has been visiting an elderly man on a weekly basis for several months now. Each week he complains of feeling awful, being taken advantage of, and living in a terrible world. This man worries about everything you can think of.

Worry stems from a lack of faith in God and is cured only by placing our faith in Him. But many people, like my elderly friend, can even worry about trusting God with their worry! It's definitely a dangerous cycle.

Worry is an inarguable mind trap. If you keep worrying, you will not make progress in life, because it will stop you from daring to make investments that could change your life. Surrender your heart, willingly place faith in God, and rejoice in the expectation that He will meet all of your needs, according to His riches in glory.

Instead of worrying and disturbing yourself over things that you cannot change, seek to do something that can actually change the situation. Paul told us exactly what to do to change our worry status.

"Be anxious for nothing, but in everything by prayer and supplication with thanksgiving let your requests be made known to God. And the peace of God, which surpasses all comprehension, will guard your hearts and your minds in Christ Jesus." Philippians 4:6-7

Prayer

Dear Father, I thank you for given me peace that passes all understanding as I cast my cares on you in Jesus' name. Amen.
Further Studies: 1 Peter 5:7

Sacrificing Entitlement

"Anyone who loves his father or mother more than me is not worthy of me; anyone who loves his son or daughter more than me is not worthy of me; and anyone who does not take his cross and follow me is not worthy of me. Whoever finds his life will lose it, and whoever loses his life for my sake will find it."
(Matthew 10:37-39, NASB)

" deserve it!" Have you ever uttered these words? Unfortunately, these three words have become a major part of the mindset of Christians when it comes to the issue of entitlement.

Even though the Word of God expressly teaches that we should lay our lives down for others, we often do so based on the amount of sacrifice that is required of us. If it requires too much sacrifice or too much discomfort, we tend to choose another route.

"And when he had called the people unto him with his disciples also, he said unto them, Whosoever will come after me, let him deny himself, and take up his cross, and follow me".
Mark 8:34, NKJ

The truth is that when we make decisions that we feel will benefit us instead of others, we're only looking at the short-term benefits, but there is always a greater reward when you sacrifice your own comfort for the sake of others.

We have a choice to make each and every day, which is that we're faced with serving our own comfort versus serving the needs of others. We would do well to remember the long-term benefits that comes from obeying the Word of God and putting the needs of others first.

Prayer

Dear Father, I thank you for the promise of an eternal reward for every single sacrifice I make on earth for your name's sake in Jesus' name. Amen.
Further Studies: *Mark 10:20-31*

Adopted

*"The Spirit you received does not make you slaves, so that you live
in fear again; rather, the Spirit you received brought about your
adoption to sonship. And by him we cry, 'Abba, Father.'"*
(Romans 8:15)

I f you have not fully appreciated what God accomplished when He adopted us and made us His children, the definition of adoption below will help you understand.

Adoption is a process whereby a person assumes the parenting of another, usually a child, from that person's biological or legal parent or parents, and, in so doing, permanently transfers all rights and responsibilities, along with filiation, from the biological parent or parents.

Adoption paints a powerful picture of salvation. God willfully chose us and paid the sum of His own life to make us joint heirs with His Son. Through Jesus' blood, we become part of a heavenly bloodline! And on top of that, God has even put His own Spirit in our hearts, so there can be no question to whom we belong! We have the very blood and spirit of our Father to testify to our adoption!

We are no longer slaves, but we have become "sons" through the spirit of sonship and adoption. So as you engage with God, embrace Him as your Father: **Abba -** God the Father, our Father!

Prayer

*Dear Father, I thank you for adopting me into your family. I am so grateful
that now my spirit can cry out Abba Father with confidence, and I know
that because you love me, you will answer in Jesus' name. Amen.*
Further Studies: *Ephesians 1:2-7*

Where is God?

*"I have set the LORD always before me: because [he is]
at my right hand, I will not be moved."*
(Psalms 16:8, NKJ)

For someone to be at a person's right hand in the scriptures means that they're in the place of authority (i.e. Jesus sitting at the right hand of God), or it could mean that they are in "the preferred" position, which is easily accessible.

In our opening verse, David declares that he put the Lord in front of him always. Where are you in relation to God? Do you think of Him before you make decisions—large or small? Is He the first person you strive to please with the way that you live your life?

Because David knew that God was always near to him, he did not worry about being defeated. He was safe as long as the Lord was at the forefront of his life.

Turn away from all the things that seek to steal that position that only God should have. God does not want to be your last resort; He doesn't want to be the person you run to when all else have failed. He wants to have the first place in your life.

Honor God today by giving Him the first place in your life. Place God at your right hand by giving Him the preeminence in your life.

Prayer

Dear Father, I give you the first place in my life. From today onward, your word will have the preeminence in my life in Jesus' name. Amen.
Further Studies: *Psalm 34:18*

Nesting in God

"He will cover you with his feathers, and under his wings you
may seek refuge: his truth is a shield and buckler."
(Psalms 91:4)

When I was growing up, my mother had a collection of small poultry. During the day, the hens would peck around the yard while their chicks ran and played somewhere nearby. They never strayed too far from their mother.

One of the things I remember from those days is how the mother hen would gather her chicks under her wings during the cold season. She would call out to her chicks, they would come scampering up to her, and then she would cover them with her wings

God often uses analogies to form mental pictures that give us a clear understanding of His Word. In this verse, He relates to Himself as a mother hen: "feathers" and "wings" and to His truth as "shield" and "buckler."

You may have limited knowledge about shields and bucklers, but if you have cared for ducks or chickens you will understand this. When a hen hatches her clutch, she becomes attached and devoted to her chicks. She protects her chicks under her wings; her strongest feathers making a sort of armory around her chicks, the soft interior beneath her wings creating a warm, safe place.

This picture reflects God's protective love for us.

Prayer

Dear Father, I am safe in your presence. You are my shield and my buckler. I refuse to be moved because I know that you jealously watch over me. Glory to your name forever!
Further Studies: *Psalm 27:1-3, Psalm 32:7*

Fruit Of your Wisdom

"The fear of the LORD is the beginning of wisdom; all who follow his precepts have good understanding. To him belongs eternal praise."
(Psalms 111:10)

In Genesis 2 we find the account of a woman who wanted to be wise, but because she sought wisdom apart from God, it ended badly for her. This verse reminds us that wisdom comes only when we fear the Lord and employ understanding and obedience to His commands.

The fruit derived from David's wisdom in this scripture is everlasting praise, but Eve's fruit was death due to disobedience. Consider the fruit of your wisdom. Is it more like Eve's or David's? Does the fear of the Lord guide your decision-making process?

You can judge the fruit of your wisdom today from the results of your decisions or actions. If you have being functioning with the wisdom of God, your life will show the fruits, but if it's otherwise, you need to change.

Have reverential fear for God. Honor Him by keeping His word, and the fruit will be wisdom. The more you know God's Word and give Him preeminence in your life, the more His wisdom will fill your heart.

Prayer

Dear Father, I thank you for giving me wisdom to deal wisely in the affairs of this life. I acknowledge your word as my source of wisdom and I give your Word the first place in my life in Jesus' name. Amen.
Further Studies: *Proverbs 2:3*

Battling for your Children

"Be on your guard; stand firm in the faith; be courageous; be strong."
(1 Corinthians 16:13)

Temptations to compromise on godly motherhood responsibilities are all around. There is the issue of Christian or secular education, the issue of who your children should be socializing with, and there are even choices regarding what you should and should not allow your children to view on the internet and television.

Because children don't always understand your rationale behind some of the decisions that you make, they may oppose you. Even some of your friends and family will stand against you, as they may not have the same convictions that you do.

In your most stressed moments, you may be tempted to just compromise on your convictions, but you are called to make difficult decisions, to stand firm in your convictions.

God gave your children to you as a gift, and He charges you with the responsibility of raising them properly. So even when everyone in the world is doing something different or they claim that your methods are "weird," you must stand firm in your faith.

Stand in the gap for your children; continually make intercession for them. Pray for them to make the right decisions and to imbibe the Christian culture that you teach them every day. Stand fast in your desire to raise your children for the Lord even when easier alternatives are presented each day.

Prayer

Dear Father, thank you for giving me wisdom to raise my children in a way that pleases you. Give me the strength to put a stop to negative influences in their lives in Jesus' name. Amen.
Further Studies: *Proverbs 22:6*

May

Strong Arms

"She sets about her work vigorously; her arms are strong for her tasks."
(Proverbs 31:17)

The interesting thing about a mother's arms is that they can be both strong and soft at the same time. As a child, my mother's arms were one of my favorite places to be. Whether we were just sitting together and cuddling or she was covering me with them during the middle of a late night thunderstorm, there was something so peaceful and calming about being wrapped up in her arms.

At the same time there was no one that could take care of the household chores like my mother. Her strong arms could endure hours of scrubbing the bathroom or the dishes, and she did it all as a labor of love.

Sometimes I would stand and watch her and wonder how she could possibly continue working so hard day after day, or why she didn't just take a break, but she took her role as the keeper of the home very seriously and worked hard to ensure that we lived in a home that she could be proud of.

The truth is, after watching all that my mother did to care for house and home, I think I was more proud of her. And as you continue to do the same within your own home, I'm sure your family will say the same of you.

Prayer

Dear Father, thank you for giving me a home to take care of and two arms that I can use to work hard in Jesus' name. Amen.
Further Studies: *Proverbs 6:6*

Pure Joy

"Consider it pure joy, my brothers and sisters, whenever you face trials of many kinds, because you know that the testing of your faith produces perseverance."
(James 1:2-3)

The book of James is considered the Proverbs of the New Testament. Here, James writes about trials and temptations. Some Christians think of sin and all the wrong things they have done each time they are faced with the trials of life, but the Apostle James shows us that the testing of our faith is actually for our own good because it produces perseverance.

You may have lost a child or suffered a miscarriage and your world came crashing down. Bits and pieces lie strewn all around, and some of them are unrecognizable, unseen. How do you come back together after all of that? And how should you count it all joy?

Pure joy is found in the arms and promises of Jesus. He knows, He sees, and He understands EVERYTHING that you go through. Trust Him to heal, restore and give you pure joy. Remember the story of Job. He lost everything and was afflicted unto the point of death. His wife abandoned him, and his three friends that came to console him ended up blaming him for his misfortune. At the end of it all, Job got everything because even in his affliction, He never took his eyes off of Jehovah.

"After Job had prayed for his friends, the LORD restored his fortunes and gave him twice as much as he had before." Job 42:10

Prayer

Dear Lord, I know that my trials are for a moment and that all things will work for my good. Father, I choose to remain stayed in you in times of trials in Jesus' name. Amen.
Further Studies: *2 Corinthians 4:16-18, Job 42:10-17*

Chastening

"Those whom I love I rebuke and discipline. So be earnest and repent."
(Revelation 3:19)

Jeanette had tears running down her cheeks. She had just received a spanking from her dad because she had gone outside without supervision after he had told her not to. Jeanette couldn't believe her dad could be so mean. Looking back at that incident several years later, Jeanette could finally understand that at that time young girls were being abducted, so in an effort to keep her safe, her father had given an instruction. When she disobeyed him, he spanked her because he loved her.

We all love the result of discipline, but no one actually likes to be disciplined. We all love those well behaved and respectful kids, and we all wish for our children to be disciplined and morally excellent. But in order to achieve those results, you have to go through the ringer with your children first.

Our opening scripture is a portion of Christ's letters to the churches of Sardis, Philadelphia, and Laodicea. This same instruction applies to us today. Jesus loves us so much, and His chastening is actually an expression of His love for us. We can trust His intentions for us; they are for good and not for evil.

Prayer

Dear Lord, I thank you for the privilege to be corrected by you. I know that your corrections and disciplines are for my good. Lord, I receive all corrections with joy in the name of Jesus. Amen.
Further Studies*: Proverbs 3:11-12, Hebrews 12:6-11*

Love, Love, Love

"As the Father has loved me, so have I loved you. Now remain in my love."
(John 15:9)

Something that interests me about the ministry of our Lord Jesus is His love and willingness to help the sick, poor, and downtrodden. In the Old Testament, there were several prophets that came to the aid of the people in times of need, but there are none that can be compared with Jesus. He had so much compassion and love.

He was so filled with compassion and love that He even prayed for forgiveness for those who had nailed Him to the cross (Luke 23:34). Our opening scripture here expressly tells us why Jesus loved so much and why He expects us to love others in the same way. *"As the Father has loved me, so have I loved you."*

The love of the Father begets the love of the Son, and it is natural for the love of the Son to beget that same love in the fruit of the Son. Your mother loves and cares for you, you love and care for your daughter, and she loves and cares for your grandchild. Love begets love, love reciprocates love. Jesus' love for us naturally causes us to love others; His continuous love for us persuades us to continue the chain of love.

Love, love, love. The ability to love others the way Jesus loves us is in our nature. Just let it flow from within you.

Prayer

Dear Lord, thank you for loving me as much as you love Jesus. I am a native born of love, and I naturally love others the way you have loved me in Jesus' name. Amen.
Further Studies: *John 13:35*

God Answers

"Hear, O LORD, when I cry with my voice: have mercy also upon me, and answer me."
(Psalms 27:7, NASB)

Your pillow knows the story very well. On many occasions it has been filled to capacity with tears, groans, moans, whimpers, and wails. Maybe you've tried talking to others about your troubles, but they don't seem to understand or even care about what you are going through.

As women, we know that shedding tears really cannot do much to improve our situation, but they do provide a bit of release for our souls. God created humans that way, so it's good to cry, but we aren't just to cry for the sake of crying; we are to cry to God.

I have always told people that I hardly cry; I do not cry for anybody under any circumstance. I only cry when I have a problem that seems insurmountable. At such times, I cry in worship and adoration to the God that can do all things, the God with whom all things are possible, the God that will never leave me nor forsake me.

"And call on me in the day of trouble; I will
deliver you, and you will honor me."
Psalm 50:15

I do not cry like one who is helpless; I cry in worship and total surrender to my God who always answers. Stop crying and wailing like one without hope, help or a helper. He has promised to answer, and He surely will.

Prayer

Dear Father, thank you for hearing and answering me
every time I call in Jesus's name. Amen.
Further Studies: *Zechariah 10:6, 2 Chronicles 7:14, John 14:13-14*

Crown of Life

"Blessed is the one who perseveres under trial because, having stood the test, that person will receive the crown of life that the Lord has promised to those who love him."
(James 1:12)

Whenever a traumatic event occurs, there will surely be a host of onlookers that gather around to see what is going on. Let's say Timmy falls into a manhole. Of course the whole neighborhood will come out to see what's going on. When the firemen finally pull Timmy out to safety, what will happen? More than likely they will be met with wild applause and cheers from the onlookers. Everyone will want to let the boy know how happy they are that he made it out of the terrible ordeal.

As it turns out, God responds the same way with us when we overcome our own trials and tribulations. The moment we emerge from the fires of this life and stand before Him on judgment day, He is there to greet us not only with joy unspeakable, flowing from His heart, but with a crown of life; our reward for our perseverance.

Christ has gone before us, enduring many trials much more difficult than anything you and I could ever face, and He has received the reward of being crowned King of the earth. As His followers, we also receive a crown for our endurance. This crown will stand as an everlasting symbol, that through the power of the Holy Spirit, we have overcome.

Regardless of the temptations that you are facing right now, you can and will overcome to receive your crown of life.

Prayer

Dear Father, thank you for constantly being with me to help me endure through the trials I have faced in this lifetime. I continue to look to you for strength in Jesus' name. Amen.
Further Studies: *Revelation 2:10*

The Way, Truth and Life

"Jesus answered, 'I am the way and the truth and the life.
No one comes to the Father except through me.'"
(John 14:6)

There are many religions in the world today, but the beautiful thing about Christianity is that though it may be classified as a religion, it stands out from the rest because it is so much more than that. Religion can be defined as man seeking a way to make contact with God, but Christianity is the pulsating life of God in man. Christianity is God's established order to bring man back into fellowship with Him.

No wonder the Apostle Paul declared, *"The Spirit you received does not make you slaves, so that you live in fear again; rather, the Spirit you received brought about your adoption to sonship. And by him we cry, 'Abba, Father'"* (Romans 8:15).

Because of Jesus, we have access to this wonderful promise of eternal life in God. Jesus is THE WAY; the only way. In Him is the truth concerning God, and He is the Life of God. He indwells you through salvation, and you become a member of the family of God.

Anything or anyone else who offers a way to God is false. This is one of the reasons why we must preach the gospel, fund gospel projects, and create enabling environments for the spread of the gospel in our offices, homes, and various spheres of influence. Jesus is the ONLY WAY, THE ONLY TRUTH, AND THE ONLY LIFE.

Prayer

Dear Father, thank you for not allowing me to grope in the dark. I
have Jesus and I have life. I do not walk in darkness or confusion
because Jesus is my light. In His name I pray. Amen.
Further Studies: *John 1:4, John 8:12, Acts 4:12*

Your Crown

"I am coming soon. Hold on to what you have, so that no one will take your crown."
(Revelation 3:11)

On the Day of Judgment, we will be held accountable for the lives that we have lived while on this earth. Did we influence our world for Jesus? Did we support the course of our great King? Did we truly love our neighbor as ourselves?

In our opening scripture we are counseled to hold fast to the promise of eternity with God even in the face of pain, shame, and suffering. As hard as such a statement may sound, there is hope. It is those that are still standing in the end that will receive a crown of glory.

> *"And when the Chief Shepherd appears, you will receive*
> *the crown of glory that will never fade away."*
> *1 Peter 5:4*

As Christians, we must hold fast to the faith we have in Christ until He returns. "Soon" is relative a term, and our understanding and interpretation of that word is different from that of God's, so don't get caught up in the time aspect of this scripture, but hold firm to the promise that one day Jesus will return.

Hold on to the promise that one day you will receive your crown, your reward of endurance, and everything you have gone through for the sake of Christ will be worth it. Your relationship with Christ and your sacrifice for the body is worth holding on to; guard it dearly so that no one takes your crown.

Prayer

Dear Father, I thank you for the crown of life that awaits me
on Christ's return. I will maintain my stand and keep my faith
against all odds and opposition in Jesus' name. Amen.
Further Studies: *James 1:12, Revelation 2:10*

Supreme Wisdom

"Do not forsake wisdom, and she will protect you; love her, and she will watch over you. Wisdom is supreme; therefore get wisdom. Though it cost all you have, get understanding."
(Proverbs 4:6-7)

The book of Proverbs is filled with much entreaty for us to get wisdom. As a Christian woman, you need the wisdom of God in order to relate with others and to build a Christian home where Jesus is enthroned.

To have wisdom means to be able to make sound decisions that are grounded in truth and understanding. There is no way that we can possibly make sound decisions, if we do not have the word of God stored up in our souls; therefore, we must be diligent in our study of the word if we truly want to obtain wisdom.

There's something interesting about this particular verse as it refers to the attainment of wisdom. It says that it will "cost all you have." If that is the case, then wisdom is a valuable trait for us to have, indeed!

Gaining wisdom will cost you your time and attention. Instead of spending your time on activities, chores, or leisure, you have to choose to spend your time in the Word. Even if you're spending your time on your family, which is totally honorable and good, you must remember that you need the wisdom of God to guide you as both wife and mother.

Examine your time to see how you can spend more time searching the scriptures and meditating on the word of God, and then choose today to get wisdom and understanding.

Prayer

Dear Father, I thank you for giving me your word to be my light in Jesus' name. Amen.
Further Studies: *James 1:5*

Today

"Jesus answered him, "Truly I tell you, today you will be with me in paradise."
(Luke 23:43)

Some people are in the habit of postponing everything until tomorrow. Whether it's homework, housework, hobbies, or following through on promises they've made, such people will convince themselves that they can take care of it another day.

Sadly enough, there are those that have even adopted this attitude towards salvation. When you preach the gospel to them, they may look convicted, but when you ask them to make the decision for Christ, they will tell you, "tomorrow." There are too many other things they want to do before they come Christ.

But we have not been promised tomorrow, so to postpone salvation can be a truly disastrous choice. I'm sure that we all know of people who have put off salvation for another day, but they never made it that far. It's truly a tragic situation.

As tragic as that situation is, it is also tragic for believers to feel the conviction of the Holy Spirit to make a certain change in their lives, yet they continually put it off to deal with it later. If the Holy Spirit brought something to your attention, He did so for a reason! Listen to Him!

Today is the day of salvation and repentance. Use it wisely.

Prayer

Dear Father, thank you for the salvation I have in Christ Jesus. Lord, forgive me for any way I've put you off for the sake of other things in Jesus' name. Amen.
Further Studies: *2 Corinthians 6:2*

Rest in the Lord

"Be still before the LORD and wait patiently for him; do not fret when people succeed in their ways, when they carry out their wicked schemes."
(Psalms 37:7)

It can be incredibly disheartening to be praying for something only to watch someone else receive the very same thing that you requested. It's even more disheartening when that person is someone who does not follow God or honor His commands. We'd like to believe that we're righteous enough to see the blessing of God in our lives, but when the wicked are the ones prospering, it can be enough to make us question our faith.

King David had been anointed to be the king of Israel when he was a young man, but it took 25 years before he saw the fulfillment of that promise. In the meantime he had to watch an insane king, a man who was no longer following God, rule for all that time. The following scripture gives us some insight into his perspective:

"Hope in the Lord and keep his way. He will exalt you to inherit the land; when the wicked are destroyed, you will see it. I have seen a wicked and ruthless man flourishing like a luxuriant native tree, but he soon passed away and was no more; though I looked for him, he could not be found."
Psalm 37:34-36

A woman who knows who she is and whose she is can rest easy in the Lord, because she understands that He takes care of all things in His time. Let us take hold of this faith and believe that just as God will deal with the wicked in due time, He will answer your need in due time.

Prayer

Dear Father, my faith is in you, and I trust that you will fulfill your word concerning me in Jesus' name. Amen.
Further Studies: *Hosea 12:6*

A Cheerful Giver

"Each of you should give what you have decided in your heart to give, not reluctantly or under compulsion, for God loves a cheerful giver."
(2 Corinthians 9:7)

I remember going to the farm with my grandpa when I was growing up. One of the things I remember is that grandpa taught me how to sow good seeds. He would always say, "Honey, if you plant a good seed, you will get a good harvest."

I remember separating the maize grains one day, when my mum asked me what I was doing. I told her that I wanted to plant the best looking grains so that I would get good harvest. When I had turned 13, I began to study the Bible, and when I came across this scripture, I knew that grandpa had taught me a principle that I would use for the rest of my life.

Anything that we give away to someone else can be viewed as a type of sowing. A good seed refers to something that is of the highest value or standard. Oftentimes, when we want to give money or donate clothes or bless someone with furniture, we only give if it's something that we don't really want, need, or care much for.

But what if God asked you to give someone that brand new jacket you just bought the other day? Would you do it? More importantly, would you give it cheerfully? That can be a hard pill for many of us to swallow, which is why this scripture encourages us to really search our hearts in terms of the type of offerings we give. Search your heart today as you endeavor to be a cheerful giver.

Prayer

Dear Father, thank you for teaching me to give and to give cheerfully in Jesus' name. Amen.
Further Studies: *Proverbs 11:25*

A Bright Face

"Wisdom lights up a person's face, softening its harshness."
(Ecclesiastes 8:1, NLT)

The other day I came across a friend who appeared very sad and gloomy. I asked her, "Julie, what is the matter with you? Why are you looking so sad and depressed?" She replied by telling me all of the things that she was going through with her family. Essentially, her children were becoming uncontrollable, and her husband was blaming it all on her.

When we're going through tough times, it generally shows in our countenance whether we want it to or not. People can look at our faces and immediately sense that something is not right. When this woman first came to me, her countenance was very downcast.

But after I had taken some time to counsel her, her face became radiant. You could literally see hope entering her soul. It was such a beautiful thing to see. This is what Solomon is talking about in our opening scripture.

A blind person sometimes moves his hand over a person's face to "see" who they are. By doing this they feel the contour and texture, but they can also get a good idea about the person's personality or emotions. Take the time today to look at yourself in the mirror and ask God to fill your countenance with the radiance of His glory.

Prayer

Dear Father, I refuse to walk in darkness in any aspect of my life. I take advantage of your wisdom to guide and instruct me today. Thank you, dear Lord, in Jesus' name. Amen.
Further Studies: *James 1:5*

Cause for Rejoicing

"But we had to celebrate and be glad, because this brother of yours was dead and is alive again; he was lost and is found."'
(Luke 15:32)

The Lord Jesus gives us the parable of the Lost Son, as recorded by Luke. We know how it feels when we lose something and then find it; it makes us happy and celebratory, especially if it is something dear to us.

So too in the Kingdom of God, when a sinner turns or returns to the Kingdom, it is cause for great rejoicing! Angels in heaven rejoice over one sinner that repents, so should we too join rejoice when people come to Christ. Being in sin makes us dead, but coming to Christ makes us alive. That's a pretty big deal!

I first heard this parable explained when I was in children's church, but I never really understood it to mean salvation. As I got older, when I started reading the Bible, it all came back to me, and I saw that I had been called to win others to Christ.

I remember walking into a church service where pastors were gathered, when someone came yelling and running down the aisle. It was a young man that I had preached to about 5 years earlier. He ran straight from the back and came to hug me. I was embarrassed but kept my cool. When he eventually calmed down, he narrated how I had led him to Christ, and all of the pastors praised God. I was so happy that day and rejoiced at God's work in this young man's life. Imagine what will happen when we get to heaven.

Prayer

Dear Father, I choose to continually bring joy to heaven by leading men and women into salvation. Thank you for your grace in Jesus' name. Amen.
Further Studies: Luke 15:10

Sons of God

"Dear friends, now we are children of God, and what we will be has not yet been made known. But we know that when Christ appears, we shall be like him, for we shall see him as he is."
(1 John 3:2)

One of the greatest mysteries in this life is probably what is yet to come; what will become of us after this life ends. Everyone has, at one time or another, pondered death and what happens after we release our final breath.

For those who do not have a relationship with God, this thought can be a very scary one. Maybe all they can picture is an empty void or maybe they envision the horrors of hell. There is no hope for anything of substance after death apart from Christ.

But for believers, we have two very great assurances. As we walk the earth, we have the assurance that we are the children of God. So we see His involvement in our lives each and every day and we testify to the truth of God being alive and active in the world today.

Being able to witness God's movement as His children instills us with a great and glorious hope that one day, when this life ends, God is going to be faithful to transform us into the image of His son and fit us with eternal bodies so that we can truly fulfill the prophecies and live with Him eternally.

If you know someone that doesn't have this hope today, consider sharing it with them. No one should have to end this life without the hope of eternity with Jesus.

Prayer

Dear Father, I thank you because I will be transformed into the image of your son at his appearing in Jesus' name. Amen.
Further Studies: 1 Peter 1:7

The Power of God

"For the message of the cross is foolishness to those who are perishing,
but to us who are being saved it is the power of God."
(1 Corinthians 1:18)

I used to tell people that Christianity is the simplest life to live on earth, and it's the truth. Everything you need has already been provided for you through Christ Jesus, and on top of that, you also have help from the Holy Spirit of God to do all that God commands. It makes total sense, right?

Well, that might be true for believers, but for nonbelievers, what we believe sounds totally foolish. To believe that someone died, came back to life, and then became the gate through which everyone on earth can enter into an eternal destiny almost sounds like the plot to a sci-fi movie.

That is one reason why we constantly see Jesus telling His disciples throughout His teachings on earth, "He that has an ear, let Him hear what the Spirit is saying." It is only those with spiritual ears that can perceive the truth of the gospel; those without spiritual understanding just hear gibberish.

The gospel we preach may not make sense to those who live in the realm of reasoning, but it sure will make sense to those who choose to believe. Therefore, we must continually pray for our friends and neighbors to be receptive to the gospel, because it will produce salvation in them when they believe.

Prayer

Dear Father, I open my spiritual hears to hear your words and the truth
therein. Thank you for the efficacy of your word in Jesus' name. Amen.
Further Studies: *Isaiah 55:11*

Path of Life

"You make known to me the path of life; you will fill me with joy in
your presence, with eternal pleasures at your right hand."
(Psalms 16:11)

There are several paths available to us in this life, and there are several people who claim to know the one true path that everyone should follow. There may even be certain pathways that look pleasing to the eye, but that ultimately lead to destruction. Here the psalmist shares that only God can reveal the path that leads to life.

The path of life that God takes us through consists of fullness of joy in His presence and pleasures at His right hand for all eternity. We can be full of joy even when walking into unfamiliar territory if we know that we're following the path that leads to life.

This scripture is the very first prayer I taught my kids, because I know that only God can lead them in the path of life. I always tell my children that God will teach them all they need to know in life, and He will guide then.

"I will instruct you and teach you in the way you should
go; I will counsel you with my loving eye on you."
Psalm 32:8

Like the psalmist, we ask God to show us "the path of life." Not just any path, but the ultimate life-giving path; a path that is only found in God's presence. Use the stepping stones of encouragement, praise and worship, strength, humility, prayer and obedience to stay on the path of life each day.

Prayer

Dear Father, I trust your guidance in life and I know that by
obeying you I will dwell in safety in Jesus' name. Amen.
Further Studies: *Isaiah 48:17*

Party in Heaven

*"In the same way, I tell you, there is rejoicing in the presence
of the angels of God over one sinner who repents."*
(Luke 15:10)

The streamers are in place, a few balloons have been placed here and there, colorful lights flash around the room, and there is food, dancing and music! This is the scene of a party. Let your imagination run wild for a bit. If this is what an earthly party looks like, can you imagine the angels at a party in heaven?

Every time someone receives Christ, there is rejoicing, there is joy, and there is a party in heaven. A party is the celebration of a special occasion, and everyone that attends a party is usually filled with an overwhelming sense of joy.

Accepting Christ is the most important event in your life, and it is worth celebrating every single time someone else believes in Jesus. As Christians, our efforts in sharing the Gospel result in a continuous party in heaven. We can keep this party alive by constantly leading people to Jesus.

Matthew 28:19-20 is known as the great commission, so you do not need to be specially called to be a soul-winner. You also do not need any special training to win others to Christ. The testimony of your conversion is enough gospel, so make it your goal to fill heaven with constant celebration.

Prayer

*Dear Father, I thank you for the privilege to cause a continual
rejoicing in heaven. Precious Father, help me to be committed
to the work of evangelism in the name of Jesus. Amen.*
Further Studies: *Matthew 28:19-20*

Incorruptible Inheritance

"...into an inheritance that can never perish, spoil or fade.
This inheritance is kept in heaven for you."
(1 Peter 1:4)

always wonder what the world will be like 50 years from now. Maybe your present house will be a bank, a school, a church, a dumping site or maybe an industrial plant. Ownership of land and properties always changes from one generation to another.

The vehicles we were used to in the early 90s and even 2000's are now old models, and some of them are nowhere to be found because earthly treasure always decay and rot with time. No wonder Jesus counseled us to lay up treasures in heaven.

There is an inheritance in heaven, and not just "any" inheritance, but one that is not susceptible to corruption, especially by bribery, nor is it subject to death or decay; it is everlasting. This inheritance is what we have been called to inherit in Christ Jesus, and that is why the world and all its treasures mean nothing to us anymore.

We become heirs to this inheritance because of the resurrection of Jesus Christ from the dead, He is the living hope. Our inheritance cannot be plucked away; its value cannot change, no one else can claim it. If you have not yet made Jesus your Lord, then accept Him now so that you can claim your incorruptible inheritance. If He is your Lord, then praise God for Jesus Christ.

Prayer

Dear Father, I thank you for the incorruptible inheritance I have in Christ Jesus. I set my eyes on you and your infallible word of promise in Jesus' name. Amen.
Further Studies: *Matthew 6:19-20*

Divinely Feminine

"And He answered and said, 'Have you not read that He who created them from the beginning made them male and female,' and said, 'For this reason a man shall leave his father and mother and be joined to his wife, and the two shall become one flesh'? 'So they are no longer two, but one flesh. What therefore God has joined together, let no man separate."
(Matthew 19:4-6)

Creation indicates that gender is a divine ordinance made by God, not a mistake in human development. When God made male and female, gender was part of the grand design.

In God's picture of marriage, two persons who are divided by vast differences become one fruitful, complementary image. How is the unity in your marriage? As you conform to God's role for you as a woman, you will find it easier to complement and unite with your husband.

If, as a woman, you find it hard to blend in with your husband, turn to the scriptures to wrestle through what it teaches about our roles as women. It is more than child bearing and managing a household; we actually help our husbands fulfill their God-given calling while we fulfill our own calling and raise godly seeds.

My husband and I have come to realize that neither of us would have been successful if we had not been working together in unity. He always says, "Honey, I owe my success in life to Jesus and to you." I usually will just chuckle and say exactly the same words to him.

Prayer

Dear Father, I thank you for making me a woman. I take my place and fulfill my call in Jesus' name. Amen.
Further Studies: *Ephesians 5:25*

Called to Conquer

"For everyone born of God overcomes the world. This is the victory that has overcome the world, even our faith."
(1 John 5:4)

God originally created man to be lords over everything in the earth, but when Adam and Eve sinned, the whole of humanity became a slave to the devil and sin. So when God devised a plan for redemption, His idea was to create or give birth to a new man that is superior to the devil, the world, and its systems; essentially restoring His original plan for mankind.

As we walk out our Christian lives of faith, the world and our flesh constantly wage war against our spirit in an attempt to take control of our lives and disqualify us from our destiny in God. Therefore, to become an overcomer of the world, we must not adhere to the ways of the world, but we must operate by the higher laws and principles of the Word of God.

Now, this may be easy to say, but not so easy to do. If our bodies naturally desire the things of the world, it can be difficult to know how to live contrary to our natural desires. The best example of overcoming the world is seen in Christ. Study the Word to discover how He dealt with sin and overcame the temptations of the enemy.

The only way we will overcome the world and partake of the resurrection is by our faith (1 John 5:4). We are called to conquer and be victorious through our faith in Christ, who has already overcome.

Prayer

Dear Father, I thank you for calling me into the life of an overcomer. I am born of you, Lord, and I overcome this world and its systems in Jesus' name. Amen.
Further Studies: *John 16:33*

Attitude Adjustment

"Praise the LORD. Blessed is the man who fears the LORD,
who finds great delight in his commands."
(Psalm 112:1, ESV)

Praising the Lord is an action can never be exhausted. You can never run out of reasons to magnify the Lord! He deserves to be praised and is worthy to be lifted up all over the world through the praises of His people.

Praise and worship always revive in us the right attitude. When we engage in them, they help to keep us on the right track. Notice the psalmist in this verse. He begins with praise, acknowledges fearing the Lord and ends in taking "great delight" in God's commands. God's commands lead to life; they are the road map to eternal life.

Take a quiet moment today to praise the Lord and acknowledge the love of God through His commands.

Maybe you are going through a tough time in your life today and you are wondering if there is really any reason to thank God. Well, the best time to praise God and give Him glory is when you are in the midst of the storms of life. The Bible records for us the account Paul and Silas who praised God in the prison. The result was deliverance.

Remember that *"God is faithful; he will not let you be tempted beyond what you can bear. But when you are tempted, he will also provide a way out so that you can endure it."* 1 Corinthians 10:13.

Prayer

Dear Father, I choose to praise you irrespective of my prevailing circumstance because I know that is working for my good. I choose to delight myself in you in Jesus' name. Amen.
Further Studies: *Isaiah 50:15, Psalm 37:4, James 1:2-4*

Strength to Care

"For God hath not given us the spirit of fear; but of power, and of love, and of a sound mind."
(2 Timothy 1:7, NKJ)

There are so many reasons to be afraid and to worry. Even so, there are 366 "Fear Not" statements in the Bible; statements where God encourages us to shun the influence of the spirit of fear in our lives.

Because of our natural nurturing capacity, women tend to be the "go-to" for some of the most difficult situations. If you are a caregiver, you know the pressure of handling many issues without falling apart.

When God tells us He has not equipped us with fear but with power, love, and a sound mind, He reminds us that He supplies our needs for every situation. Whether we're in need of provision or protection or anything else, God has it under control.

We need not depend on ourselves, but on Him to give us power to endure, love to forgive, compassion where needed, and a sound mind to give advice and encouragement to those who depend on us most.

Instead of allowing fear and its crippling effects into your heart in times of pressure, choose to praise the Lord, and He will surely guide you on what to do. David said, "The Lord is my shepherd, I shall not want." Refuse to let fear control your life and put your hope in Jesus.

Prayer

Dear Father, I refuse to fear. As I trust you today, I receive strength to care for those who depend on me and I receive wisdom to give wise counsel to in times of need in Jesus' name. Amen.
Further Studies: *Proverbs 3:5-6, Psalm 18:2, Psalm 28:7*

Balanced Discipline

"Through love and faithfulness sin is atoned for; through
the fear of the LORD evil is avoided."
(Proverbs 16:6)

The truth is we've all sinned and we all deserve a penalty, but because of mercy, God does not give us the wrathful punishment we deserve. God's mercy inspires us to turn away from evil, and the truth of His Word cleanses us. Mercy, truth, and the fear of the Lord allow us to depart from wrong doing.

God disciplines us in a way that speaks of the true nature of our sin, the mercy of forgiveness, and the desire of wanting to personally depart from evil.

"And you have forgotten the exhortation which is addressed to
you as sons: "MY SON, DO NOT REGARD LIGHTLY THE DISCIPLINE
OF THE LORD, NOR FAINT WHEN YOU ARE REPROVED BY
HIM; FOR THOSE WHOM THE LORD LOVES HE DISCIPLINES,
AND HE SCOURGES EVERY SON WHOM HE RECEIVES."
It is for discipline that you endure; God deals with you as with sons;
for what son is there whom his father does not discipline? But if you
are without discipline, of which all have become partakers, then
you are illegitimate children and not sons. Furthermore, we had
earthly fathers to discipline us, and we respected them; shall we
not much rather be subject to the Father of spirits, and live?"
Hebrews 12:5-9, NASB

Consider your response to God's discipline in your life. He disciplines you because He loves you. Are you responding rightly to it?

Prayer

Dear Lord, from this day on I choose to receive your correction, because it is prove of
your love for me. Help me to receive your correction with joy in Jesus' name. Amen.
Further Studies: *Proverbs 3:11*

Temptation is the Trouble

"Watch and pray so that you will not fall into temptation.
The spirit is willing, but the body is weak."
(Matthew 26:41)

Notice in this verse that Jesus does not say, "Watch and pray that you will not fall into sin," but He says, "Watch and pray that you will not fall into temptation." Temptation is the catalyst to sin. We fall prey to temptation before we fall prey to sin.

For example, before someone commits adultery, they must first give into the temptation to look lustfully at another person or the temptation to entertain inappropriate thoughts. The reality of the matter is that we cannot sin until we have first given into temptation. This is why it is so important for us to be on our guard against temptation.

The Apostle Paul counsels us in 1 Thessalonians 5:2 to "abstain from all appearances of evil." *To abstain means to hold oneself back voluntarily, especially from something regarded as improper or unhealthy.*

Jesus says that while our spirit is willing to obey His commands, our body is weak. Our flesh is always prone to want to do the wrong things, so to be victorious and strong in your bodies over temptation, you must watch and pray.

Watch and pray so you do not fall.

Prayer

Dear Father, I thank you for the strength to withstand all advances of evil
and to remain standing in the face of lurking evil in Jesus' name. Amen.
Further Studies: *1 Corinthians 10:13*

Pearls of Purity

"Do not give dogs what is sacred; do not throw your pearls to pigs."
(Matthew 7:6a)

Because many women are relationship-driven, pleasing the people in their lives can be a matter of high priority. When you live your life to please others, it goes without saying that there are often times that you will be required to compromise your own beliefs or values.

For someone women, that may mean compromising their physical purity. The Bible makes it very clear that sex before marriage is a sin, and yet our culture tells us something very different.

The argument to engage in such activities against the Word of the Lord can be very compelling and can lead many women astray, but in the concluding part of our opening scripture, Jesus explained what will happen if we give those things which are most precious to us to people who do not care: *"If you do, they may trample them under their feet, and turn and tear you to pieces."*

God has set you apart—He desires you to be holy! This great jewel that He has given you must be safeguarded. Just as swine do not recognize the value and significance of pearls, being yoked to someone who hasn't taken the time to discover the jewel hidden inside of you can ultimately misuse you.

Do not settle for less than what God has ordained for you. You are worth every bit of it.

Prayer

Dear Father, I thank you for giving me this body. I pledge to take care of it and keep it holy for you in Jesus' name. Amen.
Further Studies: *Proverbs 4:23*

Tangible Faith

"Now faith is the substance of things hoped for, the evidence of things not seen."
(Hebrews 11:1, KJV)

Have you believed in a particular scripture or trusted in a promise from God's word? Most likely you have. If you don the title "Christian," it should actually be part of your lifestyle in Christ. A Christian's life is a walk of faith.

We must walk by faith in God, and we must also walk by faith with the head of our home. By faith we trust that the head of our home has our best interest at heart, that he will provide for us, and that he will make decisions that are God-honoring.

There are times when he will make a poor decision that will affect the wellbeing of the family, and maybe you know in your heart that it's not the best decision. What do we do in these circumstances?

We must have faith that God will take care of us and our families, and favor us in the circumstance. God honors a woman who honors her husband, so as you put your faith in God, honor your husband by entrusting him and your family into the hands of God, and by emboldening him to operate in the grace of God.

Look with expectancy, God WILL be faithful!

Prayer

Dear Father, I thank you for the ability to believe in your word. Help me to trust you even when my circumstances and leaders seem doubtful in Jesus' name. Amen.
Further Studies: *2 Corinthians 5:7*

Reassurance

*"Burst into songs of joy together, you ruins of Jerusalem, for the
LORD has comforted his people, he has redeemed Jerusalem."*
(Isaiah 52:9)

This verse presents such an interesting visual image. Imagine the ruins of
Jerusalem strewn across a vast expanse of land with smoke rising from the
ashes. An invading army has just come through and completely ransacked the
entire city, leaving the people destitute and homeless.

And yet, the word of the Lord to those ruins is to burst into songs of joy.

In our own view, a sight such as the one described would be cause for great sorrow
and mourning, but according to this scripture, God calls for a response of joy.
Why? Well, the second part of the verse says because the LORD has comforted
and redeemed His people. He had seen them in their distress and responded to
them. That alone should be cause enough for celebration!

This verse gives a very powerful description of how we should respond when we
feel as though our lives are in ruin. We should respond in praise and rejoice in
the salvation of our Lord with the knowledge that not only is He right there to
comfort us, but He will redeem us from whatever situation we're facing and turn
our ashes into something very beautiful.

Prayer

*Dear Lord, I thank you for comforting me in the midst of my struggle.
I rejoice in you, the hope of my salvation in Jesus' name. Amen.*
Further Studies: *2 Corinthians 1:3, 2 Corinthians 13:11*

Feast of the Hungry

"For he satisfies the thirsty and fills the hungry with good things."
(Psalm 107:9)

Moms know that the cries of a baby's hunger will not be satisfied by anything but milk. A pacifier may work for a while, but once that baby recognizes that the object in his mouth is not food, he is going to let you know that he is still hungry! If you are breastfeeding, your baby knows that no one else will be able to nurture and meet his needs but you.

Babies can recognize that they are hungry, and they know from experience what can satisfy their hunger. In our case, as is typical of adults, we also know what can satisfy our spiritual hunger, but we often search for other things to pacify us in the meantime (i.e. relationships, material possessions, or substances).

Engaging in such activities can be satisfying for a moment, but that moment is fleeting. The only lasting satisfaction we can find comes from the hand of God alone.

In keeping with this analogy, just as the child knows that when he cries someone, namely his mother, is going to respond, we know that when we cry out, the Lord will avail Himself to fill our mouths with good things. Babies are helpless when it comes to taking care of themselves, and they recognize that. It's about time that we acknowledge that reality as well. We who desire to be forgiven of our sin know that nothing else will suffice; good works may ease our conscience a little, like a pacifier, but they will not give us peace with God.

If we will hunger for Him, He will feed us.

Prayer

*Dear Father, forgive me for looking to anything else for satisfaction
when I know it comes from you alone. Teach me to lift my eyes
to you whenever I am in need in Jesus' name. Amen.*
Further Studies: *Psalm 19*

Hospitable Housewives

"But God, who comforts the downcast, comforted us by the coming of Titus."
(2 Corinthians 7:6)

For the most part, women like to be close to people. We love having someone we can talk to about our innermost thoughts and feelings, and we enjoy the feeling of togetherness we get when we're around people that we love. It is especially nice to have people around when we're hurting or in need of support.

This aspect of our nature mirrors the ministry of the Holy Spirit. As our confidant, He is a very present help in time of trouble. Likewise, the simple act of being near to someone may be all it takes to bring that person through one of their darkest trials. They say that misery loves company, and though that statement is typically used negatively, it also points to the fact that we need people to be with us in the moment of our pain.

In Paul's case, he writes that Titus' visit and good report about what God was producing in the Corinthians was just the medicine he needed because it assured Paul that his labor and suffering were not in vain. Titus may not have known that he was providing such encouragement to his spiritual father in the faith, but God did.

In His infinite wisdom, God often causes our paths to cross with others who need to hear a word from Him. Why? Because we are His mouthpiece. We only have to avail ourselves to His Spirit so that we can hear what He is saying. There are other times when He simply desires that we bring His presence with us wherever we go. Maybe no words need be spoken, but through your nearness to the broken hearted, His presence can be felt.

Prayer

Dear Father, thank you for comforting me in my times of grief.
Help me to be comfort to others in Jesus' name. Amen.
Further Studies: *1 Thessalonians 5:11*

The Altar of Creation

"You shall not make for yourself an image in the form of anything in heaven above or on the earth beneath or in the waters below."
(Exodus 20:4)

Creation is beautiful. Just take a moment to step outside and enjoy the divine creativity of the world in which you live. Everything about nature points us to the sovereign God that created it. It not only allows us to see God's creativity, but it also allows us to get a glimpse into the beauty of His majesty.

However, it is easy to become blinded by the magnificence of what has been created and forget the One who created it. Think about the gods of the Egyptians and the way each god represented a creature that God himself created. Think about Hinduism and the way that cows are revered as sacred. These and many other religions have bypassed the Creator in order to worship something He created.

Though you may not know people that actually worship graven images, remember that there are plenty of religions out there that do. Pray for those who are involved in such religions to get a glimpse of the one, true and living God. Pray that they would see Him as the creator of all and reject whatever idols they've worshiped, then ask God if there are any graven images in your life that you have been worshipping.

Worship the Creator, not the created.

Prayer

Dear Father, you alone are God and there is no one beside you. May you be glorified as the maker of heaven and earth both now and forevermore in Jesus' name. Amen.
Further Studies: *Leviticus 26:1*

Limits of Prayer

"This is the confidence which we have before in Him, that, if
we ask anything according to his will, He hears us."
(1 John 5:14, NASB)

There are only two parameters to our prayers: God's will and our confidence that the requests we bring to Him matter to His heart. Part of the process of growing in a relationship with God is learning how to tell the difference between what we want and what He wants. Sometimes the line can be difficult to navigate. As His children, we often come to Him making requests of our own accord, just like our children would with us, but as children of the *King of Kings*, there is a particular protocol we must follow.

How can we be certain that we are praying according to God's will? Praying His Word is the first place to start. Everything we need to know about the will of God can be found in His Word. He's given us a very detailed manuscript of His heart, His will, and His desires. If we take His words and His promises and repeat them back to Him, we can be assured that we are praying His heart.

Now, because God's ways are higher than our ways and His thoughts are higher than our thoughts, what we assume will fit into His plan may be vastly different than what He truly wants, but that is why we have the Holy Spirit. Rely on the Holy Spirit, who searches the deep things of God as well as the deepest places of your heart, to reveal the right way to pray. There is no better person you could refer to about the will of God than the Holy Spirit.

As we pray about a need, let's surrender our hearts to accept God's way of meeting the need. He will meet our needs according to His riches in glory.

Prayer

Dear Father, help me to discern your will above mine or the will of others.
Teach me to continually pray as Your Spirit leads in Jesus' name. Amen.
Further Studies: *1 Corinthians 2:10-16*

June

Open Arms

"She opens her arms to the poor and extends her hands to the needy."
(Proverbs 31:20)

Whenever we want to know what it looks like to authentically live a Christian lifestyle, we should look to the Word. Within its pages we can discover not only the commands the Lord has given us, but also real examples of what living those commands out should look like.

It is clear from the Old Testament to the New Testament that God has a huge place in His heart for orphans, widows, and the poor. He made provisions for them in His law, and took it very seriously when His people neglected those laws. When Jesus came to the earth, He also demonstrated the heart of His Father, as He constantly ministered to those who were in need.

Now, when we hear the word *needy*, we typically think of homeless people. Though that demographic definitely fits the qualifications of being in need, there are many other ways that we can find and serve the needy in our lives. People can be in need financially, emotionally, spiritually, and even momentarily.

When someone's spouse dies and they need help with food or childcare, offer your services. When you see a child go to school in the same clothes multiple days in a row, donate some clothing. When an elderly woman is struggling to carry her groceries up the stairs, help her.

Ask God to show you where the needy are, within your sphere of influence, and how you can serve them best today.

Prayer

Dear Lord, thank you for the privilege to be a blessing to others in my world. Lord, my heart is open to hear the cry of those hurting and to help them in Jesus' name. Amen.
Further Studies: *Proverbs 19:17*

Motivator

"Do everything in love."
(1 Corinthians 16:14)

Love is synonymous with serving. If you love someone, you will naturally serve them with your time, your abilities, and your attention. To do all things in love means to consider others before yourself or to esteem others as you would esteem yourself.

Most parents' motivation for doing things for their children is love. This is the same motivation that causes spouses to go out of their way to please each other. Love is a great motivator that spurs us on in our ambition to be like Christ.

Imagine a world where every action is motivated by love, kindness, and affection. What an amazing world that would be. And it can be so in your "little" world, as you allow your motive, reason, enthusiasm, and deciding factor for doing everything to be guided by the principle of love. Jesus said, *"Therefore, whatever you want men to do to you, do also to them, for this is the Law and the Prophets"* (Matthew 7:12).

Imagine what would happen if every one of us started treating people the way we want to be treated; if you would respect and revere your husband the way you want him to revere you; if you would relate with your neighbors the way you want them to relate with you. This is how you create an atmosphere of love, kindness and affection in your little world. By deciding to live in this manner, we can change the world.

Prayer

Dear Father, thank you for teaching me to consider and esteem others as myself. I choose to live everyday doing to others what I wish they would do for me in Jesus' name. Amen..
Further Studies: *Luke 6:27-36*

First Love

"We love because he first loved us."
(1 John 4:19)

First love. These two words may bring back sweet or bitter memories for you, but either way, your first love is the kind of love you don't forget easily. When you feel an emotion like love for the first time in your life, it can definitely leave a lasting impression and greatly influence who you are and the way you love others.

God is our first love because He loved us first. Before you even knew about Him, before you were born, before the beginning of time, before your grandparents met, He was the initiator in your relationship with Him. He loved you FIRST!

That's the kind of love every woman desires. He made ALL the necessary provisions for you, He fights for you, He protects you, He delivers you, and He favors you above all. Therefore, your ultimate response should be to love Him in return.

> *"For God so loved the world that he gave his only begotten Son, that whosoever believeth in him should not perish, but have everlasting life."*
> John 3:16

This first love is authentic, so embrace it, receive it, and reciprocate it by living for Him, loving Him back, and living your life as an example that will bring others to Him.

Prayer

Dear Father, I thank you for your love that you have poured on me.
Lord, I accept and appreciate your love. Jesus is the Lord of my life
and the center of my affection, in his name I pray. Amen.
Further Studies: *Romans 5:8*

Growing Wise

"He who walks with the wise grows wise, but a companion of fools suffers harm."
(Proverbs 13:20, NASB)

It's been said that birds of a feather flock together. The next time you see a flock of birds flying together, if you check their silhouettes, you will see that they are all the same type of bird. You're not likely to see sparrows, crows, and seagulls flying in the same flock.

In the same way, you will be influenced by the associations you keep. None of us is an island. Most of the things we are today are the result of character traits and attitudes we picked up from different friends.

When I had just started going to prayer meetings, I really didn't know how to pray. But before long, I began to build a prayer vocabulary by listening to others pray. Though we don't want to imitate others for the sake of being as "holy" as they are "holy," it is a good idea to learn from those who have been where you are trying to go.

So too, in following the example of the birds, we should "fly" with the wise in order to grow wise. Growing wise requires a concerted effort, but the rewards are worth their weight in gold. The results will last for eternity. Flock with the wise and become wiser. If you have kept any company that is not relevant to your Christian walk, it is time to let go. You will always benefit more if you lose something in order to gain Christ.

Prayer

Dear Father, I thank you for guiding me into your wisdom through the examples of other Christians in the name of Jesus Christ. Amen.
Further Studies: Psalm 1

Good Courage

"Yes, we are of good courage, and we would rather be away
from the body and at home with the Lord."
(2 Corinthians 5:8, ESV)

Do you feel as though you are someone who can claim this verse to be true of your life? Are you at a place where you would rather be at home with Lord, or are there still things here on this earth that you desire more?

As much as we'd all like to say that we'd prefer being with Jesus, the way that we live our lives may tell a very different story. There is a quote I read once that said something to the effect of, "How can you claim you want to spend eternity with Jesus, when you do not even have the desire to spend one hour with Him here on earth?"

For the Apostle Paul to have made the statement in this verse demonstrates just how consumed he was with loving and living for God. Anyone who truly pines for the day that they can be united with their heavenly Father is undoubtedly living a similar lifestyle.

To be in the Lord's presence 24/7/365 is so much better than anything we could possibly experience now, even in the little pockets of heaven on earth. We just need to get a proper glimpse of the greater joys that await us in eternity.

While we wait, let us resolve to keep the hope of seeing Jesus as the ultimate goal for this race. Do not live as though life ends on earth, but live with eternity in view; focus on the things above.

Prayer

Dear Father, I am full of good confidence, because I know that to be absent in the flesh is to be present with you. Thank you Lord for this great hope in Jesus' name. Amen.
Further Studies: *Philippians 3:3*

Be Watchful

"Jesus answered: "Watch out that no one deceives you. For many will come in my name, claiming, 'I am the Messiah,' and will deceive many."
(Matthew 24:4-5)

Right from the days of Jesus, we have been warned of false prophets and false messiahs. I have come to the conclusion that those who will easily be deceived are those who are looking for what God will do for them; those who want Christianity to be like fast food. They want to run into God's house and get quick miracles and then run away until next time.

But our growth in Christ is no quick fix. Once you are saved, you must, *"Work out your own salvation with fear and trembling"* Philippians 2:12.

After your salvation, you must sit and study God's word, learn how to pray and meditate, learn to act on God's word, and then start applying your faith to the Word to get the answers and results you need.

In order to identify counterfeit money you need to handle the real money, get to know its features and how it feels. To know Jesus we must spend time with Him, get to know his characteristics, and read His word in order to know how He operates and what He would say.

Imitators will arise claiming to be the Messiah, so we need to be watchful. Our personal relationship with Him will help us to avoid being misled. You will only be able to distinguish between sound doctrine and doctrines of devils if you know the word of God.

Prayer

Dear Father, I thank you for the awesome privilege of knowing you by experience. I keep my heart on your word. I will never be deceived in Jesus' name. Amen.
Further Studies: *Matthew 7:21, Acts 20:29-30, 2 Timothy 4:3-4*

Living Hope

"Praise be to the God and Father of our Lord Jesus Christ! In his great mercy he has given us new birth into a living hope through the resurrection of Jesus Christ from the dead,"
(1 Peter 1:3)

When I think of the term "living hope," I think of something perpetual. God be praised for His great mercy which affords us new life through the resurrection of Jesus from the dead.

It all hinges on the fact that Jesus not only died, but He rose from the dead, thereby defeating death.

The death of Jesus was enough to pay for our sins and redeem us, but when God raised Him from the dead, He accomplished more than just redemption. Through the resurrection of Jesus Christ, we were brought into a place of justification before God.

> *"But also for us, to whom God will credit righteousness—for us who believe in him who raised Jesus our Lord from the dead. He was delivered over to death for our sins and was raised to life for our justification."*
> *Romans 4:24-25*

His resurrection is the very reason for our justification, and now we are free to live with Him for eternity. No wonder Peter calls it A LIVING HOPE. This is one of the reasons we must strive to live by God's word and standards against all odds.

Each day may be filled with its own baggage, but thanks be unto God, we are born again into a perpetual hope because Jesus conquered it all. Praise God.

Prayer

Dear Father, I thank you for the hope that I have in Christ Jesus to live eternally with you in Jesus' name. Amen.
Furthers Studies: *1 Corinthians 15:19*

Ministering to Jesus

*"There were also many women there, looking on from a distance
who had followed Jesus from Galilee, ministering to him."*
(Matthew 27:55, ESV)

Ministering to one another is very big component of being part of the body of Christ. It has to do with being able to give up your comfort for that of others in order to provide for the needs of other Christians and the needs of the church.

Jesus spent most of His days ministering to others, but it's not very often that we read in the Bible that others ministered to Him. The only two groups of people that we're explicitly told ministered to Jesus were the angels and various women.

What an awesome privilege we have as women to be the ones known to have had the insight and compassion to minister to Jesus! The truth is, we all need to be ministered to, and those who are involved in ministry need it the most!

We often like to believe our pastors and church staff have everything together, so we typically take as much as we want from them, but just as we are all members of one body, the brain cannot function if you don't feed it. Leaders need to be fed too.

Your service to and partnership with those in leadership will not only lead to the expansion of the kingdom, but it will result in thanksgiving to God from those you minister to.

Prayer

*Dear Father, thank you for the revelation of your word. I choose to
be very committed to my ministry of partnering with those you have
called into full-time work in your house in Jesus' name. Amen.*
Further Scriptures: *Luke 8:1-3, 2 Corinthians 9:12*

The Savior

"But our citizenship is in heaven, and from it we await a Savior, the Lord Jesus Christ."
(Philippians 3:20, ESV)

"This world is not my home, I'm just a-passing through." These words are the first line of a song Jim Reeves sang many years ago. We may live on earth, but our citizenship is in heaven. This Kingdom has a Savior who is our reigning King. He's not just a Savior, He is *the* Savior!

There are those who wonder at us and say, "Who do they think they are?" What makes them think they are special?" We are citizens of heaven, and Jesus made that possible when He died to wash us clean of our sins, and was raised again for our justification.

Our Savior has not only redeemed us from sins and saved our souls, but He has also made provision for our day to day struggles. He can rescue us from daily dangers and difficulties, He is our very present help in times of need, and He preserves us from eternal destruction and death. He's no ordinary person; He is the Son of God!

There are those who do not understand the salvation that Jesus brought to the human race, and it is our responsibility to tell them. Tell the untold about Jesus our Savior and keep your hope alive, because He is coming to take us home. Glory to God!

Prayer

Dear Father, I thank you for saving me from destruction and preserving my life in Christ Jesus in His name I pray. Amen.
Further Studies: *John 3:16*

Do not Judge

"Therefore judge nothing before the appointed time; wait until the Lord comes. He will bring to light what is hidden in darkness and will expose the motives of the heart. At that time each will receive their praise from God."
(1 Corinthians 4:5)

One of the anthems of this generation is the phrase "Only God can judge me." Although this statement is true, people most often use it as an excuse to do whatever they want. What they don't realize is that God really will judge them for their behavior, so while they may have discouraged someone else from calling them out on whatever they're doing wrong, God will bring their sin into the light one day.

We must understand that nothing is hidden from God. He knows EVERYTHING, including a person's heart. At best we presume from what we can see and what we understand based on our limited knowledge. This is why we're admonished not to judge others. There's a whole lot of story beneath the surface that we may not be privy to.

Imagine going to court and having the judge make a ruling based on only half of the evidence. Would the ruling be fair or just? Probably not. She would need all of the facts and evidence before she could make a proper ruling. The same goes for us. We cannot judge anyone's righteousness, because we don't know the whole story.

So does this mean that we cannot call people to order when they go wrong, or that we cannot settle disputes among ourselves when they arise? No, Paul is simply asking us to trust God to reveal all things in His own time.

Prayer

Dear Father, I know that there is nothing hidden from you and that you see the hearts of all men. I trust you, and I know that your justice will always prevail in Jesus' name. Amen.
Further Studies: *1 Peter 3:12, 2 Chronicles 16:9a*

Eternal Life

"Whoever believes in the Son has eternal life, but whoever rejects the Son will not see life, for God's wrath remains on them."
(John 3:36)

The wages of sin is death. You've heard that before, right? When we go through life with sin weighing us down, it can keep us from experiencing the joys of eternal life with Christ, our Lord and Savior. But what is eternal life and what is so special about it that we need to change the way that we live our lives?

Let's start by looking at a river as an example. Rivers are ever on the move, renewing themselves. If you throw something into the water, the water just carries it away. If you heap dirt into it, with time it will carry all the dirt away, and the water will become fresh again. It keeps recycling, purifying and healing, and giving life to every hungry man, beast, and plant.

You will never find a dead plant or tree by a river. Even if you cut down a plant, the continuous water supply enables it to bud again and grow back to life. Eternal life is the very life and nature of the Almighty God that is transmitted to us at the new birth. It heals and refreshes, cleans, sanctifies, and makes us alive unto God.

Unlike the river that can be traced to a particular origin by man, Eternal life cannot be traced because it originates from God. God is Eternal life and the very source of it. This is the life that is available for us in Christ. Make the choice of eternal life.

Prayer

Dear Father, I thank you for giving me eternal life, your very life and nature. I live everyday conscious of my sickness proof, death proof and ever refreshed life in Jesus' name. Amen.
Further Studies: *1 John 5:9-12*

Your Reward

*"Look, I am coming soon! My reward is with me, and I will give
to each person according to what they have done."*
(Revelation 22:12)

I t was a joy to see the graduates, especially my niece, as they marched up to receive their certificates. Five years of hard work had finally paid off. A mixture of events and emotions filled those five years; some were good while others were bad, but that day they were being awarded.

When Christ returns, He too will reward us for the work that we have done, whether good or bad. What will your reward be? The investments we make each day determine the kind of reward we will receive. What will it be?

The Bible tells about the judgments of Christ, and the apostles reveal two distinct types I want us to look at. They are the great white throne judgment, and the judgment seat of Christ.

The Great White Throne Judgment is for the condemnation of those that rejected the salvation of God through Jesus Christ (Revelation 20:11-15). The Judgment Seat of Christ is for the distribution of rewards (2 Corinthians 5:9-10). What will you be rewarded for?

How has your life contributed to the expansion of God's kingdom? Is your money, education, influence, skill and talent relevant to the gospel of Christ in your community or work place? Our eternal reward will be based on our investment in the gospel.

Prayer

Dear Father, I thank you for the privilege to be relevant in the gospel of Christ. I choose to invest in your work and receive a great reward in Jesus' name. Amen.
Further Studies: *2 Corinthians 5:9-10*

A Cup of Water

*"Truly I tell you, anyone who gives you a cup of water in my name because
you belong to the Messiah will certainly not lose their reward."*
(Mark 9:41)

Attributes of the Christian include hospitality, resourcefulness, humility, enthusiasm, generosity, flexibility, and gratefulness.

Everything we do for Christ will be rewarded. Whether it's commonplace tasks such as cooking and cleaning for your family, or it's something that requires a little more thought such as offering a cup of water to a stranger or visiting some in the hospital or prison; these things are what we do in the name of Christ.

*"And let us not be weary in well doing: for in due season we shall reap,
if we faint not. As we have therefore opportunity, let us do good unto
all men, especially unto them who are of the household of faith."*
Galatians 6:9-10

Never ignore the call to help a needy Christian. You have been blessed to be a blessing to others. As much as possible ensure that you lend a helping hand to a Christian, not because it will be convenient but because of the gain, the harvest, and the doors such simple actions could open to you.

*"Do not forget to show hospitality to strangers, for by so doing some people
have shown hospitality to angels without knowing it."* Hebrews 13:2

Prayer

*Dear Father, I thank you for teaching me to be a blessing to others. I know that
through this, I am glorifying the name of Jesus, in His name I pray. Amen.*
Further Studies: *Matthew 25:36-48*

Love One Another

"These things I command you, that you love one another."
(John 15:17)

n 1986 Sandi Patty sang a song written by Jon Mark Mohr & John Phillip Mays called "Love in Any Language." Some of the lyrics of the song are as follows:

Je t'aime
Te amo
Ya ti-bya lyu blyu
Ani o hev ot cha
I love you

The sounds are all as different
As the lands from which they came
And though the words are all unique
Our hearts are still the same

Love in any language
Straight from the heart
Pulls us all together, never apart

I do believe this little song helps us understand love in a unique way, and this is an encouragement to carry out Jesus' command. Love one another; anything less is unacceptable and if we claim to love Jesus then we must love others as He said we should.

Prayer

Dear Father, I thank you for the commandment to love. I walk in your word and will today and because I love you, I do your word in Jesus' name. Amen.
Further Studies: *1 Corinthians 13*

Heavenly City

"Instead, they were longing for a better country--a heavenly one. Therefore God is not ashamed to be called their God, for he has prepared a city for them."
(Hebrews 11:16)

Abel, Enoch, Noah, Abraham, and Sara are listed in this honor roll that we like to call the Hall of Faith. They died in faith as pilgrims sojourning to the heavenly city that God prepared for them.

They were the "greats," schooled in the halls of faithfulness, but don't be perplexed; you too have the hope like these great men and women, of entering the heavenly city. Your desire for a better place will be materialized, your place has been prepared and it is secure.

"Therefore, since we are surrounded by such a great cloud of witnesses, let us throw off everything that hinders and the sin that so easily entangles. And let us run with perseverance the race marked out for us."
Hebrews 12:1

The patriarchs and saints are the great cloud of witness that Paul made reference to in Hebrews 12:1. They are waiting for us and as such we must live by faith in preparation for Eternity with God.

Our final destination is to live with God forever, and these saints that have gone before us are presently in heaven watching and cheering us up to victory in Christ Jesus. Let that encourage you today to keep running the race and fighting the good fight of faith.

Prayer

Dear Father, I thank you because I know that my destiny is to live in eternity with you. I thank you for this great hope in Christ Jesus, in His name I pray. Amen.
Further Studies: *Philippians 3:20*

In The Love Of God

"How sweet are your words to my taste, sweeter than honey to my mouth!"
(Psalm 119:103)

One of the commands of the Lord to us is to keep ourselves pure and unspotted from the world (James 1:27). We can try to be upstanding citizens and be as good as we want to be, but there is only one way we can truly please God.

Our efforts to keep ourselves will be daunting. It is only in the cocoon of His love will we be kept. Someone may be wondering, "How do I keep myself in the love of God?"

Keeping yourself in the love of God comes simply as the result of living by His word. Jesus came to earth and lived victoriously. He gave us His secrets of success. His success was hinged on doing the word of God, doing the will of the father.

Likewise, we should treat the Bible like food to our souls and meditate on its truth day after day. Let it ruminate in your soul and guide you through each and every day of your life. It has the power to not only transform your life, but the lives of everyone around you.

Live by His word today and every day of your life. By doing so you will take His love and wrap it around yourself, for it's our hope and it's His mercy that ushers us into eternity. Glory.

Prayer

Dear Father, I thank you for the privilege of having your word and your love to keep me. As I live every day by your word, I keep myself in your love in Jesus' name. Amen.
Further Studies: *Jeremiah 15:16*

New Heaven And Earth

"Then I saw "a new heaven and a new earth," for the first heaven and the first earth had passed away, and there was no longer any sea."
(Revelation 21:1)

This is John's vision of the New Jerusalem.

The book of Revelation can be confusing, but it ends with Christ as the victor, and sometimes that is all you really need to know and understand.

This new heaven and earth will not be consumed with sin as we now know it. It's something to look forward to after all that we have seen and experienced on this present earth. The old will no longer be relevant; the new will rule and dominate. There will be no wars, no death, and there will be peace forevermore in this new heaven and earth.

Our life on earth today is a preparation, training to reign in the new heaven and earth. The world as we know it today is governed by the devil, which is not God's intention for us. Having redeemed us from sin and death that is in this world, God will not leave us here in a world of sin.

This is why you must live your life by God's word daily, because in the New Heaven and Earth where Jesus will be our Light. Glory to God!

Prayer

Dear Father, I thank you for your word that prepares me to live eternally with you in the new heaven and earth. May I live ever conscious of my preparation to reign in the life after in Jesus' name. Amen.
Further Studies: *Isaiah 25:8-12*

Treasure

"The kingdom of heaven is like treasure hidden in a field. When a man found it, he hid it again, and then in his joy went and sold all he had and bought that field."
(Matthew 13:44)

There are some people that make a pretty decent living by going to flea markets, estate auctions, and garage sales, and searching for objects of value, and then selling them for their true market value.

Not only does the previous owner of the item miss out on the wealth that object could have provided, but so do all the countless people that walk by it, not knowing its worth. It takes a very keen eye for someone to be able to discover these hidden treasures.

In the same way, you and I have discovered the hidden treasure within the kingdom of heaven. Whereas the people I mentioned before would buy their treasures for a fraction of the cost, when it comes to the kingdom of heaven, we give up everything we have.

No price is too great for the sake of the kingdom, including our lives. In fact, that is what is expected of us. In order to obtain the riches of the kingdom of heaven, we have to give up our lives. But the hope in all of this is that when we give Him our lives, we receive something of far greater value in return.

We receive the hope of an everlasting kingdom.

Prayer

Dear Father, I thank you for the teaching me to live with eternity in view. Help me to prepare for my life with you in eternity from this day in Jesus' name. Amen.
Further Studies: Matthew 13:45-46

Control

"A person's wisdom yields patience; it is to one's glory to overlook an offense."
(Proverbs 19:11)

Being unforgiving could be considered to be one of the greatest issues plaguing the Body of Christ today. We have many people that treat us badly within our personal spheres, but there are some Christians that experience great torture and even death.

It can be easy to take what is done to us to heart, and to respond out of hurt. As the saying goes, "Hurt people hurt people." But whether we have been offended or not, we are never given license by God to hurt others or to repay the evils that have been done to us.

As sober, sensible people, we need to be mindful of compassion, patience, and love in our dealings with others. Do not act or respond before you think or consult with the Spirit of God. Self-control is of the utmost importance.

No matter how urgent and pressing the situation is, learn to consult with God first. Learn to listen to Him; allow His wisdom to flow into your heart to guide you before making that decision. Choose to forgive instead of reacting, choose to let go when they expect you to hold onto that wrong.

Let them refer to us as fools for overlooking wrongs, it is Christ that we emulate, and to Him we ultimately answer. Whether we know it or not, our actions are a witness tool for winning others to Christ who bore the wrath of God in our place.

Prayer

Dear Father, I thank you for giving me the grace to live in such a way that other people may come to the knowledge of your Son in Jesus' name. Amen.
Further Studies: *Galatians 5:22-23*

Help

"Two are better than one; because they have a good reward for their labor."
(Ecclesiastes 4:9)

E cclesiastes is a book for times when life seems senseless. This verse addresses togetherness and partnership. Some people are always of the opinion that they can make it on their own, and so many of such folks are out of business because of frustration. We were created for one another; you need me as much as I need you in order to succeed.

If you work in an office, you and your boss have joined forces; you are now on the same team, working for the same cause. Alone, the boss cannot accomplish every task that needs to be done, and you would not have a job if it were not for your boss. As women, we have joined forces with our husbands to build our families, and the future of the human race by nurturing godly children.

Partial words of *No Man Is an Island* aptly states, "We need one another, so I will defend each man as my brother, each man as my friend." You will never make it alone successfully; joining hands makes work lighter and yields much more reward. Continue to help others. Even in prayers, Jesus gave us the secret to the effectiveness of prayer when it is done by two people: *"Again, truly I tell you that if two of you on earth agree about anything they ask for, it will be done for them by my Father in heaven."* Matthew 18:19

Prayer

Father, teach me to work together with others, whether in my marriage,
in my workplace, or wherever I may go, in Jesus' name. Amen.
Further Studies: *1 Corinthians 12:12-13*

Perfected Love

*"No one has ever seen God; but if we love one another, God
lives in us and his love is made complete in us."*
(1 John 4:12)

Have you ever been able to see Jesus through the way other Christians treat you? I should hope so! That is how it's supposed to be. The Bible tells us that the world will know that we are Christians not by the way we preach or how often we go to church, but by our love.

It is important to note that we do not love simply because it's a command we were given. Remember those days when you did something bad to a sibling or a friend and your parents made you apologize? How genuine do you think that apology felt to the person you were speaking to? Probably not very. So it is with love.

If we force our love, people know, so we should be careful of loving just for the sake of loving. All we have to do is rely on our nature as Christians to love and live in love. For you not to love is to live a life contrary to your Christian nature. Love is a demonstration of the very life and nature of God in us. It is proof that God lives in us because God is love.

*"Let your light so shine before men, that they may see your
good works and glorify your Father in heaven."*
(Matthew 5:16)

Your life is a message to those around you. You may not necessarily preach the gospel to people, but if you live by the word of God, the world around you will see your life and glorify your father who is in heaven. Let your life reflect His love, excellence, glory and grace.

Prayer

*Dear Father, thank you for living in me and perfecting your love in me on a daily basis.
My life of love reflects your grace, beauty and excellence every day in Jesus' name. Amen.*
Further Studies: *John 13:35, Matthew 7:16*

Prophet's Reward

"Whoever welcomes a prophet as a prophet will receive a prophet's reward, and whoever welcomes a righteous person as a righteous person will receive a righteous person's reward."
(Matthew 10:41)

The church today has little to no understanding of the concept of the prophet's reward, because hospitality and honor of the prophetic office aren't as valued in our culture as they were in the Jewish culture back then.

There is a very interesting account in the Bible that explains the prophet's reward. There was a famine in the land and the Prophet Elijah had come across a widow who only had enough food in her home to cook one last meal before she and her son would die. Nevertheless, Elijah instructed her to make him a cake and bring him water to drink.

From the meager supplies she had reserved for her son and herself, she obliged the prophet, and the rest is history. Miraculously, her supplies never ran out again, and not only did she receive food, but she received a new, abundant life.

The woman in this story received more than she could have ever imagined. That's a prophet's reward; the fullness of God's riches poured out in our lives. Whether you believe in the office of a prophet in this day and age or not, the heart of the matter is whether or not you give to your brothers and sisters, even during times of poverty. The heart of the matter is whether or not you will serve. What will your response be to those in need today?

Prayer

Dear Father, I choose to give in obedience to your word, and I receive in accordance with your word in Jesus' name. Amen.
Further Studies: *Luke 6:38, 1 Kings 17:8-24*

Compassion

"If anyone has material possessions and sees a brother or sister in need but has no pity on them, how can the love of God be in that person?"
(1 John 3:17)

The proof of love is giving. You cannot love without giving up something. If you really love someone, you will give your time, resources, ideas, money, and materials. In most cases for us women, we gave up our freedom and our family names as proof of our love for our husbands.

Here in 1 John 3:17, the apostle is teaching us about being compassionate, which means letting God's love flow through you and becoming as source of supply to others. The love of God dwells in you and me by compassion; it spurs us to respond to the needs of others.

Compassion and love can be seen through the way you give. The extent of your love is demonstrated in the value of the gifts you give. Here God is asking us to lend a helping hand.

God has blessed you to be a blessing, and this is a wake-up call for you to stop neglecting the poor in your environment. Compassion is a call to care about what others are going through, not to turn our backs or a blind eye.

You and I have been recipients of compassion; somebody helped you to get to where you are today. God has opened doors for you, and now it's your turn to help others too.

Prayer

Dear Father, my ears are open to the cry of the needy, and my heart is quick to respond to their needs in the measure of your blessings upon me in Jesus' name. Amen.
Further Studies: *Ephesians 4:32*

Pure Religion

"Religion that God our Father accepts as pure and faultless is this: to look after orphans and widows in their distress and to keep oneself from being polluted by the world."
(James 1:27)

Christianity is not a religion; it is God living in, among, and through people. As much as it is in our human nature to want to boil Christianity down to a bunch of rules to follow, we would do well to remember that to be a Christian literally means to be a "mini-Christ." We are examples to the world of what it looks like to have Jesus living inside of us.

Jesus was the least religious man to walk the face of this earth. Even when He was here, he often butt heads with the religious people of the day. Instead, Jesus had a heart for the orphan and the widow, just like His Father.

As we look through both the Old and New Testaments, we find that just as God made numerous provisions in His law for the less fortunate, so Jesus instructed His disciples to care for the vulnerable in society as well. This is a subject that is very near and dear to their hearts, so it should also be for us who claim to be their followers.

It is important to note that we shouldn't serve the needy out of simple adherence to a rule that God set forth for us. We don't love others because we have been commanded to. We should practice this pure form of religion because it is what is in our hearts. Our ultimate goal should be to serve others in love and to demonstrate the love of our Father to the watching world.

Prayer

Dear Father, I thank you for teaching me to practice pure religion and thank you for the blessing of doing your word in Jesus' name. Amen.
Further Studies: *Psalm 82:3*

The Happiness Myth

"My sacrifice, O God, is a broken spirit; a broken and
contrite heart you, God, will not despise."
(Psalm 51:17)

Christian women are often erroneously encouraged to put on a false display of happiness at all times, as an expression of their faith. Without this display they can be harshly judged as being contentious or unbelieving.

Let the burden of your heart be eased; know that God does not expect you to come to Him with your, "I can handle this, what's going on in my life is not bigger than my abilities to handle" attitude.

He wants you to come to Him with your heartbreak, sorrow, shame, and guilt. He is looking for someone who will approach Him with humility, not happiness. Be genuine with God every day.

One of the things I learned earlier in my life is that I cannot hide anything from God; He is omnipresent, which means He is present in all situations and at all times, so there is actually no point hiding anything from God.

Instead of hiding things from Him, I am of the opinion that you should cry to Him and tell Him everything about how you feel and what you feel. I actually feel free each time I cry to God, because I know that He can handle it all. He will not despise your contrite spirit.

Prayer

Dear Father, I thank you for always listening to me when I call.
From this day, I will cast all my worries and cares on you because
I know that you can handle it all in Jesus' name. Amen.
Further Studies: 1 Peter 5:7

A Simple Hello

*"If you greet only your brothers, what more are you doing
than others? Do not even the Gentiles do the same?"*
(Matthew 5:47, NASB)

God's intention was for salvation to change everything about us, even our social graces. In this verse, we are asked to explore how godly we are by observing whether or not we are being exclusive in whom we choose to greet and whom we pass by.

Why is this a big deal? Because *every* individual is made in the image of God. Just as God does not favor any one person over another, He does not want us to develop cliques and thereby exclude people.

I became a jovial person for the sake of the gospel. It dawned on me that I needed to be cheerful and learn how to start conversations so that I could get people to listen to me. One of the ways I do that today is by greeting people cheerfully.

Greeting people cheerfully can bless them, put smiles on their faces, and open doors of opportunity for us to preach the gospel.

Instead of building cliques, build moments of compassion with people, as this could make a lasting impact on their perception of God.

Prayer

Dear Father, I thank you for this principle of relating with everyone cheerfully. I acknowledge that we are all your creation and as such I will relate to everyone in my world as my sisters and my brother. Thank you, Lord, in Jesus' name. Amen.
Further Studies: *Proverbs 15:13*

Little is Much

*"Truly I tell you, anyone who gives you a cup of water in my name because
you belong to the Messiah will certainly not lose their reward."*
(Mark 9:41)

Multiple times, when Jesus interacted with those who needed His help, the scriptures tell us that He was "moved with compassion." The repetition of this statement should be a clear indication to us that aside from the Holy Spirit, one of the driving forces behind our actions should be compassion. There should be an overwhelming desire to help someone escape from whatever trouble they're in, whether emotional, physical, or spiritual.

Sometimes housewives feel that they are unable to do anything for the Gospel's sake because the nature of their lifestyle keeps them isolated from the world. They may even feel like they are insignificant to God. Not so. Every choice you make to do the right thing, no matter how small or grandiose, matters to God.

*"For I was hungry, and you gave Me something to eat; I was
thirsty, and you gave Me something to drink; I was a stranger,
and you invited Me in, naked and you clothed Me; I was sick,
and you visited Me; I was in prison, and you came to Me."*
Matthew 25:35-36

We tend to believe that when Jesus made this statement He was only referring to the homeless or people who are complete strangers to us, but "the least of these" can also be your children or your husband. Every act of compassion you extend to them is an act of kindness unto Christ. Take comfort in how valuable you are to God. You are laboring daily for the Gospel through patience and diligence, showing love to the Lord and your family.

Prayer

*Dear Father, thank you for showing me how valuable my daily
service to my family is to you in Jesus' name. Amen.*
Further Studies: *Matthew 25:31-46*

Growing Up

"Because you know that the testing of your faith produces perseverance."
(James 1:3)

No one enjoys going through trials. They're called trials for a reason: they *try* your patience, and that just isn't a fun process. It is, therefore, very easy for us to look upon trials as negative experiences, but James urges us to do otherwise.

The trials of our faith are critical for revealing the true nature and maturity of our faith in Christ. A lot of times people like to think that God puts us through tests so that He can see where we are at spiritually, but the truth is that God is already knows. He's sovereign, remember? He gives us the tests so that *we* can see where we're at in comparison to where we should be. They show us how strong our faith truly is. Trials are not only revealing; they push us to grow.

Patience is the measure of how firm our convictions are. Let's compare this process to a sauna. The longer you sit in one, the more uncomfortable you feel and the greater the urge you may feel to bum rush the door. People who have never been in one before or who don't understand the purpose of one will likely succumb to temptation and leave after a few minutes. But those who understand that the heat from the sauna aids in the release of toxins will patiently sit for the full allotted time, trusting that the detoxification process is worth the discomfort. As you go through the fiery trials of life, endure and wait patiently for the Master to complete His good work in you.

Prayer

Dear Father, thank you for the trials I have already faced and overcome as well as the ones that are yet to come in Jesus' name. Amen.
Further Studies: *1 Peter 1:6-8*

The Word of God

"In the beginning was the Word, and the Word was with God, and the Word was God."
(John 1:1)

We live in a day and age where everywhere you turn, someone is trying to refute the validity of the Bible or negate its relevance in our current society. But regardless of what the world says or does in regards to the Bible, we know that God's Word is living and active, sharper than any double edge sword, piercing the hearts of men. In fact, that is one of the biggest reasons people try to silence the influence of the Bible – it has the power to bring conviction, and that makes people very uncomfortable.

For a Christian, on the other hand, daily saturation in the Word of God is a must. We must seek out its contents to find inspiration as well as conviction, as both will serve to help us grow. When we read the Word of God, we open ourselves to the whisperings of His Spirit who brings wisdom and revelation.

But not only will we receive personal edification from the contents of the Word, but it will influence others as well. You may encounter people on a daily basis that would never pick up a Bible on their own, but when they see your actions, they can "read" what you do as the embodiment of scripture. They can learn about Jesus and His commands through the way you live your life each and every day.

Let the Word of God permeate every area of your life for His praise, honor and glory.

Prayer

Dear Father, thank you for the gift of your Word. May I never cease to fill the reservoir of my heart with its contents in Jesus' name, Amen.
Further Studies: *Hebrews 4:12*

Feeling or Faith?

"When I am afraid, I put my trust in You."
(Psalm 56:3)

There are times in our lives when we can honestly say that we do not feel like trusting God. In those moments we may be struggling with offense, fear, anger, or even hatred, and pursuing those emotions may seem to be more satisfying and easy than trusting God. If we are completely honest with ourselves, we would have to acknowledge that more often than not, our feelings control a lot of the decisions that we make.

If someone were to keep a tally, how often do you think they would record you saying "I don't feel like it" or "I feel like..." on any given day? It is probably more often than you think. Yet the psalmist does not say that we should put our trust in God when it's easy or when we feel like it. Instead, we are to trust God when it is hardest, when our minds are clouded with doubt, and when our emotions are awry.

Now, this isn't to say that God wants us to shut down our feelings entirely only to engage in blind faith. He created our emotions, and they are not bad in and of themselves, but we must be careful of allowing them to control our decisions. Women are emotional creatures by habit, so we really have to struggle to keep our emotions in check so that our spiritual nature can be free to influence our decision making process. To do this, we need a lot of help from the Holy Spirit!

What is keeping you from putting your faith in God? When the odds are stacked against you, you can trust Him and rest assured that He will not disappoint you.

Prayer

Dear Father, I know that you have my best interests in mind.
Help me to keep my faith steady and to trust in you regardless
of how I may feel at the moment in Jesus' name. Amen.
Further Studies: Psalm 20:7

July

No Fear

"When it snows, she has no fear for her household; for all of them are clothed in scarlet."
(Proverbs 31:21)

How many times do you think your mother called for you to grab a jacket before you went outside to play? How many times do you think she made sure you had sunscreen slathered all over before you dove into the swimming pool? How many times have you done the same to your children?

Though as children it can be annoying to have your mother butt in and "smother" you, there is always a method to a mother's madness. God gave us the incredible ability to be intuitive and anticipate our family's need before they happen. Even our husbands often benefit from this gift as we help him to prepare for various responsibilities or tasks he must complete.

This is a beautiful sign of strength as a mother, as your preparedness allows you to relax in peace. As the scripture says, even if a snowstorm were to come, you would have peace of mind in knowing that you've already taken care of the needs of your children. That's definitely a kind of peace we should all pursue!

Prayer

Dear Father, thank you for giving me the gift of a mother's intuition. I will use it use well to ensure that my family is well taken care of in Jesus' name. Amen.
Further Studies: *1 Thessalonians 5:6*

Not Angels

"To which of the angels did God ever say, 'Sit at my right hand until I make your enemies a footstool for your feet'?"
(Hebrews 1:13)

As majestic and powerful angels are described to be in the Bible, they are our servants. They were sent to minister to us because we are joint heirs with Christ Jesus, who is exalted high above all principalities and powers, and has authority over all things, even the angels (Hebrews 1:14, Romans 8:17).

Think of a footstool that is placed under your feet when you sit in a chair. If the enemies of the Son of God will be made His footstool, this means that they will be subdued. We are hid with God in Christ, and it is His enemies that will be subdued. Because we are hid in Christ, our enemies are also subdued. Whoever contends with us contends with God and is brought to naught.

This is one of the reasons we do not fight or contend with those who have set themselves as our enemies. *"For this is what the LORD Almighty says: After the Glorious One has sent me against the nations that have plundered you--for whoever touches you touches the apple of his eye"* (Zechariah 2:8). God guides us jealously, and anyone who decides to be an enemy will have to contend with Him.

A greater truth is that we cannot even be touched by any one because we are seated with Christ in the heavenly places, far above all principalities and powers. The world and its systems are subject to our authority. We rule and reign as kings in this world. Glory to God!

Prayer

Dear Father, thank you for exalting Jesus and His body (the Church) far above all powers, in Jesus' name. Amen.
Further Studies: *Ephesians 1:19-23, Genesis 15:1*

Fearfully and Wonderfully Made

"For you created my inmost being; you knit me together in my mother's womb."
(Psalm 139:13)

One thing that creation reveals is that God is very thorough and detailed. He is a master craftsman that is very fond of His creation. He created everything with absolute precision and attention to detail, giving everyone and everything a unique identity.

In our opening scripture, King David talks about God's perfect knowledge of man, the works of His hand. Every intricate detail about you was planned even before your mother met your father. Every birthmark, freckle, and shade of coloring has been chosen as part of His design for you. So regardless of what you've heard, or what anyone has said about you and to you, God made you SPECIAL.

He plotted the course of your life and knew the path that you would choose, where you would be born, and the experiences you would have. You are fearfully and wonderfully made, so live like it! Instead of trying to be someone else, be the best you. You are God's dream, so changing your personality will mean losing your uniqueness.

No matter how you look or what you have accomplished, people will definitely have something to say, something they will want you to change and so on. But keep your head up high, pride yourself in your uniqueness, and praise God for the way you are.

Prayer

Dear Father, I thank you for my uniqueness. I choose to pride myself in your creation and live to fulfill my potential in Jesus' name. Amen.
Further Studies: *Psalm 139*

Strong & Courageous

"Have I not commanded you? Be strong and courageous. Do not be afraid; do not be discouraged, for the LORD your God will be with you wherever you go."
(Joshua 1:9)

Moses, the servant of God and deliverer had died, and the mantle fell on Joshua who had been Moses' aide. Though he had followed Moses and learned a lot from him, acting in the place of Moses was a different game entirely.

Joshua inherited Moses' ministry alongside the troubles and oppositions from some factions among the Israelites, and at that point in his life he needed courage, assurance and strength to accomplish the great task of leading God's people. In that very desperate time, God spoke to Joshua, encouraged him to stand, gave him strategies to lead the people, and empowered him for the task ahead. Above all, God promised to be with him in all his journeys.

The tapestry of our lives is woven from the many paths that we have trod. As we look back and move our hands over the textile, we stop at various intervals to reminisce about how a word from God gave us the strength and courage to make it through.

It doesn't matter what you are faced with today. God has promised to be with you in all you are involved in. Do not let fear rub you of your confidence. Strength and courage, YES. Fear and dismay, NO! God is with you every step of the way. It's a command He gives, He is faithful!

Prayer

Dear Lord, thank you for being my strength, my ever present help in times of need. I face life with courage and boldness today, because I know that you are with me in Jesus' name. Amen.
Further Studies: *Hebrews 13:5-6*

Grace

"Grace be with all them that love our Lord Jesus Christ in sincerity. Amen."
(Ephesians 6:24, KJV)

My mother was always showing off her most precious, delicate vase. "Don't touch it," she would always say. But it was too beautiful not to touch. I just wanted to feel how smooth it was and see it up close.

One day, the next thing I knew, when I came to myself, the vase lay in fragments all over the ground. My first thought... Where can I hide it? I was terrified. But alas, there was nowhere and no time to hide it, so when she got home, I sullenly took the broken pieces to her, expecting the worst.

To my surprise, she hugged me and said, "It's okay." That, my friends, is grace. I knew how important the vase was to her and I broke it, so I deserved to get in trouble. I fully expected it. What I got instead was forgiveness and a slate that was wiped totally clean.

Paul's letter to the Ephesians is a revelation and reflection of the grace of God that he had personally experienced. Whenever he wrote an epistle, you'll notice that if he's not talking about grace throughout the letter, he at least greets the churches with the word. It goes without saying, then, that grace was a pretty big deal to him.

Paul recognized that without grace he would still be that sinner condemning Christians to death, who was himself condemned to hell. Take a moment to reflect on your own life. Where would you be without grace?

Prayer

Dear Father, thank you for your grace. It is by your grace that I received my salvation and it's by your grace that I live each day. Help me to never forget that in Jesus' name. Amen.
Further Studies: *2 Corinthians 5:14*

No Fear

"There is no fear in love. But perfect love drives out fear, because fear has to do with punishment. The one who fears is not made perfect in love."
(1 John 4:18)

Have you ever been in a romantic relationship where you were not able to express yourself because of fear of what the man would do in response? The beauty of such situations is that when you do tell him how you feel, he responds in a way that immediately removes all fear and doubt. So it is in our relationship with God.

Love and fear cannot co-exist. When love shows up, fear disappears. If you are in love and there is fear, then that love is far from perfect, because the two do not go together. In our relationship with God, there is no fear because of His provision in times of our weakness and flaws.

"This is how love is made complete among us so that we will have confidence on the Day of Judgment: in this world we are like Jesus."
1 John 4:17

The antidote for fear is love. Oh, how you and I NEED something to counteract the unpleasant feeling of fear! The fears that torment and paralyze us; holding us captive and unfulfilled.

Suzan knows that she has walked out of line in her relationship with the Lord. She is ashamed, but she also knows that no one else can help her, so she repents, goes back to the Father, trembling at first, but pushing forward until there is no fear. She received forgiveness and restoration, and you will too.

Prayer

Dear Father, thank you for loving me beyond my sins. I will not allow fear, torment or accusation from the evil one to stop me from enjoying your perfect love in Jesus' name. Amen.
Further Studies: Isaiah 41:10

The Source of Soundness

"Jesus answered, "It is written: 'Man shall not live on bread alone,
but on every word that comes from the mouth of God."
(Matthew 4:4)

What is the source of your understanding of God? What informs your belief on who He is?

Can your beliefs be explained explicitly from Scripture? For many women, theology comes from a coffee cup, a greeting card, a calendar, a movie, a book, or sometimes from another religion.

When Jesus said that we are to live by every word that comes from the mouth of God, He meant it! Our understanding of God and the world should come from the source who is Truth himself.

There is no one that knows a product more than the manufacturer. The Bible contains all the information that we need to live on earth. If your information of who God is and what life is all about is not from the Bible, then you've got it all wrong.

Jesus said we should live by the very information and principles of the word of God. If what you believe about God or life is not founded on the revealed scriptures, then it's time to set those things aside and start believing in the scriptures and the scriptures only. Surrender to the authority of God's Word which is the source of all truth and garner all of your thinking from it.

Prayer

Dear Father, I thank you for the revelation of your word. I choose to believe in your
word and your word only is my source of information in Jesus' name. Amen.
Further Studies: *Psalm 119:11*

Hunger that will be Satisfied

"Blessed are those who hunger and thirst for righteousness, for they will be filled."
(Luke 6:35)

Have you ever had a craving for something to the point that it almost caused you pain because you wanted it so badly? No matter what you tried to do to satisfy the craving, nothing else sufficed?

God wants us to desire righteousness in this manner. We should be obsessed with doing the right thing simply because we know that it brings God glory. Nothing in the world should pacify the intensity of this craving.

There is none of God's creation that is independent of its source. Fish depend on water, the plants depend on the sun, and man depends on God. There is a craving in us, a vacuum that only God can satisfy.

The satisfaction that mankind seeks will only come from the creator. Seeking God early will save you the stress of seeking for satisfaction and fulfillment in the wrong places. Develop a hunger and a longing for God today, and His promise is that He will fill you up.

Has your desire for God ever slipped?

Stimulate your desire for Him again with praise for His goodness during times of personal worship in His Word. He will fill you; He will fill your hunger and thirst because He fills the hungry soul.

Prayer

Dear Father, I thank you for satisfying me with good things and filling me up with your very own self. Glory to you, Lord in Jesus' name. Amen.
Further Studies: *Psalm 63:1, Psalm 42:1*

Preparing to Worship

"God is a Spirit: and they that worship him must worship him in spirit and in truth."
(John 4:24)

When you rush to get out the door to attend church, you typically run the risk of forgetting to prepare your heart. Oftentimes, the pre-church scene in many homes contains the woman barking at the children, getting testy with her husband, and suffering from a general irritation with others.

It's likely that most of us have committed numerous sins by the time we get to church. Then by the time we get to church to join in and sing **"All Things Bright and Beautiful,"** our actions seem hypocritical.

Worshipping God is a genuine lifestyle of demonstrating deep love for God with our whole heart, body, and mind, even as we are faced with tests of patience, personalities, and other trials.

Worship is an attitude and positioning of your spirit, soul, and body. You must condition your soul and spirit and make them ready to bow before God in holy reverence and adoration before you enter a place of worship.

Ask God to help you develop a lifestyle of true worship. He is the one that requested that we worship Him in spirit and in truth, and He alone can teach us how to do so.

Prayer

Dear Father, I thank you for teaching me to worship you in spirit and in truth. Lord, I ask that you teach me to worship you as I should in Jesus' name. Amen.
Further Studies: *1 Chronicles 21:24*

Manipulation

"Do not let your heart envy sinners, but live in the fear of the Lord always."
(Proverbs 23:17)

Women are incredibly powerful creatures. We have the ability to manipulate situations and people at will, quite easily. With a snap of the finger, a pout of the lips, or a sway of the hips, many women can get whatever their heart desires.

It is difficult not to look at them enviously and think, "If only I could just copy a little bit of what they do, I would get the respect and opportunities too." That is the very mistake a lot of women have made, and today they live to regret it.

Our opening verse admonishes us to fear God always. Never envy the people of the world, because there is really nothing to be envied in their lives. It may seem like they are making progress now, but the truth is that all that we see them enjoying today will grow wings and just fly away.

It is better to be Lazarus here on earth and inherit life eternal, than to be the rich man and burn forever in hell. Through every trial we must remember that God is there and we should respond in a way that pleases Him, and not allow our hearts to envy sinners.

Prayer

Dear Lord, I put my hope in you, and I refuse to compromise my faith in the face of temptations. I know that you are able to make my life beautiful for your own purposes in Jesus' name. Amen.
Further Studies: *Psalm 37:34-40*

Ignoring the Warning

*"If we say that we have no sin, we deceive ourselves, and the truth is
not in us. If we confess our sins, he is faithful and just to forgive us
our sins, and to cleanse us from all unrighteousness. If we say that we
have not sinned, we make him a liar, and his word is not in us."*
(1 John 1:8-10)

In our desire to be perfect or to make people think that our lives our perfect, we have the tendency to cover up our sins and pretend like nothing is going on. In such situations, God's gentle warnings of our need for repentance can easily go ignored. We continue in our sin until we reach a point where we think, "I've gone too far."

It doesn't have to be that way though. If we would first acknowledge our faults and confess our sins to God in a prayer of repentance, we would effectively remove the power of sin over our lives and put ourselves back in right standing with God.

The Bible says that Christ ever lives to make perpetual intercession for us in heaven (Hebrews 7:25). We may slip, but underneath us are His everlasting arms (Deuteronomy 33:27).

God's mercy holds us together as a thread does fabric, and He keeps us from failing and falling; therefore don't ignore the warning! Always remember that He has made provisions for your sins and it should not be taken for granted.

Prayer

*Dear Father, thank you for your loving kindness and tender mercies.
I thank you for always forgiving and restoring my relationship
with you each time I fall in Jesus' name. Amen.*
Further Studies: *1 John 2:1-2*

Do You Love Him?

"He who has My commandments and keeps them is the one who loves me;"
(John 14:21)

Every mother knows how foolish and hurtful it can be for a child to use confessions of love to escape doing what they are told. When a rebellious child professes to love his mother, he communicates a message of disregard and apathy towards her by disobedience. This is not love.

Likewise, when we refuse to obey God and look for opportunities to serve Him in self-gratifying ways, we are like that child who says "I love you," but shows disregard and apathy toward God and His Word.

The test of our love is this: if we love Him, we will obey Him and keep His commandments. As rote and boring as keeping commandments may sound, when you truly love someone, all you want to do is to make them happy; therefore we keep God's commandments because we want to make Him happy.

Do you love Him? Do not answer the question by words. From today, prove your love to God by your actions. Let Him know how much you love Him by keeping His word and doing His biddings.

Prayer

Dear Father, I thank you for loving me enough to give Jesus to die in my place. I prove my love for you from now henceforth by doing your will and keeping your word. Father, help me to accomplish this by the power of your Spirit in Jesus' name. Amen.
Further Studies: *Matthew 7:21*

Pride and Prejudice

"Humble yourselves therefore under the mighty hand
of God that He may exalt you in due time."
(1 Peter 5:6)

Pride robs women of their godly design.

Instead of nurturing their child's development, pride focuses on keeping the house clean out of fear of what others might think or say.

Instead of diligently investing time in building relationships, pride creates an unapproachable, too-important-for-you attitude.

Instead of being a helpmate to their husbands, pride reverts to needy attention-seeking and helplessness.

"Likewise, you who are younger, be subject to the elders. Clothe
yourselves, all of you, with humility toward one another, for
'God opposes the proud but gives grace to the humble.'"
1 Peter 5:5 (ESV)

Unfortunately, even Christian women fall into the trap of believing that prideful behaviors will actually propel them upwards toward a greater more fulfilling life. What a mistake! The only way to go upward is to go down—through humility. Only with humility you will be promoted by God.

Prayer

Dear Father, I thank you for teaching me to humbly discharge my duty as a wife and mother. Lord, help me to put away every trace of pride in my life in Jesus' name. Amen.
Further Studies: *Proverbs 16:18*

A Fruitful Witness

"So faith comes from hearing, and hearing by the Word of God."
(Romans 10:17, NASB)

This is one of the greatest principles in the word of God revealed in the New Testament. Most of the things you know to do today were communicated through words. So is faith in God; it is communicated by reading, listening to and hearing God's word.

Are you living in a home with unsaved loved ones? Pushing and pulling them to come to faith is a vain effort. As women we have the unique capability of setting the atmosphere of faith in our homes. We set it by making God's Word encouraging, exalted, ever-present, and ever-obeyed.

Only God's Word saves. The more it is heard in a favorable light, the more conducive the atmosphere will be for salvation by faith. Therefore be diligent at it.

In 2005, I had this friend who just would not get saved no matter how hard I tried. I invited her to church services, camp meetings, and house fellowships, but she never showed up for anything. As I was praying one day, I got an idea from the Spirit of God. The idea was to make her listen to the word of God with me.

I arranged for her to visit me more often, and in each of those visits I ensured a message was playing. Before long, because of hearing the word and our relationship, she gave her life to Christ, and she is still walking with God today. It is not only God's written word but also the "word" of our actions that acts as a fruitful witness.

Prayer

Dear Lord, I thank you for helping me to bring others into your kingdom by your word and my actions in Jesus' name. Amen.
Further Studies: *Romans 10:14-15*

A Promise

"Now the LORD was gracious to Sarah as he had said, and the LORD did for Sarah what he had promised. Sarah became pregnant and bore a son to Abraham in his old age, at the very time God had promised him."
(Genesis 21:1-2)

Sarah and Abraham were old and way past the childbearing stage, but God gave them a promise, and even though they doubted God, He was faithful in fulfilling His promise to them. Something you must understand as a Christian woman is that God is faithful, even to a thousand generations, and His word to you will never fail.

The Bible is replete with God's faithfulness, and the account of the birth of Abraham and Sarah's son Isaac is a particularly interesting one. God took what was considered impossible and blew everyone's minds.

I want to assure you that He is the same God today, and He is still very faithful, just as He was in the days of the Bible. His word to you will never fail or fall to the ground, so you must believe.

You may not get an explanation from God, as to why the fulfillment is taking so long, BUT you will definitely get a promise which will sustain you until its fulfillment. The only thing that is expected of us is that we believe He is faithful and will do all that He has promised. Trust the promise that God has given you. He is FAITHFUL to perform it!

Prayer

Dear Father, your word to me is enough. I know that your word has never failed and it will not fail in my time, in Jesus' name. Amen.
Further Studies: *Isaiah 55:11*

Our Advocate

"My dear children, I write this to you so that you will not sin. But if anybody does sin, we have an advocate with the Father—Jesus Christ, the Righteous One."
(1 John 2:1)

Anyone in social work or foster care should be familiar with the term *advocate*. In most cases, whenever there is a child whose parents are not able to speak for them, the court will assign an advocate to the case; someone to fight on behalf of the child.

In this scripture the apostle John explains that when failure occurs in our lives, we are not doomed. We do not have to hang our heads in shame or abandon the path of righteousness. We are bound to fall many times in this lifetime. God knows very well that we are prone to weakness, but thankfully, He appointed an advocate for us.

Jesus Christ is our advocate. Our path is surely going to be filled with stumbling blocks, but that should not deter us from getting up and continuing the journey. When the accuser of the brethren rears his ugly head and begins to throw condemnation our way, we have an advocate who fights on our behalf, who holds our hand, and who leads us on.

He is on your side. He is not angry at you, so tune out the accusations of the enemy and free yourself from the guilt of your past. Jesus has already plead your case before the Father and pleads for you daily, so there is nothing in this world that can separate you from the loving gaze of your Father God.

Prayer

Dear Father, thank you for making provisions for my mistakes in my walk of righteousness. I thank you for Jesus who always makes intercession for me, and I take advantage of your grace to live in righteousness continually in Jesus' name. Amen.
Further Studies: *Hebrews 4:15, Hebrews 7:27*

Safety

"Fear of man will prove to be a snare, but whoever trusts in the Lord is kept safe."
(Proverbs 29:25)

Imagine the reality of a life lived in fear. One where you're always looking over your shoulder, fearful of what could be lurking around the corner. That would not be much of a life indeed. Every decision you make, and every step you take, would be based on fear.

It is easy for us as women to develop fears: fear of men (especially if you've had bad experiences with them), fear of the future, fear of death – to name a few. Our opening scripture encourages us not to be entrapped by fear, but to put our trust in God and lay hold of safety in Him.

> *"This is what the Lord says: 'Cursed is the one who trusts in man, who draws strength from mere flesh and whose heart turns away from the Lord. That person will be like a bush in the wastelands; they will not see prosperity when it comes. They will dwell in the parched places of the desert, in a salt land where no one lives.'"*
> *Jeremiah 17:5-6*

We must rely on God because we have assurance of His promise, guidance, provision, and protection. He is the only one who has never and will never fail us, and the only one who is capable of thwarting the plans of the enemy for our life.

Now imagine the peace that rules one's life when their hope and trust is in God Almighty, who knows the beginning from the end and has all power and authority to rule heaven, earth, and everything under the earth. It is only in God that we have protection from the adversities and troubles of life.

Prayer

Dear Father, you are my refuge and my shield. Lord, I trust completely in you for my protection and safety. Thank you for keeping safe in Jesus' name. Amen.
Further Studies: *Proverbs 21:31, Psalm 27*

Steadfast

"God is in the midst of her, she will not be moved; God
will help her when morning dawns."
(Psalms 46:5, NASB)

For those dealing with pain and illness, personal dilemmas, or fears and doubts, night time is often the hardest. Why? Well, because during the night we are not able to distract ourselves.

Let's say you were verbally attacked by someone you had considered to be a close friend. During the day, if you don't want to think about it, you can make yourself busy with cleaning and cooking or spending time with your kids. But at night, without anything to distract us, we are left alone with our thoughts and tend to mull over what's going on in our lives.

It is in the night hours that our suffering can sometimes be at its worst, and we can begin to feel as though we're suffocating in our troubles. But this verse gives us great hope to be able to get through the night. God is with you, and nothing the enemy can throw at you can change that! Though you may feel overwhelmed in the night, God will be your strength as the next morning dawns. He will gird up your legs and help you to walk. He will be your peace who has broken down every wall. He will protect you.

No matter what dark night of the soul you may be experiencing, remember that God is with you, and though you may not be able to see Him in the thick of the night, the light of day will reveal to you that He was standing with you all along.

Prayer

Dear Lord, you are my help and I trust you completely, in Jesus' name. Amen.
Further Studies: *Psalm 46:1, Hebrews 13:5-6*

Hope

"And hope does not put us to shame, because God's love has been poured out into our hearts through the Holy Spirit, who has been given to us."
(Romans 5:5)

Life in Christ isn't easy. If any of us got into Christianity thinking that it would be easy, it probably wasn't very long before we were in for a real shock! Nevertheless, life in Christ does offer an abundance of peace and joy. This is the fruit of a hope-filled life in Jesus.

One of the many promises God gives to those who follow Him is eternal life with Him in a place more beautiful than any eye has ever seen, or ear has ever heard. Hope for this future with God is to be our daily fuel. It should be what gets us through those difficult days; knowing that one day our perseverance will be worth it.

As a young girl, you may have put your hope in someone and ended up disappointed. Then, as you grew older, maybe you became a little more cautious about being too hopeful, but God is not a man that He should lie. Whatever He has promised, He will bring to pass, and He will never put you to shame. No one whose hope is in the Lord will ever be put to shame!

That means that you can not only trust Him to keep His promise to give you the reward of eternal life, but you can trust Him to keep any other promise He's ever made you regarding your future, the future of your husband and children, or any other issue you may be facing. Continue trusting Him, because He is faithful.

Prayer

Dear Father, thank you for rekindling the fires of hope in my soul. I pray that the flames continue to burn until the day I see you in eternity, in Jesus' name. Amen.
Further Studies: *Hebrews 10:23, Proverbs 10:24*

Everlasting Life

"For God so loved the world, that he gave his only begotten Son, that
whosoever believeth in him should not perish, but have everlasting life."
(John 3:16, KJV)

Most people live as though life on earth is all there is, but you must understand that man is a spirit, so when our flesh returns to the earth where it came from, our spirit will continue living. Our life here on this planet is only preparation for eternity. What you do on earth will determine where you will live for eternity.

God, being a loving father, has made provisions for the whole world to live with Him in eternity, and that is why He sent Jesus to give us everlasting life. Our opening scripture reveals that, *"whosoever believes in Jesus should not perish, but have everlasting life."* What do you think will happen to the man or woman who refuses to believe?

"Whoever believes in him is not condemned, but whoever
does not believe stands condemned already because they have
not believed in the name of God's one and only Son"
(John 3:18).

Condemnation here is eternal separation from God. It is eternal suffering, eternal pain in the lake of fire. This is why we must preach the gospel of Jesus Christ to everyone in our world. The death of Jesus Christ made eternity with God possible for mankind, but the choice of where to live eternally is still our very own to make.

Note that if you were the only woman in the world, God would still send His Son Jesus to die for you. That's how much God loves you.

Prayer

Dear Father, thank you for the privilege of living with
you for eternity in Jesus' name. Amen.
Further Studies: *John 5:24, Matthew 25:46, 1 John 5:9-13*

Call on the Name of the Lord

"And everyone who calls on the name of the Lord will be saved."
(Acts 2:21)

You may recall back when you were a kid the way you responded whenever you were in distress. If you hurt yourself, who did you call? Mom. If you got sick to your stomach and needed someone to take care of you, who did you call? Mom. If you were afraid of things that go *bump* in the night, who did you call? Mom.

In times of deep distress and sorrow, sometimes it's only the whisper of the name of the Lord that can get one through turmoil. Take for instance one of the powerful accounts of King David:

"In my distress I called upon the Lord, and cried to my God for help; He heard my voice out of His temple, and my cry for help before Him came into His ears. Then the earth shook and quaked; And the foundations of the mountains were trembling and were shaken, because He was angry... Then the channels of water appeared, and the foundations of the world were laid bare... He took me; He drew me out of many waters. He delivered me from my strong enemy, and from those who hated me, for they were too mighty for me. They confronted me in the day of my calamity, but the Lord was my stay. He brought me forth also into a broad place; He rescued me, because He delighted in me."
(Psalm 18:6-19)

Whatever the situation you are facing, remember the Lord delights in you. Call on His name, and you will be saved.

Prayer

Dear Father, I trust that as You did for David, You will come through for me in Jesus' name. Amen.
Further Studies: *Psalm 145:18*

Poor but Rich

"Listen, my dear brothers and sisters: Has not God chosen those who are poor in the eyes of the world to be rich in faith and to inherit the kingdom he promised those who love him?"
(James 2:5)

When you meet people who would be considered poor in the eyes of the world, you'll discover that they don't hold onto their possessions very tightly. In fact, they don't derive much pleasure from their "things" at all. What they do value, is their belief that God is watching out for them and providing for every single need that they have.

I remember hearing the story of a missionary who had met a woman in her early twenties. This woman had given birth to a child, but the father of the child had recently died of AIDS, which he had also given to her. The woman was forced to await the fate of her own mortality as well as that of her child's.

As the missionary had prayed with and encouraged the woman, she asked her if she wanted a Bible. The young woman yelped, "Yes!" When the Bible was revealed, the woman hungrily grabbed it and began flipping through the pages and jumping up and down. You would think the Bible was some kind of treasure the way she lovingly held it to her chest.

Even though the young woman's world was crumbling around her, the one thing that brought her joy was her faith – God's Word was literally food to her soul. The world may not think much of her now, but one day she will be exalted to a high place in the kingdom of God for her strong and continual faith. Let's be challenged by the faith of this woman and those around us who maintain their love for Jesus in spite of their poverty.

Prayer

Dear Father, please help me to remember my spiritual poverty in Jesus' name. Amen.
Further Studies: *Matthew 19:30*

Led by the Spirit

"For those who are led by the Spirit of God are the children of God."
(Romans 8:14)

Back in the Old Testament, everyone knew that the Israelites were God's children because there was an obvious pillar of cloud that led them through the wilderness during the day, and a pillar of fire during the night. It was hard for the world not to notice who they belonged to! I believe God used this as a symbolic example of what He would do for future generations.

Today, the Holy Spirit's guidance is what helps us as believers make it through each day. He whispers directions into our hearts and keeps us from going down the wrong path or from making bad decisions. The Holy Spirit's job is to help us navigate the many pathways of life and to bring us to full maturity in Christ. There's no better source for us to get our directions from than the very spirit of the Living and Almighty God!

Just as all the people in surrounding areas could see the pillars of cloud and fire and know that the people following those pillars belonged to the Lord, so does the evidence of the Holy Spirit within us show people that we are children of God. People who follow the guidance of the Holy Spirit embody His fruit: love, joy, peace, patience, kindness, goodness, faithfulness, gentleness, and self-control. They serve others above themselves; they share the Good News of Jesus. In all we do and say, we show the world that the Holy Spirit lives in us, and those in the world will know that we are Christians by our love.

Thank God for the precious Holy Spirit who counsels us. Allow the Holy Spirit to help you today.

Prayer

Dear Father, thank you for sending your Holy Spirit to counsel me. I will incline my ear and listen to what He has to say in Jesus' name. Amen.
Further Studies: *Isaiah 30:21*

Created

*"So God created man in his own image, in the image of God he
created them; male and female created he them."*
(Genesis 1:27)

t is likely that when you were a kid you wondered about what God looked like. Maybe even as an adult you still wonder. No one has even seen the face of God, so it's hard to say exactly what He looks like, but if there's anything we can definitively say about the appearance of God from the Bible, it's that He is resplendently beautiful.

Having been made in His image, it should be impossible for us or anyone else to declare anything else about ourselves. When you look at yourself in the mirror, do you see the image of God in you? If you don't, it's time to get a shift in perspective. Even though all you may be able to see at times are your faults and flaws, they do not define you. You are defined by the fact that you look just like your Daddy: beautiful.

What's cool about this verse is that after we're told that we're made in the image of God, we're also told that He made two versions of Himself: male and female. If God's beauty can be translated into different sexes, it can even be translated into 7 billion different types of people; each uniquely reflecting the beauty and glory of God.

The glory of God dwelling inside of us is what makes us beautiful. So often we look to our outward appearance and believe that that is what defines our beauty, but it isn't. Beauty is something inward, something spiritual. If you can't see it yet, trust that God will give you new perspective and allow you to see you into the awesome woman He already sees you to be.

Prayer

*Dear Father, thank you for creating me in your image and likeness in
Jesus' name. Help me to see this truth all the more each day. Amen.*
Further Studies: *1 John 4:9-10*

One for All

"For I am not ashamed of the gospel, because it is the power of God that brings salvation to everyone who believes: first to the Jew, then to the Gentile."
(Romans 1:16)

There was a time in the Apostle Paul's life that his mission was to torture Christians for their faith in Jesus Christ. Now, imagine the audacity that it took for him to become a believer and stand against everything he had believed in before. Imagine the confidence that he had to have in Jesus in order to write this verse and to declare to the world that he was no longer ashamed of the gospel of Jesus Christ, the Messiah and the savior of the world.

Paul could speak with such confidence because he had himself seen and experienced the Messiah for himself in his "come to Jesus" moment on the road to Damascus. There was no way he could deny that Jesus was the Son of God from that point on!

Paul had another reason to be confident in his belief: Jesus had forgiven him a great debt. To have had a hand in the murder of many followers of Christ, Paul had to have felt as though he would be the last person Jesus would want on His team, and yet Jesus came to him directly and called Paul to follow Him.

What is your story? What makes you confident in the gospel of Jesus Christ and unashamed to share it with the world? We each have our own personal testimonies, but we are not meant to keep them to ourselves! Just as Paul did, we should share the gospel with the world, because freedom and salvation come only by the preaching of the gospel of Jesus Christ.

Prayer

Father, I thank you for the gospel of Jesus Christ that brings salvation. As I speak to people today, help me to present them with the salvation that comes to all who believe in Jesus' name. Amen.
Further Studies: *Acts 4:12*

One in Christ

*"There is neither Jew nor Greek, there is neither slave nor free man, there
is neither male nor female; for you are all one in Christ Jesus."*
(Galatians 3:28, NASB)

Has anyone ever made you feel special? Or acknowledged your strengths irrespective of your ethnic background or gender? If so, you undoubtedly felt loved and appreciated by their actions.

So it is in Christ. We are special. Everyone is special and unique; nothing changes that: not your height, the color of your eyes, the color of your skin, NOTHING. It is not about the rules, for by faith we are one in Christ.

If you read the verse before our opening verse, Paul says it is only being a new creation that matters. *"So in Christ Jesus you are all children of God through faith, for all of you who were baptized into Christ have clothed yourselves with Christ"* (Galatians 3:26-27).

Some men may want to intimidate you because you are a woman. In some churches and Christian circles, women are not allowed to handle certain responsibilities because they are women. It can be hard for women to really grasp their value in such settings.

But never let anyone intimidate you because you are a woman. In Christ Jesus, we are all one. Once you give your life to Christ and receive salvation, you have equal right with everyone, including men. There is neither male nor female in Christ.

Prayer

*Father, I thank you for the revelation of your word that I am a new creation
in Christ and that that's all that matters in Jesus' name. Amen.*
Further Studies: *Romans 2:11*

New Creation

"Therefore, if anyone is in Christ, he is a new creation; the old has gone, the new has come! All this is from God, who reconciled us to himself through Christ and gave us the ministry of reconciliation."
(2 Corinthians 5:17-18)

The concept revealed in this chapter is something that you must understand if you want to win as a Christian. Most times, we are accused of or reminded of our unpleasant past; things that we did before we became born again.

Until you understand the concept of the new creation, you will continually live in guilt because the devil will keep bringing up your past just so he can discredit your salvation (Revelation 12:10). To be a new creation means you have no past; you were miraculously disconnected from your past the very day you received salvation. You are altogether a new person.

2 Corinthians 5 can be referred to as "Paul's Hope of Eternal Glory," because in this chapter the apostle revealed some hard and sacred truth about our present realities as Christians. A new creation has no past; your life began the day you got born again.

There's a story of a man who suffered a massive heart attack and was pronounced dead, but God restored his life. Sometime afterward, his blood work test revealed that he had a new DNA, which showed no connection to having had a heart attack. That's what God does. He makes us new creations. Honor Him with your life today.

Prayer

Dear Father, I thank you for the new life I now have and enjoy in Christ Jesus. The mistakes of my past life cannot have a hold on me, because I am completely disconnected from my past and a new woman in Christ Jesus. In His name I pray, amen.
Further Studies: *2 Corinthians 5:16-7, Colossians 1:13-14*

No Greater Love

"Greater love has no one than this, that he lay down his life for his friends."
(John 15:13)

According to this scripture, laying down one's life for a loved one is the highest demonstration of love. That is exactly what Jesus did. He took our place of sickness, condemnation, and death so that we could have life and have it to the fullest.

Isaiah 53:4-6 gives us a better picture of what Jesus did for us:

> *"Surely he took up our pain and bore our suffering, yet we considered him punished by God, stricken by him, and afflicted. But he was pierced for our transgressions, he was crushed for our iniquities; the punishment that brought us peace was on him, and by his wounds we are healed. We all, like sheep, have gone astray, each of us has turned to our own way; and the Lord has laid on him the iniquity of us all."*

Today we may not be required to lay down our physical lives for loved ones, but there are other ways we can show such sacrificial love to those around us. It's when you have to deny yourself some kind of pleasure or comfort so that someone else can have something they need.

Let's take Jamie for example. She feels and looks like the odd one out among the other women. You become friends with her because you know what it feels like; you've been there. No acts of heroism, really. That's how you demonstrate love. You put her needs above your own so that she may experience the love of Christ. Who in your life needs to experience the love of Christ?

Prayer

Dear Lord, thank you for loving me so much to give your son for me. I am a dispenser of your love to a hurting world. I dispense your love everywhere in Jesus' name. Amen.
Further Studies: *Leviticus 19:9-18*

Inheritance

*"Then the King will say to those on his right, 'Come, you who are blessed by my Father;
take your inheritance, the kingdom prepared for you since the creation of the world.'"*
(Matthew 25:34)

This scripture serves to remind us that life is beyond this earth; all you see is not all there is. The Lord Jesus told us in John 14:2-3, *"In my Father's house are many mansions: if it were not so, I would have told you. I go to prepare a place for you. And if I go and prepare a place for you, I will come again, and receive you unto myself; that where I am, there ye may be also."*

This is beyond a promise, but it has serious implications. After reading our opening scripture and scriptures like it, you must pause and meditate for a while. The Master left us here with instructions on how to live and what to do while He is away, and one day very soon He will return and we will be required to give account of all that we have done in His absence.

Let's say your boss has been away for months and upon his return he summons you to a meeting. In his absence you have worked diligently, guided by the principles and instructions he left. Even though you were sometimes weary, you continued to do and act in the rightful manner.

He will undoubtedly express his profound gratitude to you for holding down the fort and for being instrumental in the growth of the company. So too will your inheritance be from the King of Kings, as His sheep. Choose to be diligent in your work of the ministry.

Prayer

Dear Father, I thank you because I have an inheritance in Christ Jesus. I have hope beyond this world, an incorruptible and imperishable inheritance in the world to come.
Further Studies: *Matthew 25:14-31, 1 Corinthians 15:19*

Rooted & Grounded

"That Christ may dwell in your hearts through faith, and
that you [be] rooted and grounded in love..."
(Ephesians 3:17)

The words "rooted and grounded" readily bring to mind the image of an old tree that has stood the test of weather and time. Over the years its root system has plunged deep into the bedrock of the earth, and it cannot be moved.

Whenever a storm passes through a park, you can get a pretty clear picture of which trees have a good root system and which ones don't. The ones with shallow roots will be knocked over, but the ones with roots that go deep down into the ground will remain standing tall.

There are many things in life that can represent a storm: difficulties with your spouse, children, friends, co-workers, health, etc. Without Christ and His love dwelling in our hearts, keeping us rooted and grounded in Him, we would easily topple over. The only thing that can ensure our ability to remain steadfast in Him is our faith.

Another great point about the analogy to roots here, is that roots are not only good for stability, but they also pull nutrients from the ground. The deeper our roots go down into Christ, the more we can draw out of Him. The very essence of God is love, so imagine how much love we can amass, when we stand tall as oaks of righteousness.

Prayer

Dear Lord, thank you for granting me according to the riches of your glory, to be strengthened with might by your Spirit in the inner man, rooted and grounded in love, and able to comprehend with all the saints what is the width and length and depth and height of the love of Christ which passes knowledge in Jesus' name. Amen.
Further Studies: *Ephesians 1:16-19*

Blessed Hope

"...we wait for the blessed hope--the appearing of the glory
of our great God and Savior, Jesus Christ."
(Titus 2:13)

What hope can be as pleasant as the appearing of our Lord, Master, and Savior? We must live every day with the blessed hope of Christ's return, because that will be the end of all of our troubles on this earth.

We know that when He shall return, we will not only enter into our rest, but we will receive rewards for our labor of love and life of obedience. This is why it is such a blessed hope. Paul looked forward to this day and recounted some of the gains we will receive on that day.

"Now there is in store for me the crown of righteousness, which the
Lord, the righteous Judge, will award to me on that day--and not
only to me, but also to all who have longed for his appearing."
2 Timothy 4:8

It's like sitting on a veranda, looking out every day, waiting to see your mother coming home from work. You never get tired, and she is always bringing something special for you. Even if she does not, just to hear her soothing voice and feel her warm embrace is good enough.

So too, as God's daughters, we wait, looking out for the blessed hope of His appearing, our great God and Savior. He blesses us all the time, and His words of promise are priceless!

Prayer

Dear Lord, I thank you for the blessed hope of your return in glory.
I live every day with faith on your word and in anticipation of your
return that will usher me into eternal rest in Jesus' name. Amen.
Further Studies: *Colossians 1:5*

August

Clothed with Strength and Dignity

"She is clothed with strength and dignity; she can laugh at the days to come."
(Proverbs 31:25)

Imagine that back in medieval times, a farmer had a bone to pick with his king about a particular matter. Angrily, he would stomp to the castle, wait in line for his turn to air his grievance, and then when his turn finally arrived, he would spout off all of the ways he planned to get back at the king.

Do you think the king would be bothered by these declarations? Not at all. He's the one with the power, and he knows it, so the most the farmer would probably get out of the king would probably be a good hearty laugh.

This is the same kind of confidence that we should have when it comes to our own lives. Because we have Jesus on our side to strengthen and emboldened us to go up into higher heights of glory, daily, we have no reason to be afraid, even when we hit hard times.

No matter what situations you may face in life, when you know who you are and who you belong to, you can literally laugh in the face of danger.

Prayer

Dear Father, thank you for giving such a powerful inner peace that I can laugh in the face of storms and trials. You are my peace who has broken down every wall, and I stand firm in you in Jesus' name. Amen.
Further Studies: *Philippians 1:6*

A Vow to One

"You shall not commit adultery."
(Exodus 20:14)

As the subject of adultery is listed among the initial commandments God inscribed on the tablets that He gave to Moses, we can be assured that the sanctity of marriage is a topic that is dear to His heart. As believers, we are the bride of Christ, and He is jealous for our love and affection. One can imagine then, why our unfaithfulness in our earthly covenants with our spouses grieves the heart of God. Our marriage covenants are a mere shadow of the Holy Communion that Christ desires to have with us, so the act of breaking our covenant is not something He takes lightly.

An intimate physical relationship with someone other than your spouse is typically defined as adultery; however, Jesus set the standard even higher in His Sermon on the Mount, as He compared looking at someone with lust in your eyes to adultery. According to Christ, it is not with our bodies that we commit adultery, but with our hearts. Therefore, we must search our hearts in order to determine where our affections lie.

For many women, adultery can be an emotional relationship with someone other than their spouse. Women typically connect with men emotionally, long before the physical aspect of a relationship ever comes into play. As such, if there is an emotional deficiency of some sort within a marriage, the woman must be careful to communicate that to her husband, and trust God to meet the voids and fill the needs she has, instead of seeking satisfaction from relationships with other men.

Adultery is a sin that affects both single and married women. Single women can encourage married men to commit adultery by engaging in flirtatious behaviors or intimate friendships with them, and married women can commit adultery by forming personal relationships with other men. Infidelity usually isn't premeditated, but it gradually progresses over time. For that reason, be diligent with setting boundaries as you honor the Lord by loving your husband.

A vow to one: your husband isn't debatable.

Prayer

Dear Father, thank you for my husband and the covenant of love we have established with you. Help me to love, respect, and honor him so that our marriage can bring glory to your name in Jesus' name. Amen.

Further Studies: *Mark 10:1-12*

A Holy Name

"You shall not take the name of the Lord your God in vain; for the Lord will not hold him unpunished who takes His name in vain."
(Exodus 20:7, NASB)

The way that we speak a name says a lot about how we feel about a person in that moment. For instance, you probably remember *that tone* in your mother's voice whenever you were in trouble. Or when women value a relationship with an individual, they often use pet names.

However, when the relationship is strained, they tend to revert to a first name or title basis with the individual. Whether we realize it or not, that tiny change in the way we address others means a lot, and people pick up on it.

Likewise, if we use God's name dishonorably, it is not only an indication that the relationship is strained, but it is also a tell-tale sign of something much more serious. Time and time again, we read throughout the Bible that the name of the Lord is holy; it's sacred because it represents His very nature. All of the many names used to describe God say something about His character and worth, and every name has just as much power as the next.

A number of ways we can take the Lord's name in vain are outlined in the Bible. A few examples are as follows: making a promise in His name and then going back on your word, or claiming to be a follower of Christ and then deliberately disobeying His commands.

When we use His name flippantly or dishonorably, essentially discounting the truth about His character, we take His name in vain. It shows a lack of respect, and as the illustrations above demonstrate, it shows that the reverence we are to have for the Most High King is far from our hearts.

There will come a day when every person that has ever lived will hear the name of Jesus and fall to their knees in worship. Why wait until the last day to honor His name? Why not honor His name today?

Prayer

Dear Father, your name is holy just as you are holy. Help me to honor you daily as I live up to the standard of your name in Jesus' name. Amen.
Further Studies: *Isaiah 57:15*

Favor From the Lord

"He who finds a wife finds a good thing and obtains favor from the LORD."
(Proverbs 18:22, NASB)

During the time of Solomon, when women were essentially sold and used like property, and generally disrespected, such a statement as this one could be considered to be quite counter-cultural. Instead of claiming that women were created simply for procreation and cleaning purposes, King Solomon identifies us as a source of favor from the Lord, thereby affirming the value of women and their role in marriage.

Though women are not treated in exactly the same manner today, this is a reassuring promise for our culture as well. Within the context of certain homes, there are women who are merely seen as a glorified house help. That certainly is the perspective in many countries around the world.

But the role of a wife is important, and she is a blessing to the union of marriage. The favor of God goes with her and brings His blessing to not only her marriage, but everything she puts her hand to. In that way, God has given women great intuition and sensitivity to His Spirit to be able to discern people and events, so when we walk in that anointing, our marriages and families prosper.

Throughout the ages, men have benefited from the wisdom of women. Before a lot of men make decisions, they may consult their wives because of the complementary gift that God has given them, and more often than not, the advice of a woman turns out to be in line with the wisdom of God.

If men would choose to take on the perspective of Solomon when it comes to their wives, they would truly be able to see how their wives can be a helpmeet to them, both inside and outside of the home. The value of a good wife in the home is priceless.

If you are desirous of getting married, it is advantageous to aspire to become all that you were created to be as a wife. When your husband finds you, he'll find a treasure and he'll also be endowed with favor from the Lord.

Prayer

Dear Father, you have created me with such care and wisdom. As I step into a deeper understanding of who I am in you, please grant me the eyes to see how I can be a support to my husband in Jesus' name. Amen.
Further Studies: *Proverbs 31*

Expecting

"But in keeping with his promise we are looking forward to a new heaven and a new earth, where righteousness dwells."
(2 Peter 3:13)

The expectation of acquiring something has the power to change the way we live our lives. When we are expecting a baby, we change the way we eat, sleep, and even the activities that we choose to engage in. Every decision we make revolves around our expectation of delivering a healthy child.

In Hebrews 11 we are presented with what many people like to call the "Hall of Faith." In this chapter, Paul lists off several men and women of the Bible who maintained their faith even in the face of danger, trial, suffering, and great loss. He goes through each of their stories and points out how their faith carried them through their given situations. Though their stories all differ from one another, one thing remained the same: their expectation.

> *"All these died in faith, without receiving the promises, but having seen them and having welcomed them from a distance, and having confessed that they were strangers and exiles on the earth. For those who say such things make it clear that they are seeking a country of their own. And indeed if they had been thinking of that country from which they went out, they would have had opportunity to return. But as it is, they desire a better country, that is, a heavenly one. Therefore God is not ashamed to be called their God; for He has prepared a city for them."*
> *Hebrews 11:13-16*

The one thing that kept their faith from wavering was the expectation that one day they would return to their heavenly home. When Paul challenges believers to run the race and press on to receive the prize, he is urging us to set our expectations on heavenly matters and on the finisher and the one who perfects of our faith. Once we've established the eternal as our prize and set our expectations in that way, it will change the choices we make and the way we live our lives.

What are you expecting?

Prayer

Dear Father, you are the joy set before me, and eternity with you is my ultimate heart's desire. I choose today to set my expectations upon you in hope that one day I will receive them in full in Jesus' name. Amen.
Further Studies: *Hebrews 11*

Vision of the Pure

"Blessed are the pure in heart, for they will see God."
(Matthew 5:8)

Have you ever engaged in conversation with someone that you can tell has bad intentions? Their lips may be saying one thing, but by their body language or the tone of their voice, you are certain that they are thinking or wanting something else.

God made it very clear in His Word how He feels about people who honor Him with their lips but whose hearts are far from Him. It grieves His Spirit. It is no wonder then that the people He would choose to reveal Himself to are the ones who are pure in heart.

To be pure in heart means to be blameless, clean, or without spot or wrinkle (to put it another way). The pure in heart are single-minded in their pursuit of pleasing God with their body, mind and soul. God is holy, so He requires that we pursue holiness. The achievement of that command is to be pure in heart.

"Who may ascend the mountain of the Lord?
Who may stand in his holy place?
The one who has clean hands and a pure heart,
who does not trust in an idol
or swear by a false god."
Psalm 24:3-4

On many occasions in the Bible, God relates our sin to the act of adultery. In the same way that adultery is betrayal of a marriage covenant, so is sin a betrayal of our covenant with Christ. As Christian women, we are betrothed to Christ, which, according to Jewish tradition, is not much different than being married. We are to be received by the King on our wedding day as a pure, spotless bride. The best of life from the world's viewpoint is nothing to be compared with the happiness experienced by the pure in heart, who will get to join in the wedding feast with the King of all kings.

Prayer

Dear Father, give me clean hands and a pure heart; prepare
me for your presence in Jesus' name. Amen.
Further Studies: *Psalm 51:10*

For His Glory

"I am writing to you, dear children, because your sins
have been forgiven on account of his name."
(1 John 2:12)

Though salvation is the greatest thing to ever happen to humanity, and it is a very personal gift that we each receive from God through the sacrifice of Jesus, God's gift of salvation is not only for us, but it is for His glory. After all, that is what we were created for, right? To bring glory to His name.

Sometimes it is easy for us to get caught up in the "For God so loved me" aspect of salvation and forget that God's ultimate goal is for every knee to bow before the Lamb who was slain before the foundation of the world. Yes, Jesus loves us and gave himself as a ransom for us, but one day He will receive the reward of the suffering He endured.

Part of working out our salvation requires that we recognize this truth about why we have been saved. In fact, seeing Jesus recognized for the king that He is should be a desire of our hearts.

There are many in the world that would like to discount the truth of Christ and His power in our lives, essentially giving Him a bad name. When we receive Jesus as our Lord and Savior and become ambassadors of the kingdom of God, part of our responsibility is to declare the truth about who He really is. We declare His love, His kindness, faithfulness, and goodness. Because of the forgiveness of sins, the name of Jesus is shared, adored, sang about, reverenced and exalted on every continent.

Now, not only are we forgiven of our sins for His name's sake, but we are also to continue in holiness for His glory, remembering that the way we live our lives is a direct reflection of the nature of Christ. We are Christ's ambassadors—for His glory and name's sake we must show the world that sin can be overcome through the blood of Jesus Christ.

Prayer

Dear Father, your name and renown are the desire of my heart.
May you always be gloried in my life and through all believers
now and throughout eternity in Jesus' name, Amen.
Further Studies: *2 Corinthians 5:20*

Stealing life

"You shall not murder."
(Exodus 20:13)

God is the creator of all things, including mankind. When he formed Adam from the dust, He breathed a single breath of life into his flesh, and that breath has sustained all of mankind for generations. As our creator, it is only right that He be the only one with the authority to remove our breath, but since the days of Cain and Abel, men have been claiming that right for themselves. This particular verse is applicable to everyone, but has been adopted by the pro-life movement to condemn abortion—and rightly so. Scripture makes it clear that life begins at conception:

"For You formed my inward parts;
You wove me in my mother's womb.
I will give thanks to You, for I am fearfully and wonderfully made;
Wonderful are Your works,
And my soul knows it very well.
My frame was not hidden from You,
When I was made in secret,
And skillfully wrought in the depths of the earth;
Your eyes have seen my unformed substance;
And in Your book were all written
The days that were ordained for me,
When as yet there was not one of them."
(Psalm 139:13-16)

As Christians, we should seek to uphold this command by taking a stand against abortion. God was not for it when Pharaoh killed the Hebrew babies to control the Israelite population, nor was He for it when Pilate killed the male babies to find Jesus. Now that these same types of murder are being committed on a massive scale, it is safe to say that it grieves God's heart. What will you do?

Prayer

Dear Father, I want to be a voice for those that have no voice. Give me insight on how I can help end abortion in Jesus' name. Amen.
Further Studies: *Psalm 139*

Commit your Children

"By faith Moses' parents hid him for three months after he was born, because they saw he was no ordinary child, and they were not afraid of the king's edict."
(Hebrews 11:23)

Moses' mother lived through an ordeal no mother would ever wish would happen to her greatest enemy. Pharaoh was on a bloodthirsty rampage to reduce the Jewish population by killing their male babies. Thousands of babies were being slaughtered in front of her, and her son was next in line. If she, a godly woman had confessed to giving birth to a son, he would have been killed by the authorities. Imagine the horror she must have felt. But what she did demonstrated quite a huge step of faith... she hid him.

As Christian mothers, we will encounter circumstances where we must decide if we are going to give our children to the world and its systems that kill them spiritually, or if we are going to shelter them for God and His purposes. What has become the cultural norm these days is typically antithetical to what God outlines as good and right in His Word. In these days it is very common for society to call what is evil, good and what is good, evil.

Children are very impressionable, very much like wet cement. The younger they are, the easier it is to make a significant mark in their lives. The older they get, the harder the cement, and the less chance you have of making an impression. Therefore, it is imperative that parents actively seek to protect their children and teach them the ways of the Lord early on. That way when they grow old, they will not depart from it.

There will be times that your child will experience situations in life that will be completely out of your control. You will undoubtedly feel like all hope is lost, but it's okay, because nothing is out of God's control, and nothing is too difficult for Him. If you have done your job and filled your child with the knowledge of God, you have nothing to fear. The only thing you need to do is trust.

Commit your children to the Lord and trust Him.

Prayer

Dear Father, I submit my children to your care, knowing that you are more than capable of keeping them safe. Raise them up to be men and women of your Word in Jesus' name. Amen.
Further Studies: *Proverbs 22:6*

Promise for the Persecuted

"Blessed are those who are persecuted because of righteousness, for theirs is the kingdom of heaven."
(Matthew 5:10)

When Jesus walked this earth, He was surrounded by people who loved Him, but He was also surrounded by those who wanted nothing more than to see Him dead. Long before He was sentenced to death on a cross, He was hounded by the Pharisees. They would heckle and taunt Him when He spoke, and they often tried to forcibly detain Him. Their final act of persecution was to kill Him.

After He ascended into heaven, this reality was transferred to those who took on the name Christian (mini-Christ). The disciples endured great hardships simply because they bore Christ's name on their hearts. Like our Master and those who followed Him before us, we have those who want to silence the message of the Good News. We share in the suffering of Jesus as persecution is part and parcel of the Christian life.

Injustice is not easy to endure peaceably. To be denied the opportunity to testify of your own innocence can be a hurtful and embittering experience, more so without Christ. With Christ however, persecution can bring us great joy. 1 Peter 4:14 says that persecution is a rewarding experience because God's glory and spirit rests upon you. We see this best in the example of Stephen, the first martyr for Jesus. Though he found himself at the mercy of scoffers, in his last moments He caught a glimpse of heaven. He saw the Lord seated at the right hand of the Father, and he surely received his eternal reward.

If you find yourself in a situation where you are called to endure injustice for Christ's sake, utilize the experience well. Do not seek escape from the trials that beset you or exhibit bitterness. Jesus promised us that if we choose to follow Him, we will have troubles, but to take heart because He has overcome the world.

The kingdom of heaven is the promised for the persecuted, including you! You are blessed, be strong!

Prayer

Dear Father, I love you, and serving you is the greatest joy of my life. Help me to withstand persecution for the sake of love whenever it may arise in Jesus' name. Amen.
Further Studies: *1 Peter 4:14, John 16:33*

The Coronation

"Blessed is a man who perseveres under trial; for once he had been approved, he will receive the crown of life which the Lord has promised to those who love Him."
(James 1:12, NASB)

James begins his epistle by stressing the importance of enduring trials and tribulations and encouraging us to face such situations joyfully. We may initially read those first few verses and feel like it is a high calling, one that is too high for us, but here he reinforces his earlier statements by shedding light on the fact that there is a special reward for us when we persevere: the crown of life.

When we want our children to do something, before they are capable of obeying simply for the sake of honoring their parents, we often have to teach them to obey by showing them that there is some kind of reward waiting for them if they do as they are told. Some people may call it bribery, but it really is a principle that our Father uses with us, and it is an effective one. Why else would we run a race if not to receive a prize?

Notice that this verse is a promise to those that endure temptation, not to those who escape it. Women who seek easy fixes for every pain and escape routes by giving in will find themselves without this crown. Imagine a group of runners running a race with hurdles. Some may run and jump over every hurdle perfectly while others may knock over some of the hurdles. Regardless of how they run, if they make it to the finish line, they receive an award. Now imagine those who see the hurdle and stop running only to walk around it. What would happen to them? They would be disqualified.

We disqualify ourselves when we give up in the middle of our trials, but when we endure trials and when we refuse to bow to the sins we are tempted with, we will receive an eternal reward-in-waiting; the crown of life.

Through endurance, we are building a witness of our love and dedication for Christ.

Prayer

Dear Father, your son is my great reward and I want to live for your name. Help me to keep fighting the good fight and endure through this race so that I may reach the prize in Jesus' name. Amen.
Further Studies: *Hebrews 12:1-3*

Purged of Idols

"You shall have no other gods before me."
(Exodus 20:3)

This first commandment from God is concise, but deep. He is God alone (note the capital "G"), and there is no other god (note the lowercase "g") in heaven above or on earth below that can compare to His authority, abilities, and sovereignty. For that reason, we are to worship Him and live our lives in obedience to Him. That is what He created us for – the glory of His name.

Because we were created to worship the Lord, there is an innate desire within us to do just that: worship something. The enemy of our souls knows this and will often present a plethora of options for us to choose from. Think of how many religions there are in the world; how many false deities are worshipped. Whether these people have ever been introduced to the God of the universe or not, they understand that they are supposed to worship something other than themselves.

The very definition of a god is something or someone that has power over you. You submit to it and it dictates what you are to do. A god doesn't have to be a deity of any sort that people worship as part of a religion. Other people can become your god and you can even become a god to yourself when you allow pride, malice, hatred, and lust to govern your decisions and control your life.

This can be evident in those moments when you hear the Spirit of God telling you to forgive your neighbor for a wrong they have committed against you, but you choose to listen to your pride. At that point in time, you have chosen pride as your master over God. Without even knowing it, if you continue choosing pride whenever these situations arise, you will be establishing pride's position on the throne of your heart.

Like the psalmist, cry out to God that you might be cleaned with hyssop and keep His commandments.

Prayer

Dear Father, I was created to worship you. I repent of any other thing or person I have allowed to take your position on the throne of my heart, and I seek to honor you now and henceforth in Jesus' name. Amen.
Further Studies: *Psalm 51*

Celebration of the Somber

"Blessed are they who mourn, for they will be comforted."
(Matthew 5:4)

When your heart breaks over personal loss, there is nothing that seems like it will satisfy you more than having your loved one back. Growing close to people forms a bond between the two of you that leaves an indelible mark on your soul. When that person leaves, it can often feel as though there is a hole in your life where they used to be, and nothing can replace it.

That is what it means to mourn – it is to grieve the loss of something or someone.

If anyone could be considered to have been a target demographic for Jesus as He walked the earth, it would be anyone who was lowly and downtrodden. He said that He came to the earth not for the healthy and whole, but for the sick. His mission was to heal, comfort, and restore anyone who had need of Him.

"The Spirit of the Lord is upon Me,
Because He anointed Me to preach the gospel to the poor.
He has sent Me to proclaim release to the captives,
And recovery of sight to the blind,
To set free those who are oppressed."
(Luke 4:18)

So when we are going through hard times and struggling within ourselves to find comfort and peace, we must remind ourselves of the One whose ultimate aim for being here on the earth is to ask us to cast our burdens on Him, knowing and believing that He cares for us and every bit of grief we may endure.

Cast your cares upon Him, for He cares for you.

Prayer

Dear Father, thank you for sending your son to come and be a soothing balm for my pain and grief. You are my peace in Jesus' name. Amen.
Further Studies: *Mark 2:17*

The Foundation of your Faith

"So that your faith might not rest on human wisdom, but on God's power."
(1 Corinthians 2:5)

It is a blessed gift to have spiritual unity in your marriage. As iron sharpens iron, so can you and your spouse sharpen one another and spur one another on in the faith. In fact, this is something couples should do together. However, it can become a default for wives to rely on their husband's knowledge and faith instead of studying God's Word and depending on Him for themselves.

If this is true in your case, it may not have always been that way for you. Maybe before you got married you enjoyed an intimate, thriving relationship with God, but once you found yourself bound to another, you found your affections slightly divided, and finding time to spend with the Lord became more strained. The next thing you knew, you were spending little to no time with God and then all you were able to glean from the Word was what you got from church or what your husband shared with you.

The nature of our sin is too great a responsibility to pass on to your husband to deal with. Sin can only be dealt with through Christ on an individual basis. In order to grow in your faith, you have to engage with the Holy Spirit on a personal level and allow Him to bring conviction and encouragement through your time in personal reflection with Him, reading the Word and praying.

Knowing God's Word for ourselves is the only way to be able to rightly divide the Word of Truth and to communicate a scriptural reason for your faith in God. If you don't have personal encounters with God along your faith journey to renew your faith, how will you respond when people ask you why they should get to know Jesus?

They will be saved by the testimony of your faith.

Prayer

Dear Father, forgive me for any areas where I have neglected spending time with you. I commit myself to continually come to meet with you in the secret place and explore the depths of your love in Jesus' name. Amen.
Further Studies: *2 Timothy 2:15*

Lineage of Respect

"Honor your father and your mother..."
(Exodus 20:12)

If you grew up in the church, it is very likely that you often heard this scripture repeated multiple times in Sunday school, by the pastor in church, and even in your home. After all, if parents have been given the task of instructing children in the ways of the Lord, listening to them is essentially the main responsibility of children. But even more than simply listening, they're commanded to honor their parents. That means to treat someone with great respect.

If a child's parents are seeking to guide him in the way of the Lord, this is not a difficult commandment to follow. He can trust their leadership in his life and there is no significant reason to protest. He takes their advice, prayer, and even chastisement in confidence. Of course, because kids typically think they know better than their parents, there will always be a bit of push back, but, generally speaking, the children will understand that the parents have their best interests in mind.

However, if a child's parents have worldly ideas, getting their advice might not always be to his wellbeing. For most children, especially if they are followers of Christ and their parents are not, they may struggle with how they are to engage with their parents and what honoring them should look like. Even if they aren't believers, their children are called to respect them for the simple fact that God put them in their life to fulfill that role, and He knew what He was doing.

As a role model for your children, the way you interact with your parents will give them a great example of how they should engage with you. Do unto them as you would have done unto you. Ask them for help in their areas of expertise. Spend time with them and do things for them. Let them know that you care about them. Above all, pray for them especially through their difficulties and make it a priority in your life.

Prayer

Dear Father, thank you for the parents you have given me and their influence in my life. Help me to be a godly figure in my children's lives in Jesus' name. Amen.
Further Studies: *Ephesians 6:1-3*

Fellowship of the Merciful

"Be merciful, just as your Father is merciful."
(Luke 6:36)

Mercy is an extension of compassion towards someone who deserves punishment even though it is well within your rights or power to given them their due punishment. Mercy is a difficult virtue to display in relationships with people who perpetually hurt you. Not only is it difficult to get over the pain of what they did, but you may feel like if you give that person mercy, they will only take advantage of you and do you more harm. What's even more than that is that you may not feel as though that person deserves mercy.

When you find yourself in such a position, and extending mercy to someone is the last thing you want to do, remember the sacrifice of Jesus:

"But God demonstrates His own love toward us, in that
while we were yet sinners, Christ died for us."
Romans 5:8

Knowing full well the sins we would commit before we even existed, Jesus chose to extend the greatest act of compassion – laying down His life – towards us. We did not deserve such mercy, yet He did it anyway. We understand mercy when we understand what Jesus endured for our sins and for the sins of others. In our cases, mercy may not require a very grand gesture other than dying to ourselves, but in Christ's case, mercy meant death. If He could go to those lengths for us, we can surely extend mercy to those that have hurt us.

Now, extending mercy certainly doesn't mean letting the person hurt you continuously without setting up any boundaries, but it does require that we freely offer forgiveness and reconciliation after an offense. As hard as it may be in the moment, you will undoubtedly save yourself loads of stress and remove an opportunity the enemy has to bring the root of bitterness into your life.

The wonder of this act is that when we show mercy to others, God extends it to us as well, regardless of the offence.

Prayer

Dear Father, you have shown me what it means to extend mercy to those that are not deserving. Help me to follow suit with those who need your mercy most in Jesus' name. Amen.
Further Studies: *Matthew 18:21-35*

Why this Weakness?

"And on the basis of faith in His name, it is the name of Jesus which has strengthened this man whom you see and know; and the faith which comes through Him has given him his perfect health in the presence of you all."
(Acts 3:16, NASB)

Have you ever had a particularly bad situation happen to you in front of other people? How did it make you feel? Embarrassed? Frustrated? Hurt? Did you ever wonder why God would allow you to endure the public humiliation? Most of us probably have because in such situations, we can usually only see the matter from our perspective and through the lens of our embarrassment.

Like this man in Acts, we must understand that though trials allow the world to see how weak or flawed we are, it is not as bad as it may appear. The world, having seen our weakness, is able to be stunned by the strength of character God displays through us.

In the account of this man's healing, as well as other public healing in the Bible, their sickness gave onlookers an extraordinary opportunity to see the power of God at work. For the many years that these people dealt with all manners of sickness and disease, they probably felt the same way we do: embarrassed, frustrated and hurt. But once they received their healing, I imagine they got a good glimpse of God's perspective of it all.

One of the biggest points of attraction in Jesus' ministry was the signs and wonders He performed in public places. The amazement of what He was capable of drew people from far and near. Once they saw, they believed, and once they believed they received Him as the Messiah.

God aims to use our stories for the same purpose. With faith in Christ, the worst situations can be overcome, even as the whole world watches.

When we are weak, Christ's strength is manifested in great power.

Prayer

Dear Father, thank you for choosing me to display your power and glory to the world in Jesus' name. Amen.
Further Studies: *Acts 3:3-10*

The Topaz of Tribulation

"You intended to harm me, but God intended it for good to accomplish what is now being done, the saving of many lives."
(Genesis 50:20)

One of the most remarkable aspects of the story of Joseph is that when everything was said and done – after his brothers had attacked him and sold him into slavery where he was falsely accused of rape and sent to prison for two years – he had enough discernment to see God's plan in the midst of it all. Instead of seeing the pain that he endured and attempting to throw it all back on his brothers, we get the beautiful quote listed above: "God meant it for good."

Women who have had to live in an abusive relationship know what it's like to endure many difficult trials: spiteful actions, family members turning against them, torment, and the love they once cherished being stripped away as they become mere objects. If you have not been in the pain of an abusive situation, it may be difficult to understand how scarring it can be on a woman not only physically, but also emotionally and spiritually.

And yet, God desires to use these horrible situations to bring good to these women's lives and to save many others. It can be a hard concept for us to grasp when it comes to understanding why God allows such things to happen to His children, but just as the Father turned His face away in anguish as His son was beaten and bruised, knowing it had to be done in order for salvation to come about, He surely does the same for His other children. We are never alone in our pain and suffering.

One of the beautiful results of having gone through such issues in your life is that you will develop a sensitivity and compassion for other women in the same position so that they don't have to go through it alone. You will understand their sufferings, and by the grace of God, you can help pull them through their darkest hours. Just as Joseph realized his years as a slave were meant to put him in a position of power so that he could save God's people from famine, ask the Lord to show you what He intends of you and most importantly, to give you the faith to take the difficult but necessary steps you're faced with in the day of difficulty.

Prayer

Dear Lord, I trust in your sovereign plan for my life. Even when my circumstances seem like they will drown me, let me see your light pierce through the darkness and renew my hope in Jesus' name. Amen.

Further Studies: *Jeremiah 29:11*

Name of the Peaceable

"Blessed are the peacemakers for they will be called children of God."
(Matthew 5:9)

et's face it. Women love drama. We love a good story and a bit of gossip. How many times have you been in the middle of a conversation that you know is about to turn the gossip route, but you just can't seem to bring yourself to bring the conversation to an end because you really want to know the juicy details? Then, when you are with other friends, you again feel yourself bursting at the seams to share that juicy tidbit of information. You know you shouldn't, but there it goes, right out of your mouth and into the itching ears of women who find themselves dealing with the same internal struggle.

Whether we realize it or not, our receiving and spreading gossip only serves to stir up bitterness and dissension, and it's actually a form of slander. It's no wonder why God clearly outlines gossip numerous times in the Bible as one of the sins that He really detests. He is a God of peace and He cannot stand to see His children stirring up discord among one another. Imagine your own children and how you feel when you see them hurting each other or bickering. Our inclination to drama separates us from that peace we desperately crave.

To have peace with each other, we must first have peace with God. We must understand the peace that comes from resting in His grace, and then walk it out. Live like someone whose mind is kept in perfect peace and refuse to allow anything to remove that peace. Once you have experienced this peace for yourself, it should be your aim to help others discover the same peace. Wherever you see there is discord, anger, hatred, or jealousy, bring that spirit of peace.

And as much as it drives us crazy, our children are following in our footsteps of creating chaos. From their messes to fights with siblings, sometimes it can seem as though peace is a million miles away from our homes. Then, we must remind ourselves and our children to imitate God's actions in our relationships. In so doing, we direct our families and ourselves away from being chaos-creators to peacemakers.

Prayer

Dear Father, I want to be known to others as your child, and a sure indicator of your children is peacekeeping. Help me to model this lifestyle for my children and those around me in Jesus' name. Amen.
Further Studies: *Isaiah 26:3*

Enduring to the End

"Who shall separate us from the love of Christ? Shall trouble or hardship or persecution or famine or nakedness or danger or sword?"
(Romans 8:35)

Our love for the Lord is not determined by the amount of passion we have for Him, but by the endurance we demonstrate as part of our dedication to Him.

When most people begin a romantic relationship, they inevitably go through a phase of infatuation. All they can think about is being with that person, and most of their days are spent with that person. In the same way, when new believers first come into the faith, they often are extremely passionate and zealous about their devotional life and sharing the Good News of Jesus.

Over time though, the infatuation and the passion fade. This change occurs naturally as time, circumstance, and various distractions arise, leaving the person to figure out how they really feel and what love truly is. No matter how much you love the Lord, there will be situations that will make you waver or shrink back. And yet, throughout these times of failure, God never leaves nor forsakes you. He is fully aware of this component of our human nature, which is why He makes Himself strong in our weakness.

Though we are very aware of the frailty of our love, we can also be encouraged by the strong, enduring love of our Father. As the Scripture says, His love is so strong that nothing can separate us from it, neither height, nor depth, nor present, nor future. It was for the sake of love that He brought us into this world, it is by love the He sustains us each and every day, and it because of love that we have received the gift of salvation that ensures us of eternity with the lover of our souls.

And He will keep on loving us to the end.

Prayer

Dear Father, thank you for loving me so well. Open my eyes to see glimpses of your love around me and my heart to trust in your love even when I feel unworthy in Jesus' name. Amen.
Further Studies: *2 Timothy 2:12-13*

Sacred Rest

"Remember the Sabbath day by keeping it holy."
(Exodus 20:8)

When God created the world in six days and took the seventh day as a day of rest, He established a paradigm for all of humanity to follow. Therefore, as believers, our lifestyles should be marked by this pattern. Being good stewards of our time, we should work to the best of our ability throughout the week, but we must not forget to dedicate one day of the week to rest and reflect on the good things the Lord has done for us.

For mothers and wives, getting rest can become almost impossible. After all, there are spills to be cleaned, meals to be served, and people to be cared for every day of the week. Sometimes it can be a struggle to get five minutes alone, let alone an entire day. How then can we honor this command to take a break from our work and rest in Christ?

As many wives and mothers discover, once they transition into that new phase of life, when it comes to a devotional life, one must first choose to make personal time with Jesus a priority. If we decide that Jesus is worth the extra time and effort, no matter what happens throughout the day, we will strive to ensure that nothing takes away from the secret place.

The same could be said of our treatment of the Sabbath. Think about it. When God gave this command to His people, did the women in that day and age not have children to look after or messes to clean? Of course they did, and yet they managed to honor the Sabbath. The key back then and the key for today is in preparation. The night before the Sabbath, they would cook ahead or prep as much as they could so that nothing could cause them to break their covenant day with God.

In the same manner, if we make a point to make the Sabbath a priority and plan ahead, we can use the day to commit ourselves and our families to the reflection and study of God's words as we cease from physical work and activities that shift our focus from Him. Sacred rest is possible.

Prayer

Dear Father, I want to honor you above all else. Teach me what it looks like to honor the Sabbath and find my rest in you in Jesus' name. Amen.
Further Studies: *Mark 2:27*

The Teaching Woman

"Therefore anyone who sets aside one of the least of these commands and teaches others accordingly will be called least in the kingdom of heaven, but whoever practices and teaches these commands will be called great in the kingdom of heaven."
(Matthew 5:19)

From the Old Testament through the New, we see that God is consistently concerned with how the believer's lifestyle affects others. When He gave the Israelites His laws, His ultimate aim was that they would be set apart from everyone else. Everything they did was to be a sign and symbol to the world that they belonged to Him. Therefore, he commanded His people to forever keep His laws on their lips; to speak of them to their children when they sat at home, when they walked along the road, when they slept, and when they arose.

Likewise, Jesus condemned anyone who would lead children astray (Luke 17:1-4), and the Apostle Paul encouraged believers to stay away from any activity that would cause their brothers and sisters to stumble – even if the believer did not believe the activity to be contrary to God's word (Romans 14:13-23). No matter how we feel, we must take the time to disciple those who look to us for spiritual guidance.

When God created women, He created us with an innate desire to nurture and care for others. Because of that God-given trait, many women have a unique ability to lead children and younger women to Christ. One may even call it a woman's ministry. Whether you are a mother or a local church member, there are young people who are watching the decisions and commitments you make. Your decisions may help them form their own concepts of truth as well as develop aspirations for their own lives.

If we ignore the Word of God or believe contrary to it in any area, we will naturally teach others to do likewise. But if we diligently apply the Word to every area of our lives through daily studies and the instruction of others in truth, then we will be the recipients of great rewards in heaven.

Prayer

Dear Father, open my eyes to see those teachable moments when I can use situations I may be facing to show others your glory and to give you praise in Jesus' name. Amen.
Further Studies: *Titus 2:3-5*

Unique

*"You made all the delicate, inner parts of my body and
knit me together in my mother's womb."*
(Psalm 139:13, NLT)

Women can typically be their own worst critics. No matter how many people tell you that you look nice, you will easily spot the "flaws" on your outfit, your skin, or your body. No matter how many times you look in the mirror, your eyes will always fall onto that "problem area" you've always hated.

In this Psalm, King David reveals the uniqueness of every one of us. He reveals the fact that when God created us, He created us to be perfectly and distinctively who we are today. There is no other person like you, there has never been anyone like you, and there will never be anyone like you until the end of the world.

From the embryonic stages, God uniquely developed your inner parts: organs, cells, tissue, and your DNA. No one else comes close to your prototype, and no one ever will. Think about the intricacies, attributes, and preferences that you have as a woman who was intricately woven and orchestrated by God that make you unique.

Embrace and celebrate who you are, because it is God who has fashioned you, and He cares about you. From the womb to the tomb, He'll be there for you. Dare to live your life knowing that you are the only one of you that God made, and that each day that you wake up in the morning, just as He did in the beginning of time, He looks upon you and declares, "She is good."

Prayer

*Precious Father, thank you for creating me specially. I choose to
believe what you believe about me, in Jesus' name. Amen.*
Further Studies: *Psalm 139:1-18*

Freedom

"Stand firm, then, and do not let yourselves be burdened again by a yoke of slavery."
(Galatians 5:1b)

magine a bird has been captured and placed in a cage. Day after day it wallows in captivity until finally, one day, the cage door is opened and the bird is able to escape.

We were once captives to sin, and the law was our only means of being made right with God. But the bonds of law became a type of slavery in and of itself, because we were chained to a never-ending list of rules to follow. BUT the death of Christ and His shed blood set us free. He made it possible for us to be filled with the Holy Spirit, who would become an ever-present instructor for our Christian walk.

Sometimes it can be hard for us to live in the freedom and grace that Christ bought for us, because we want so desperately to please God. Oftentimes we believe that following as many biblical laws as possible will make us more holy and acceptable to the Lord, but why would God want us under a yoke that He had already freed us from?

"For sin shall no longer be your master, because you are not under the law, but under grace."
Romans 6:14

God would want nothing more than to see us living in the freedom that He bought for us with the blood of His only son. So the next time you find yourself beating yourself up about not getting something right, remember that it is for freedom's sake that Christ set you free, so be free of the condemnation and continue on with the Lord.

Prayer

Father, I thank you for setting me free through the death of Jesus. Now, I live freely for you as I display your virtues and glory to my world in Jesus' name. Amen.
Further Studies: *Romans 8:2, Galatians 5:1*

Good over Evil

"Love must be sincere. Hate what is evil; cling to what is good."
(Romans 12:9)

If we were to boil the entire Bible down to just one word, that word would be *love*. The Old Testament is a love story between God and His people. Everything He did was out of love for them, even when He had to discipline them (Hebrews 12:16). In the New Testament, the very reason that Jesus came to this earth was for the sake of love, and everything that He taught revolved around love.

Now, we can look at all of the commandments that God gave the Israelites and make a list of do's and don'ts, but think about it. Instead of having to be told not to kill, steal, or commit adultery, when Jesus simply tells us to love our neighbors as much as we love ourselves, it goes without saying that if our love is sincere, there should be no desire to kill, steal, or commit adultery in our hearts whatsoever.

If our love is sincere, we will naturally hate what is evil and cling to what is good. Naturally, we will seek to help the lowly and oppressed, naturally, we will forgive those that have wronged us, and naturally, we will serve others in humility. After all, it is how we would want to be treated, right?

This is love; the love of Christ who first loved us, the same love that propels us to do that which is good. Choose to walk the path of love, which just happens to also be the path of righteousness.

Prayer

Lord, I choose to activate your life in me. I choose good over evil in Jesus' name. Amen.
Further Studies: *Galatians 5:14*

Saved

"Here is a trustworthy saying that deserves full acceptance: Christ Jesus came into the world to save sinners--of whom I am the worst."
(1 Timothy 1:15)

Looking back over your life, you may shake your head and say, "Thank you, God, for saving someone like me." Only you know the intimate details of your past, but regardless of the severity of details, the basic truth of us all is that we were sinners and Christ came and saved us.

Before you came to Christ, maybe you thought you were beyond saving; too bad, too mean, or too unwholesome. But if anyone had the right to believe he was beyond saving, it was the Apostle Paul. He traveled the countryside trying to dissuade people from believing in Jesus and assisting in their deaths if they refused!

The beauty of Paul's story though, is that though he easily could have won the title of being the worst sinner of his time, Christ came to save him. Christ came to save us too. Without him we would still be wallowing in our sins, but because of Him we are free. Take some time to praise Him for saving you today.

"For God sent not his Son into the world to condemn the world; but that the world through him might be saved. He that believeth on him is not condemned: but he that believeth not is condemned already, because he hath not believed in the name of the only begotten Son of God."
John 3:17-18

Prayer

Dear Lord, I thank you for the salvation of my soul in Jesus' name. Amen.
Further Studies: Mark 16:15

Bound by Selfishness, Freed by Sacrifice

"Through him everyone who believes is set free from every sin, a justification you were not able to obtain under the law of Moses."
(Acts 13:39)

Most countries have a special day set aside to celebrate their independence. We celebrate our independence days in order to remind ourselves of what life was like under another government's thumb and to revel in the freedom that is now available to us and to our children. Unfortunately though, the further we get away from that initial day of independence, the easier it is to forget exactly what it was that we were set free from.

For Americans, our predecessors fought for independence to worship God as they pleased. They came seeking freedom of religion. Nowadays, Americans have been granted more freedoms than any other country, but instead of using that freedom to pursue relationship with God, many use their freedom to do whatever they want, even if the Bible this country was founded on calls their actions sin. Instead of celebrating their freedom from sin, they celebrate their freedom to sin.

When Jesus came and sacrificed His life for us, He removed the yoke of the law that made holiness seem nearly impossible to achieve. In its place He gave us grace – unmerited favor that pardons us from our sins. Sometimes we can treat the grace of God like a free ticket to do whatever we want, but that is not what God intended. He set us free so that we could run after Him unencumbered by our humanity. Filled with the Spirit of God – His very essence – we would therefore be enabled to scale heights that the weight of our sins could never allow us to achieve before.

Jesus made the ultimate sacrifice, and He's calling us to make a similar sacrifice each and every day. He came to this earth choosing to lay aside His rights as a Deity and to take on the nature of a servant – what an awesome sacrifice! Now He looks to us to lay aside our rights to do as we please and to humble ourselves enough to sacrifice our desires for the true freedom and purpose that comes from submitting our lives to His will.

Prayer

Dear Father, I yield myself to you in faith and obedience, knowing that justification can only be attained through Christ alone who gives me true freedom. Thank you for your Spirit that brings liberty to my life in Jesus' name. Amen.
Further Studies: *Romans 6*

The Good News about Bad News

"They will have no fear of bad news; their hearts are steadfast, trusting in the LORD."
(Psalm 112:7)

There are some days when you can watch the news and literally feel like hiding under a rock. Whether it's the presidential elections, the decay of morality, or rising tension between entire nations and people groups, the state of the world we live in today is enough to weigh pretty heavily on one's soul.

Aside from that, we have our own troubles in our personal lives to face. For some that may come in the form of a late night call about some trouble your child has gotten into or a diagnosis from the doctor that does not seem promising. But as much as we hate bad news, we must identify the benefits of its presence in our lives so we can determine how to deal with it properly.

When we receive bad news, we discover that the gravity of the situation typically pushes us to ask difficult questions about God and our faith. Better yet, it thrusts us into the capable arms of a God who knows very well the plans that He has for us. Difficult situations encourage us to seek Him for guidance not only on what to do but on how to keep worry, fear, and doubt from taking control of our minds.

Although we may be tempted like Job's wife to disassociate ourselves from God, He wants us to respond in humility and faith, accepting His will and trusting the plan He has for us. Bad news doesn't mean God has forsaken or cursed us; on the contrary, it means God has specifically chosen a trial that will bring Him glory and allow us through faith, to grow.

Remember Jesus sleeping in the boat with His disciples? The storm was enough to strike fear into their hearts, yet when they woke Jesus, He was totally unperturbed by the events that were going on around Him. He knew that God would bring them from point A to point B no matter what was going on around them. If we can harness that kind faith, we can withstand any bad news this world has to throw at us.

Prayer

Dear Father, help me to keep my eyes on you instead of the negative situations I may face in life. Thank you for being the strength I need to get through it all in Jesus' name. Amen.
Further Studies: *Jeremiah 29:11*

A New Day

"Because of the Lord's great love we are not consumed, for his compassions never fail. They are new every morning; great is your faithfulness."
(Lamentations 3:22-23)

There are many wonderful promises in the Bible for those who believe and follow in the footsteps of Christ, but the shame and guilt of sin often keep us from taking hold of those promises, especially when we need them the most. Have you ever felt like there is a distance between you and God or that He's disappointed in you and hiding His face from you? Such distance is actually only perceived.

Because we are well aware of the sins that so easily beset us, we often deem ourselves unworthy of relationship with God. We know He's holy and only those with clean hands can approach Him, so part of the way we punish ourselves is by projecting feelings of anger or disappointment on God. By doing so, we convince ourselves that because we are upset with ourselves, God is too. But that is not the case.

God has promised that His compassion for us does not "run out", but it is renewed every morning without fail — great is His faithfulness! Yes, our sins demand that we be punished – or as the Scripture implies, consumed by the fiery wrath of God – but thank God for His great compassion.

It is important for us to remember that God is a God of justice. He hates sin and He will do everything in His power to remove it from our lives. That is part of His nature, but it is only one part. When God declared His name to Moses He said this of Himself:

"The Lord, the Lord God, compassionate and gracious, slow to anger, and abounding in loving kindness and truth; who keeps loving kindness for thousands, who forgives iniquity, transgression and sin; yet He will by no means leave the guilty unpunished..."
(Exodus 34:6-7)

If sins from yesterday still hold you in guilt or shame, remember that it is for the remissions of those sins that Jesus fully paid the price. Don't dwell on past failures, but embrace God's compassion for each day.

Prayer

Dear Father, without your compassion I would be destroyed. I praise you for being a merciful and compassionate God in Jesus' name. Amen.
Further Studies: *Psalm 103:8*

Changing Every Day

"But we know that when Christ appears, we will be like him, for we will see him as he is."
(1 John 3:2)

Every day of our lives is a day of transformation. Jesus, who started the good work in our hearts from the day we declared Him to be our savior, has been faithfully working to complete that work to this day. Day after day He sloughs off the old self and teaches us by His Spirit how to act a little more like Him, talk a little more like Him, and live a little more like Him. Day by day we are transformed into His image.

Though we are becoming like Jesus, we have not reached the fullness of what it means to be a Christian ("mini-Christ"). The key to achieving the fullness of what it means to be transformed into Christ's image is to see Him as He is. While we live on this earth, our view of Him is limited. We can only see in part because our only experience with Him is what we've heard or felt, but we have never seen Him.

"For now we see in a mirror dimly, but then face to face."
(1 Corinthians 13:12a)

When Jesus returns, we will finally be able to look at the author and finisher of our faith face to face, beholding Him in all of His glory. As His bride, we should eagerly await that day when the veil will be removed, as He is our only hope of glory, but in the meantime, we press on. We press on to know Him, because knowing is as close to beholding as we can get on this earth.

Through reading God's Word, we are able to grow in our knowledge of the Lord. It tells us that we should see Him as the Creator (*John 1:3*), as Lord (*Philippians 2:11*), and as the only Savior from sin and the curse (*John 3:16, Romans 8:21*). He is also the immortal God (*Hebrews 13:8*). We can spend our entire lives searching the Scriptures and will never exhaust what it teaches about the nature of Christ, so why not spend the rest of your life trying?

Through regular time in His Word, we will learn His attributes and become more and more like Him.

Prayer

*Dear Father, I long for the day that I can see you face to face. Help
me to keep that longing alive in my heart every day that I live,
move, and have my being in you in Jesus' name. Amen.*
Further Studies: *Romans 12:2*

The Mighty Savior

For the Lord your God is living among you. He is a mighty savior.
He will take delight in you with gladness. With his love, he will calm
all your fears. He will rejoice over you with joyful songs.
(Zephaniah 3:17, NLT)

Can you imagine God living in your house with you the same way He used to dwell in the Ark of the Covenant or the Most Holy Place or even the way He used to walk through the garden with Adam? That would truly be an awesome experience.

Prior to this Scripture, we discover that the nation of Israel had committed numerous transgressions against God. Because God is a God of justice, He knew that they deserved to be punished for their sins. But instead, we see the prospect of redemption. God tells them that He has taken away their judgment and cleared away their enemies. Instead of judgment, He gives them Himself.

What's even more than giving Himself, He gives Himself in a way that demonstrates His pure delight in being with His people. He rejoices over them with singing and dancing. Imagine that!

Imagine being a child who has done something wrong. You know that when your parents find out what you did, you're going to get in trouble, so up until that moment of reckoning, you're filled with fear. Now imagine that when your parents find out what you did, they not only forgive you but praise you for telling the truth. That, my friends, has the power to calm fears.

And that is what God does with us. When we are afraid, His love conquers our fear and replaces it with peace and joy. The Mighty Savior takes delight in you gladly, His love will calm every fear that you have and He rejoices over you with joyful songs.

Acknowledge your sins daily and repent quickly. God dwells with us and desires to have delightful fellowship with us.

Prayer

Dear Father, what an awesome privilege it is to know that you are rejoicing over me.
I choose to rest in your love today and to let it calm my fears in Jesus' name. Amen.
Further Studies: *Psalm 103:13*

September

The Law of Wisdom

"She speaks with wisdom, and faithful instruction is on her tongue."
(Proverbs 31:26)

Have you ever had a friend that you always go to for spiritual advice, because you know that whatever they say is going to be full of wisdom and lead you in the right direction? That is what you would call a virtuous woman.

The Bible tells us in the book of James that the tongue is one of the hardest members of our body to control. It is also one of the most powerful. To tame it is quite a task indeed, so any woman that is considered to always have "faithful instruction on her tongue" has learned the art of being quick to listen and slow to speak, and I would even add that she is open to the leading of the Holy Spirit.

Wisdom comes from the Holy Spirit, so if you want to be that woman who can speak the mind of God instead of simply giving people a piece of your mind, you're going to want to fill your mind with the Word of God and speak it on the regular. Nothing that you speak from the Bible can lead anyone astray, because it is the very word of God himself already!

A loose and rash tongue can cut someone to the heart, but a woman who speaks wisdom builds others up to the glory of the Father. Each time you speak, consciously and deliberately choose to speak positive words. Allow the wisdom of God and the character of God to flow through you by speaking and acting as your heavenly Father.

Prayer

Dear Father, I thank you for filling me with your nature. As I deliberately act on your word, I exude your nature and character in Jesus' name. Amen
Further Studies: *Matthew 5:14-16*

Teaching

"[The older women] can urge the younger women to love their husbands and children, to be self-controlled and pure, to be busy at home, to be kind, and to be subject to their husbands, so that no one will malign the word of God."
(Titus 2:4-5)

There are many benefits to growing older: gaining loads of knowledge and experience, an ever-expanding group of close family and friends, and the opportunity to pour into the lives on women younger than yourself.

Though we should live our entire Christian lives in service to others, it's a special directive Paul gives here to older women to take the younger women in the church under their wings and to teach them about marriage so that their lives can be enriched.

What Apostle Paul admonished the older women to do here is something similar to what is practiced in some African cultures. In some places in Africa, when a young woman comes into the family through marriage, for the first few years she is made to live with the older women in that family. The older women will teach the young woman how to conduct herself, how to take care of her husband, what to do when she is pregnant, and all the necessary home making techniques. This kind of life-on-life discipleship is similar to what Paul is instructing the older women among us to do with the younger women.

If you are an older Christian woman with knowledge of God's word and many years of experience, you are a worthy guide and teacher to those who are young.

Prayer

Dear Father, I thank you for entrusting me with the ministry of teaching younger women. I will not fail in this responsibility in Jesus' name. Amen.
Further Studies: *2 Timothy 2:22-24*

Convicted Consumers

"You shall not covet..."
(Exodus 20:17)

Covetousness has become a lifestyle for many of us. We scroll through our social media accounts and are constantly bombarded with photos and statuses showing off everyone's "perfect" life. We "pin" other people's items, relationships, and even food on boards that represent aspirations we have for our lives. We watch television and we are told what's trending and what we should wear, look like, or be doing with our lives. We attend events and compare ourselves to everyone around us.

Covetousness is hard to overcome and even more so with the media depicting that our dreams can be fulfilled through the acquisition of "new" things. We may not even realizing we are coveting at first, but if we take a closer look at what it is we're actually doing, we will begin to see that behind that longing gaze at the décor in our neighbor's living room lies yearning to possess something we don't have.

We can attempt to avoid this temptation by discontinuing email and catalogue subscriptions or trying to remove whatever triggers the temptation to covet, but a change in behavior alone will not change our hearts. A change in heart can only occur if we change our perspective, and covetousness begins when we compare ourselves to others.

Two main results come from comparison: 1) You look down on others because you believe you have more than them, or 2) You look down on yourself because you believe you have less than others. One leads to pride and the other to covetousness. Neither do anything but cause us trouble; neither are pleasing to God.

Contentment is the antithesis to covetousness. It's looking at what you have and being satisfied with the way God has blessed you. Even if you have less than so-and-so across the street, you have all you need, and that should be enough. By accepting Christ's promise and presence in our lives, He fills every void and we can overcome covetousness.

Prayer

Dear Father, thank you for all that I have. I would have nothing without you. Help me to be satisfied and to quit playing the comparison game in Jesus' name. Amen.
Further Studies: *Hebrews 13:5*

Fleeing the Forbidden

"So do not throw away your confidence; it will be richly rewarded."
(Hebrews 10:35)

Everyone reaches a point in their Christian life where they grapple with whether or not their faith is based on reality. Sometimes this questioning may be the result of a tragedy – those moments when we cannot seem to understand God's sovereignty – and we project those feelings of confusion onto our faith as a whole. Other times questioning your faith may be the result of a direct challenge someone poses to your belief system – you know those arguments people like to have sometimes to prove that you don't really know what you know.

This season of questioning is especially relevant to people who were saved early in life and have built their whole life around a routine of walking in faith. Maybe they did Christian things because that's how they were raised or what they were instructed to do by other Christians they admired, but they had never quite developed a personal relationship with God. Therefore, when something happens to shake them a little bit, they wonder why they do the things they do, if it's right, and if God's Word can really be trusted.

We know from the story of Job that Satan stalks the earth looking for opportunities to trip us up. If it's a tragedy, so be it. If it's people around you who hate God and are willing do anything to shake your faith, so be it. If it's tormenting you in your mind, causing doubt to flood your thoughts, so be it. When he initially came to Adam in the garden, what was his tactic? To get Adam to believe something other than what God said. His tactic today remains the same. He want us to believe something other than God's Word. We must resist his lies.

Another phrase for confidence is "firm trust." There aren't many people that we can say have earned our unwavering trust. At some point in time, everyone is going to fail us... everyone that is, except for Jesus. He has proven Himself time and time again to be trustworthy, so let go of everything that speaks against what you know of Christ and hold fast to Him.

Our confidence in Him will be richly rewarded, so be steadfast and flee worldly pleasures.

Prayer

*Dear Father, when my faith is shaken, gird up my legs that I
may stand and not waver in Jesus' name. Amen.*
Further Studies: *Galatians 6:9*

Choosing to Lose

"He who has found his life will lose it: and he who has lost his life for My sake will find it."
(Matthew 10:39, NASB)

When a woman gets married, she loses some of the time, activities, and relationships that she had as a single person. When she has children, even more time, money, and personal interests become lost. For the sake of loving her family rightly, she can easily make those sacrifices because she knows that what she gains is well worth it. Time spent with loved ones could never be replaced by what was available to her before they came along.

When a woman makes a vow to God, she again makes a vow to "lose" her own life. That means that before she makes the sacrifice of time for her husband or her children, she should seek to honor her time with God. Many women look at the little time they have available in a day and feel overwhelmed. It is natural in those moments to want just a little "me-time" to be able to recharge and spend whatever moments you can spare doing something you enjoy. It is also natural to push time with God to the back-burner because He is not in your face demanding your attention.

Even so, Jesus says that when we give up our rights to our lives, including our time, money, personal interests, and so on, we will find a more abundant life in Him. When you give Jesus your time as a precious sacrifice (as He undoubtedly realizes how busy you are and how much you value your time), your life becomes enriched. All of the wonderful things that flow from the goodness of God – like peace and joy – become part of your life.

As you read this, you may be feeling a little tug on your heart reminding you of where you have fallen short in prioritizing your relationship with God over everything else. It's not too late to make a change. Choose God all over again and begin to make a plan for how you can offer a sacrifice of praise to the Lord in the form of your time.

If God is calling you to make a commitment for His sake, don't be afraid to lose your life for the abundant life that He wants to give you.

Prayer

*Dear Father, in you is life and life abundantly. Help me to honor
my time with you above all in Jesus' name. Amen.*
Further Studies: *Psalm 91:1*

Created Equal

*"There is neither Jew nor Gentile, neither slave nor free, nor is
there male and female, for you are all one in Christ Jesus."*
(Galatians 3:28)

This verse does not mean that gender has no value to God or that there is no difference in the ministries of male and female. No, He created each sex uniquely and diversely with very specific intentions. Each has their own gifting, abilities, and overall make up. The first book of the Bible makes that clear:

*"He created them male and female, and He blessed them and
named them Man in the day when they were created."*
(Genesis 5:2)

What this verse is saying though, is that there is no difference in the spiritual value or capacity of either sex. Regardless of our nationality, background, economic status, or gender, Jesus equally saves us, equally offers fellowship, knowledge, and virtue to everyone.

"For there is no partiality with God."
(Romans 2:11)

Although women were created as helpmates, they are not inferior. Their virtue, knowledge, salvation, and fellowship with God are equal to that of their male counterparts. Women have strengths where men are weak and vice versa. God designed it to be this way so that neither can lord their status or position over the other. We are all wretched and in need of a savior, and thankfully for us, Jesus died to save ALL.

Therefore, women can take part in the inheritance of Christ just as much as men. Women can be used by God just as much as men. And women can receive equal rewards in heaven to that of men. Here on earth women have to fight for equality, but in the heavenly realm, our stature is great. It's about time we started living like the favored ones that we are.

Prayer

*Dear Father, I am your daughter and I know that I am loved by you. Thank
you for seeing me impartially and loving me as I am in Jesus' name. Amen.*
Further Studies: *Acts 10:34*

Crossing the Lie Line

"You shall not bear false witness against your neighbor."
(Exodus 20:16, NASB)

Bearing false witness can take many forms. Let's start with gossip – a problem areas for a lot of women (and men, apparently). Gossip is considered to be reporting a story to another according to your own views instead of strictly relaying the facts. To put it even simpler than that, gossip is talking about other people's business even though it has nothing to do with you. Truthfully, most of what is shared in gossip is based on rumors or misunderstandings. That's bearing false witness against your neighbor.

Forming false judgments about people privately is another example. We all make assumptions about people based off of what we see (or don't see) and make judgments about them. You may not verbally express what you think about a person, but remember that Jesus said, "Whatsoever a man thinks in his heart, that so he is." If you are thinking it, it's no different than you saying it. You are just as guilty.

Testifying about a situation in order to incriminate someone wrongfully is also considered bearing false witness, and lying to our children, spouse, or parents is yet another example. No matter how easy it seems to tell a little "white lie" for whatever reason, God makes it clear here that false testimony should be the last thing coming out of our mouths.

Through the strength of Jesus Christ we can conquer those tendencies we have to depend on false witnessing in conversation or in our thought lives. Also, an adherence to personal penitence, and/or the recognition of our personal struggles that cloud our judgment and perspective in a situation are vital.

Ask yourself today. Am I crossing the lie line?

Stay on the right side.

Prayer

Dear Father, purge my tongue and forgive me of any guilt I may have from bearing false witness. May my mouth be an instrument of worship and peace from here on out in Jesus' name. Amen.
Further Studies: *Psalm 19:14*

Wear this Belt

"Stand firm then, with the belt of truth buckled around your waist..."
(Ephesians 6:14)

Ephesians 6 lists a number of pieces that make up the whole armor of God. Of course as armor protects a soldier in battle, so are these attributes of our faith meant to protect us against attacks from the enemy. The first article we are to wear is the belt of truth.

A belt maintains the function of stabilizing a garment. It keeps everything in its place. As simple as this may sound, just think about your personal use of belts. Sure there are times we use them simply as an accessory, to give a dress an interesting look, but think about those times you have donned a pair of jeans that just didn't fit right. Think about the way the simple addition of belt made something that was impossible to wear possible.

Now let's translate that aspect to truth. In order to stabilize our faith, we need to be rooted and grounded in truth. We cannot stabilize our faith with feeling, experience, charitable deeds, or even another person's testimony. When we find ourselves in the midst of attacks, what else can we hold onto but the truth?

The enemy will try to attack you and claim that you have no worth, but because you know the truth that God created you with purpose and that you are incredibly valuable to Him, your armor (your defense) against him remains intact. Likewise, when the enemy tries to tell you that God is not good or that's He's anything other than His true nature, the truth about the nature of God will keep you grounded against the enemy's attacks.

Scripture teaches that Jesus is the very embodiment of truth. In John 14:6, He says, *"I am the Way, the Truth, and the Life."* If we face the enemy with Jesus as our stabilizer, there is no way that we can fall.

Are you standing firm and your loins girded with this truth?

Prayer

Dear Father, today I put on the belt of truth and stand on your reality - not my own or what enemy tells me is my reality. Thank you for being my strength in Jesus' name. Amen.
Further Studies: *John 8:31*

Begin with Submission

"In the beginning God created the heaven and the earth."
(Genesis 1:1)

In the beginning there was nothing. God spoke. And there was. Are those not some of the most powerful statements about God in the entire Bible? The fact that He created the universe to operate in perfect harmony by the simple use of a short phrase demonstrates the amazing power of our great God. The details of every aspect of nature, even down to the smallest, most seemingly insignificant creature, demonstrate not only His careful attention to detail, but also His abundant love for all of the works of His hand.

We are called to submit in worship to the Sovereign God, our Creator, in whose image we are made (v. 27). When you think about it, this is truly the least we can do. It seems as though humanity can get so carried away with living our own lives that we forget our lives are a gift from God. He brought us into this world and gave us everything that we needed to survive. And yet, we forget this truth and ultimately forget to worship Him.

To worship God is to declare His worth-ship. It is simply saying that He is worthy of our adoration because of who He is and what He's done. It is acknowledging the fact that without Him we are nothing. It is acknowledging all of the wonderful things He has done in your life personally. It is acknowledging that there is no one in all of heaven above or on the earth below that is like Him.

Yet regardless, to know who we really are and what our purpose is, we go on these personal journeys attempting to "find ourselves". It is as though we believe that by looking to "created things," we can find the answers we seek, but the only one who can give us any valid insight to our true identity is the one spoke a destiny over our lives and breathed it into our lungs even before we were born, and the one who sustains us daily until we reach the fulfilment of that destiny.

As our worship goes before His throne, He will send revelation. Worship the Lord today.

Prayer

Dear Father, you are holy and worthy of all of my worship. Thank you for all that you have done for me and all that you have been in my life whether I've seen it or not in Jesus' name. Amen.
Further Studies: *John 4:24*

From Darkness to Light

"...to open their eyes and turn them from darkness to light, and from the power of Satan to God, so that they may receive forgiveness of sins and a place among those who are sanctified by faith in me."
(Acts 26:18)

Paul was commissioned to bring the Good News of the life and death and resurrection of Christ to the Jews and Gentiles of his day. Having experienced the transforming power of Jesus himself, Paul was passionately devoted to this cause. He was so convinced of the truth of Jesus and carried such compassion for those who had yet to know the truth about Jesus, that he gave his life out of service to the Great Commission.

Many people today are walking around in darkness. Some people have no idea that they are in the dark, while others are frantically searching for a way to get out. Where there is darkness, Satan has dominion. He is the father of darkness and loves to do his evil deeds under its cover.

Have you ever noticed that when you engage in sin you tend to want to keep things in the dark, hidden from the sight of everyone, including God (or so we'd like to think)? That is a tactic of the enemy. The longer we keep something hidden in the dark, the more power he has to control us. We may believe that we are protecting ourselves from embarrassment, but all we are doing is hurting ourselves.

Those who are followers of Christ <u>must</u> walk in the light. We are a reflection of the true Light, the Light of the World – Jesus. Wherever we go, we should be bringing His light and providing a way out for those trapped in darkness. Just like Paul we have been commissioned to stop taking our light and hiding it under a basket, but to display it on a hilltop for all to see.

You are light of world. Go and be the light.

Prayer

Dear Father, thank you for shedding light into the areas of my life where the enemy prevailed. Help me to be a light to others so that I can provide the same freedom you gave me in Jesus' name. Amen.
Further Studies: *Isaiah 9:2, 1 John*

Inner Strength

"Therefore we do not lose heart. Though outwardly we are wasting away, yet inwardly we are being renewed day by day."
(2 Corinthians 4:16)

If you have children or help with the care and education of youth in any capacity, you have probably come to realize how hard it is to keep up with them. Their energy levels, their physical abilities, and their zeal serve as constant reminders that we are not as young as we used to be.

Some women attempt to do whatever they can to hold onto their youth by preserving their skin through beauty and fitness routines. It is in our youth that we feel the strongest and loveliest, so it is natural to try to hold onto that feeling as time trudges on.

But the reality of the matter is that the closer we get to the grave, the more our bodies will decay. Dancers who used to have the most flexible bodies discover new stiffness when attempting to stretch, knees make climbing stairs difficult, loud noises give you headaches, so on and so forth. You know how it goes.

Even so, though the body may be not be eternal, there is something within us that is: our soul. Every day God gives our soul fresh strength and unparalleled vigor without fail. Our soul does not become aged or broken; it is strong, and remains so, until we leave this world, and it will live on eternally in the next. This inner strength has been given to help us endure afflictions with joy and patience.

No matter what we feel in our bodies or even when we are faced with death, we can have a hope that one day that eternal portion of our makeup will be free from this earthly cage and we will live eternally with Christ Jesus our Lord and Savior.

Prayer

Dear Father, I don't want to store up treasures on earth, even if that includes my earthly body. Thank you for the eternal life I have in the name of your son, Jesus. In His name I pray, amen.
Further Studies: *Matthew 6:20*

Ministry of Music

*"You are my hiding place; you will protect me from trouble
and surround me with songs of deliverance. Selah."*
(Psalm 32:7)

Throughout the Psalms, King David and other skilled poets, share the contents of their heart on paper. The Psalms are filled with real, raw emotions that we all can identify with and claim as expressions of our own grief, doubts, or joy. The psalms of David's day were actually spoken to music. Wherever you see the term "Selah", that meant a music interlude was to be played to allow for personal reflection and meditation.

God intended for music to play a special role in our lives. It is not just something that is pleasing to the ear, but it something that is pleasing to the soul. Lyrics give us a point of identification in which we can feel a special connection to the song, and the music provides a soothing melody that reaches deep down into our being. Even scientific research has shown that music can make significant changes in our brain and body, for better or worse.

Worship music helps us to remember God's goodness or visualize His presence or even express the contents of our heart to Him. Look for worship music that aligns with the Word of God and is full of good doctrine, like the songs sung by many worship leaders. These songs, like the Psalms of old, should serve to draw you deeper into the presence of God.

It is important to note that music can also be a deceptive device of Satan. It can provide a distraction or incite fear or hatred. For instance, when a girl breaks up with her boyfriend, she may feel like listening to songs that identify with the emotions she is feeling at that moment. A lot of secular music dealing with break ups speak of revenge and bitterness. When the girl listens to these songs over and over again, she will find herself becoming more upset and mistrusting of men, and may even act on some of the suggestions of the music. Definitely not a fruit of the Spirit.

Instead of filling your mind with the deception of the enemy, let God minster to you through music that will deliver and make you whole.

Prayer

*Dear Father, thank you for the gift of music and the way
is revives my soul in Jesus' name. Amen.*
Further Studies: *Psalm 150*

Love does Compassionate Things

"When he saw the crowds, he had compassion on them, because they were harassed and helpless, like sheep without a shepherd."
(Matthew 9:36)

When Jesus used to travel the countryside and teach, large masses of people would follow Him. Forgoing their daily responsibilities or plans, they would leave their life on pause for the chance to see and listen to the man from Galilee that spoke with an authority greater than the Pharisees and that healed the sick and performed miraculous signs and wonders.

Now, since Jesus wasn't planning crusades or conferences, the people would just gather wherever He was. Christ and His disciples tried to be accommodating and find nice wide open spaces, but even so, the people would have to sit on the ground or on rocks. Not comfortable seating, to say the least. As Jesus would often spend the entire day, or even multiple days, teaching, the people would become tired and hungry.

Jesus could have ignored their situation since He had never asked them to show up in the first place, but because of His compassion, because His heart ached for them, He did everything He could to take care of them – which, as we know, turned out to be more than enough.

Many people around the world hunger and thirst for godly leadership, as sheep without a shepherd yearning for someone to point them in the right direction. Do we pass by them or are we moved with compassion to do something to help them? Can you invite them to a Bible study or a church service or a conference? Is there an opportunity for you to personally mentor them? Even in marriage, women should support their husbands to help them become leaders within the family and for those who are seeking spiritual guidance.

Compassion propels us to make significant sacrifices in order to see others saved and led by God. We should also strive to be wholly dependent on God, and in so doing we will better understand how much others need Him too.

Prayer

Dear Father, it is because of your great compassion that I am saved. Instill that compassion in my heart that I may be an extension of your love to those in need in Jesus' name. Amen.
Further Studies: *Matthew 11:28-30*

Divided, We Fall

"Every kingdom divided against itself will be ruined, and every city or household divided against itself will not stand."
(Matthew 12:25)

Think about a snowflake. As it falls to the earth it is small and frail. With a simple touch of your hand, you can melt it, thereby destroying it. Now, when that snowflake joins with other snowflakes, say in the formation of a snowball, there is such power behind it that if someone were to throw it at you, you would be the one experiencing pain. In the same way, there is power in unity.

In our homes we pray for a spirit of unity to knit our family's hearts together. We mostly desire it for the sake of peace in the home, but there is more at stake when we lack unity than the mere absence of peace. There is the risk of tearing the home apart.

King Solomon states in the book of Proverbs that the contentious woman tears down her own house. Women become contentious when after enduring hurt, they want to retaliate. Part of that retaliation is evidenced by her desire to argue, nag, and nitpick. She may be looking for some kind of self-satisfaction from this behavior, but it actually results in the division of their household and instead of satisfaction, she only manages to inflict more pain on others and herself.

When you are grappling with pain or grief, especially if it was caused by your significant other, take it to the Lord. One of the main jobs of the Holy Spirit is to teach the Body of Christ how to stand together in unity and to bind our hearts together with cords that cannot be broken. Your marriage is your ministry and the Holy Spirit longs to be active in the ministry of marriage and provide the same support. So let Him be who He is in your midst and relinquish the control to Him.

Be careful not to tear down your home by inflicting hurts, but enrich it with joy, patience, and a steadfast reliance on the Holy Spirit.

Prayer

Dear Father, I know that you desire unity between your people and even in my family and marriage. Help me to be a peacemaker and not a form of division in Jesus' name. Amen.
Further Studies: *Hosea 11:4*

Secret of Relationships

"Honor all men. Love the brotherhood. Fear God. Honor the king."
(1 Peter 2:17, NASB)

To honor someone is to regard them with great respect. All relationships should be marked with honor simply for the fact that all people are made in the image of God. As Jesus once said, what we do and say to others equates to what we do and say to Christ. Even if we don't care much for someone's personality, we should honor and respect them anyway, because they are dear to the heart of our Father God.

The church is a brotherhood, and there should be a deep regard for the brotherhood in our hearts. As you have likely heard it said many times over, the church is more than a building, but it is a gathering of like-minded believers. Therefore, our relationship with the church should be marked by sacrifice and service, not just by attendance. If love means putting others before ourselves, then to love the brotherhood means to do just that: serve, give, and edify.

The second part of the scripture calls us to fear God. In His Word, the Lord tells us that to fear Him means to depart from iniquity. It is to recognize that there is nothing the Lord detests more than sin and that when we engage in it and willfully disobey Him, we bring the consequences of sin on our head. When we understand that God is almighty and there is nothing that happens on this earth that He doesn't see or deal with, we will likely think twice about our involvement in sin.

Naturally then, instead of disobeying the King, we will choose to honor Him. We do that by following His commands. God expects us to obey, respect and serve everyone in our spheres of influence and even those outside, like those who govern our country, whether they do it with righteousness or wickedness.

The secret of performing the former part of the verse is to achieve the latter. As you fear and honor God, you will naturally begin to love and honor your brothers and sisters in Christ.

Prayer

Dear Father, help me to honor you in all that I do and say and to do likewise with those around me in Jesus' name. Amen.
Further Studies: *Matthew 25:40-45*

Wolves and Sheep

"Watch out for false prophets. They come to you in sheep's
clothing, but inwardly they are ferocious wolves."
(Matthew 7:15)

Jesus gives us a word picture here to demonstrate the need for spiritual discernment in the church. Oftentimes when we hear of scandalous or deceptive events that happen in churches, you will hear many members of the congregation claim that they had no idea the person was like that. Well, that is why the Lord gives us the gift of discernment – the ability to discern what kind of spirit a person has.

The Bereans were praised in the Bible for being a people that searched the Scriptures to determine whether or not what they were being taught lined up with the Word of God. If anyone were to come and preach something that wasn't of God, they would have known immediately. Even in this day and age, men and women need to know the Scriptures and search them like the Bereans did in order to accurately determine whether the things they are being taught are true. With the advancements of modern technology and the access we have to commentary, biblical studies, and so on, there should be no excuse.

As we discover the truths of the Bible and store them away in our heart, we will notice a change in the way that we view the world. If we see things happening around us that don't quite line up with what we know to be true, a sort of alarm will go off in our spirit. That is, in part, what discernment looks like.

Women actually are often gifted with the ability to discern what's going on in any given situation, so we can be supportive and instrumental with confronting and challenging bad doctrines. This can only be done effectively however when we understand the doctrines themselves and understand what the Bible says about dealing with doctrinal discords within the church.

The importance and authority of God's Word will be preserved and it will expose wolves in sheep's clothing. We must first do our part.

Prayer

Dear Father, please give me eyes to see situations as you do and cause
your word to become alive and active inside of me so that anything that
speaks against it can easily be identified in Jesus' name. Amen.
Further Studies: *Proverbs 15:21*

The Weapon of our Warfare

"...and the sword of the Spirit, which is the word of God."
(Ephesians 6:17)

Out of all of the armor the Lord has given us to clothe ourselves, the only offensive weapon we have is the sword. Considering this is the single weapon we have to attack the enemy, it must be powerful. Generally speaking, the sword is very powerful. It has the ability to pierce through an opponent's armor straight to their heart. It can intimidate the opponents, bring them to their knees in surrender, or bring their life to an end.

Likewise, the Sword of the Spirit or the Word of God is very powerful.

"For the word of God is living and active and sharper than any two-edged sword, and piercing as far as the division of soul and spirit, of both joints and marrow, and able to judge the thoughts and intentions of the heart."
(Hebrews 4:12, NASB)

When Jesus was in the wilderness for 40 days and nights, He was met by Satan who tried to tempt Him to sin. What was His response? He used His sword, the Word of God, to drive the enemy off. With every taunting comment the enemy made, Jesus responded by quoting Scripture back to Him. After three exchanges, the enemy was defeated, and he had to retreat.

In the same manner, as we encounter attacks from the enemy in our home, at our jobs, or in our church, we must follow the example of Jesus and take up the Sword of the Spirit. We must fight this battle in a spiritual manner. No word we can speak and no action we can take can compare to the power of the Word of God when we face our enemies.

At the sound of the Word of God, the enemy is only left with three responses: 1) surrender 2) defeat 3) retreat. It is the weapon of our warfare!

Prayer

Dear Father, you have given me incredible power through your word. Thank you for entrusting me with your word and for teaching me how to use it in spiritual battles in Jesus' name. Amen.
Further Studies: *Ephesians 6:12*

Buying Back

"Do not fear, you worm Jacob, you men of Israel; I will help you,
declares the Lord, and your Redeemer is the Holy One of Israel."
(Isaiah 41:14, NASB)

Though the concept of a kinsman-redeemer is foreign to most of the Western world, it played a significant role in shaping history of the Israelites of old. A kinsman-redeemer was a next of kin male who, among other things, absorbed the debts and responsibilities of a widow. To be a kinsman-redeemer required tremendous personal sacrifice. When he married the widow, his children were considered the children of his wife's first husband and he wasn't entitled to any kind of inheritance.

In the story of Ruth and Boaz, Boaz was the kinsman-redeemer to Ruth. Ruth had married Naomi's son, but when he died, he left her a widow. She returned with her mother-in-law to her home country and did what she could to provide for her mother. As she gleaned in the fields to find scraps to eat, Ruth caught the eye of Boaz – a man who happened to be a relative of her late husband. As was custom, he married Ruth and took care of all of Naomi's financial needs and continued the line of her late husband Elimelek.

For years God promised the Israelites that He would send a Kinsman-Redeemer to free her from her debts. That Kinsman Redeemer was none other than Jesus, the Messiah. Because of His great love for Israel, He bought her back from the world and willingly paid the price for all of her debts: His life. And now He offers redemption to all who accept it. As the first born of humanity, He came and redeemed us all.

The most wonderful aspect of this story of grace is that we are redeemed not because we deserve it. No, in fact this Scripture compares the children of Israel to worms. We are but worms in comparison to the holiness of Christ, but because He is holy and compassionate and gracious, He has betrothed Himself to us and will one day come back to claim us.

Prayer

Dear Father, thank you for loving me enough to make the great
sacrifice of redeeming me in Jesus' name. Amen.
Further Studies: *Ephesians 1:7*

Prisoners of Sin

"But Scripture has locked up everything under the control of sin, so that what was promised, being given through faith in Jesus Christ, might be given to those who believe."
(Galatians 3:22)

This verse starts by saying that there are no grounds for an argument about who is a sinner or about how much power sin has over anyone. All people are prisoners of sin. Or as Romans 3:23 puts it, "All have sinned and fallen short of the glory of God." Though this reality can initially seem disheartening, there is a beautiful perspective to be gained from the fact that we are all sinners.

For a moment, imagine that you have been stranded on an island for five years. For five years you have survived on coconuts and fish – not a bad diet in its own right, but extremely tiresome to maintain for two weeks, let alone five years. Now, let's say an unopened bag of potato chips washes ashore one day. When you bite into the crispy goodness of that sliced potato, will it not be the most divine taste you could ever imagine? Why? Because the absence of something or the lack of something makes receiving it all the sweeter.

Likewise, because we are all sinners, we are in need of someone to save us from our sin. We have all tasted what the world has offered and in some causes gorged ourselves on the empty, shallow, and tasteless feast it offers. But Jesus approaches us while we are in this state and offers salvation and a new life. And the resulting taste of the salvation of the Lord is like honey, sweeter than the honeycomb on our lips.

Because of our sin, we have the opportunity to taste of the goodness of the Lord and to see that He is good. The further we were steeped in sin, the sweeter His grace appears. That is the beautiful dichotomy of salvation. Sometimes you have to know the low before you can really know how good the high really feels.

Prayer

Dear Father, I have tasted and seen that you are good, and I never want to go back to my old ways. Thank you for eternal life in Jesus' name. Amen.
Further Studies: John 10:10

No Joy in Sin

"The fear of the LORD is a fountain of life, turning a person from the snares of death."
(Proverbs 14:27)

When we engage in sin, we are demonstrating not only disobedience, but a lack of fear of the Lord. Those who fear the Lord understand that He is an all-powerful God and out of holy reverence and respect for Him, they keep His commands. Those who do not fear the Lord feel that they have the right to do whatever they may feel like doing, namely sinning.

Those who display an appropriate fear of the Lord will discover a fountain of life. If you know anything about fountains, you know that they use an abundance of water and that they never run dry. Therefore, that fountain is a representation of an abundant life here on the earth as well as an eternal life.

Those who fear the Lord will receive a life abundant of all of the goodness that God desires to pour on His children, and on top of that, they will get to enjoy that foundation of life forever, but those who do not honor the Lord and choose to continually engage in sin will experience a very different fate.

"For the wages of sin is death; but the gift of God is
eternal life through Jesus Christ our Lord."
Romans 6:23

The natural consequence of a life of sin is death. Just as we can partake of the fountain of life as we live on the earth, so it is with death. Those who sin will not only know what it's like to experience the second death, but they will also experience great loss during their lifetime.

No one can live a life of sin and sustain their happiness. God didn't create us that way. We were all created with an innate desire to be close to Him. As sin keeps us from being able to approach Him, there is no way to find spiritual fulfillment anywhere else.

Prayer

Dear Father, I want to know what the fountain of life looks like in my life, so this day I choose to fear you and to trust and obey your word in Jesus' name. Amen.
Further Studies: *Psalm 36:9*

Answer to Anxiety

"I prayed to the Lord, and he answered me. He freed me from all my fears."
(Psalm 34:4, NLT)

Throughout the Psalms, we see many instances where David is literally wrought with anxiety. He had good reason to be anxious though, considering he had to hide in a cave from an insane king who was searching the countryside to hunt him down. David faced many situations in his life that became the inspiration behind some of the Psalms we know and love today. Most of those Psalms generally begin with descriptions of David's process of dealing with anxiety.

Anxiety is a feeling of worry, nervousness, or unease, typically about an imminent event or something with an uncertain outcome. In our own lives we may experience anxiety when things go awry in our friendships, or we may experience anxiety when our children are growing up and we feel like there's not much we can do to protect them anymore, or maybe we feel anxiety when there are issues at work.

The presence of anxiety may indicate that we have not yet given up control of our lives to God. As women we like to be in control of our lives and even our children's lives. We don't like it when we don't know what is in store just as much as we don't like knowing that something inevitably bad is headed our way.

Often, in order to get rid of anxiety, we must learn to trust God. God expects us to surrender all of our fears to Him and trust Him to work for our good in every situation. There is no need to be anxious or to fear anything if your trust is put in the One to whom nothing is impossible! This requires living a life of total surrender; obedience to His Word and making lifestyle changes in order to become healthy in body and mind.

Though that may sound easier said than done, refer back to the same Psalms where David is expressing his anxiety, and you will see that in every instance where he is afraid, he encourages himself to put his trust in God. He reminds himself of the goodness of God, and that gives him the strength he needs to keep going. Follow the example of David today and pray for empowerment in times of anxiety.

Prayer

Dear Father, with you at the helm of my life, I have no reason to fear. Teach me by your Holy Spirit to trust you even more, no matter what comes my way in Jesus' name. Amen.
Further Studies: *Proverbs 3:4-5*

Guard your Heart

"...and having put on the breastplate of righteousness."
(Ephesians 6:14, NASB)

Another vital part of the armor of God Paul stresses we should utilize in spiritual warfare is the breastplate of righteousness. The purpose of a breastplate is to guard our heart and other vital organs. It is the equivalent of a modern day bullet-proof vest. Whether the enemy is throwing arrows or bullets at you, the job of the breastplate remains the same: to guard the heart.

If breastplates guard the heart and Paul compares the breastplate to righteousness, then we can assume that righteousness is an essential component of keeping the command God gives us to guard our hearts. Righteousness is defined as being in right standing with God. It means to be right in His sight. Therefore, the best protect for our heart against the attacks of the enemy is to live a life that is right in the sight of God.

As Christians, we know that righteousness cannot be earned by anything that we do, but that it is solely based on what Christ did. Yes, to walk rightly means to walk in obedience to God, so there is some element of responsibility in the role of righteousness in our lives, but it is only because of the sacrifice and constant intercession of Jesus that we are even able to come before God.

Through His payment on the cross, Jesus covered with His blood so that when God looks upon us He not only sees us without sin, but He sees the righteousness of His son. How marvelous was the sacrifice of Jesus, that He would make us righteousness in the sight of God!

To keep our faith alive we should continually guard our hearts with the righteousness of Christ and it will sustain all that is vital to and for us.

Prayer

Dear Father, my righteousness is not my own, but it comes from your Son. Help me to walk worthy, as one who is righteousness, that I may protect my heart from the enemy in Jesus' name. Amen.
Further Studies: *Romans 13:14*

Established

"Plans fail for lack of counsel, but with many advisers they succeed."
(Proverbs 15:22)

Have you ever found yourself in a situation where you needed to make a decision? Maybe you even lost sleep and your peace of mind, agonizing over what to do. Maybe you mulled it over again and again in your mind, thinking that you could work it out on your own, until you realized that the challenge was much bigger than you and your capabilities.

As women, we sometimes have the tendency to try to figure things out on our own. In some cases we don't want to bother people with our thoughts and ideas, and in other cases, we just feel like no one could understand the plan as well as ourselves. But when we try to "go it alone", we miss the opportunity to refine those ideas.

Have you ever reached out to a friend about a problem you were having and before you knew it the solution popped out of the blue? God has given us all the ability to see the world and situations from different perspectives. Sometimes we may need the perspective of someone much older and wiser than ourselves, and sometimes we may need the perspective of someone who has already "been there and done that".

God created us to be a body, not a bunch of separate, individual parts. We need each other and no matter what we're facing or where we're headed to, we should depend on one another for sound counsel.

Prayer

Dear Father, thank you for surrounding me with godly friends who will give me godly counsel in times of need in Jesus' name. Amen.
Further Studies: *Proverbs 12:15, 11:14, 13:10*

Mercy

"Blessed are the merciful, for they will be shown mercy."
(Matthew 5:7)

The principle of sowing and reaping is quite common in the Bible: give and it will come back to you (Luke 6:38), forgive and you will be forgiven (Matthew 6:14), the way you judge is how you will be judged (Matthew 7:2), and so on.

Our opening scripture applies the principle of sowing and reaping to mercy. To show mercy means that though you have it in your power to extend punishment or judgment to someone, you show them kindness, forgiveness, and compassion instead. This concept is illustrated best in the parable of the man with a large debt.

There was a man who owed the king a large sum of money. When he was brought before the king, he groveled and begged for mercy. The king extended it to him, forgave his debt, and sent him on his way. As the man left the palace, he found a fellow servant on the street who owed him a small amount of money. He had the servant thrown into debtor's prison until he could pay back the money. When the king found out about this, he was outraged and ordered that the man be tortured in prison until he could pay back his debt.

We can treat people in the same manner every day. Our situations may not be as severe as the man in the parable, but the outcome can be just as devastating. Make the choice to be kind and compassionate to others; you never know when you might be the one in need of mercy.

Prayer

Dear Father, thank you for teaching me to sow mercy, forgiveness, compassion and love to all those in my world in Jesus' name. Amen.
Further Studies: *Galatians 6:7, Luke 6:38b*

From Death to Life

"We know that we have passed from death to life, because we love each other. Anyone who does not love remains in death."
(1 John 3:14)

The Lord Jesus commanded us to love, and we discover from Gal 5:23 that love is innate in every child of God. The death of Jesus is proof of God's love for mankind. John reveals a very profound truth about love and working in love.

He said that through love we become aware and convinced that we have passed from death to life. If you do not love your fellow Christian, you are living in death. Love for us as Christians is not an option, it's not negotiable. We must love others and demonstrate God's love to a hurting world.

Some people are hard to love, we can all attest to that fact! We will not, however, remain in death, but will rise to life obeying this command to love. Our ultimate goal is to pass from death to life. In the realm of death and destruction, there is no love because the devil cannot love you and neither can he teach you to love. Love is the life and nature of God, so if we claim to be of God then we must love, because it is His nature.

Every person has a story to tell which influences their beliefs and behaviors, and we know that some people have suffered horrendous circumstances. While their behavior is not an excuse, we will not fall prey to focusing on their actions. Let us strive to love the brethren regardless.

Prayer

Dear Father, thank you for teaching me how to live in the realm of life. I choose to live in your light and life by expressing your nature of love every day of my life in Jesus' name. Amen.
Further Studies: *Romans 12:10*

Fear & Honor

"Honor all men. Love the brotherhood. Fear God. Honor the king."
(1 Peter 2:17, KJV)

To fear God is to have a holy reverence or deep sense of awe for who He is and what He can do. Normally, when we hear the word fear within the context of a relationship, we see it as a bad thing (no one wants to be afraid of a loved one), but within the context of relationship with God, fear is essential to the building up of our faith.

In Romans 3 we're given a list of sins that people typically commit against God and one another. Can you guess what the underlying component of these misbehaviors is? *"There is no fear of God before their eyes"* (Roman 3:18). When we lack fear of God, we become bold in the things of the world. That's a dangerous line to cross.

On the other hand, to honor someone is to show them proper respect. All men are created in the image of God, therefore they should be given respect for that reason. If someone is in a position of authority, whether we like them or not, we are still to show them honor.

Now, it would be in our best interest to distinguish between fear and honor and to whom each is due. The Bible makes it very clear that we are not to fear man. As Matthew 10:28 says, what's the point of fearing man when they can only destroy the body? Only God has the power to determine our eternal fate, and that is far more important.

So the next time you find yourself in a position of fearing man, remember the one who holds your very breath in His hand.

Prayer

Dear Father, you are great in the heavens and the earth and worthy to be feared by all. Let me not forget to tremble in Jesus' name. Amen.
Further Studies: *Proverbs 9:10*

Ask for Wisdom

"But if any of you lacks wisdom, let him ask of God, who gives to all men generously and without reproach, and it will be given to him."
(James 1:5)

There is nothing we require to live the Christian life on earth that has not been provided for us in Christ Jesus. To live a good life on earth you need wisdom; this is wisdom that only God can give. This wisdom will put you over in life, because it is what you require to make sound decisions and receive wise counsel.

You need wisdom to foresee trouble and hide yourself, your husband, and your children. That is why Solomon said, *"Wisdom is the principal thing; therefore get wisdom: and with all thy getting get understanding"* (Proverbs 4:7, KJV).

The wisdom of God can only come from God. That is why James implores us to ask for God's wisdom that will enable us to joyfully go through trials of all kinds. Wisdom is defined as the quality of having experience, knowledge, and good judgment; the quality of being wise. There are two types of wisdom: intellectual and godly.

Godly wisdom comes only from God, of course. If you don't have it, ask for it as directed in this verse. To overcome trials, we need God's wisdom, which allows us to discern what the right thing to do in any situation is. Therefore, let us ask for wisdom.

Prayer

Dear Father, I thank you for all your provisions for me to have a good life on earth. I ask for wisdom to live wisely and make sound decisions that will keep me and my family safe in Jesus' name. Amen.
Further Studies: *Proverbs 16:20, Matthew 10:16*

Holding Back

"A fool always loses his temper, but a wise man holds it back."
(Proverbs 29:11)

This is one reason the Apostle James counsels us to ask for wisdom. A foolish woman does not know when to be quiet and when to speak. You need patience and temperance to be a good wife and mother.

Patience and temperance are two very important virtues I would like to point out here. *Patience is the quality of bearing provocation, annoyance, misfortune, or pain without complaint, loss of temper, irritation, or the like.*

Temperance is defined as moderation or self-restraint in action, statement, etc.; self-control.

For Alison, it seemed like the perfect time to vent her feelings. She had been hurt, abused and misused. It was time to set things right! But before she could speak, she heard a whisper saying, "I will take care of you, be quiet." She was startled, but she knew the prompting of the Holy Spirit all too well.

When Alison listened to the Holy Spirit and walked away, resolutions came shortly after, in a manner that astonished her. She was happy with herself for holding back and being wise. If she had angrily said all that was on her mind, she could have ruined everything.

You need wisdom to know when to speak and when to hold back. The Holy Spirit is always there to guide you. Don't be foolish by ignoring His counsel, and don't lose your temper!

Prayer

Dear Father, I thank you for granting me wisdom to deal wisely in the affairs of this life. I am patient and temperate in all things in Jesus' name. Amen.
Further Studies: *James 1:19*

To be Wise

"Do not be wise in your own eyes; fear the LORD and turn away from evil."
(Proverbs 3:7)

There is the wisdom of this world and there is the wisdom of God. Most of the knowledge we gain through academics and life experiences only leads to the wisdom of this world. Though there is nothing necessarily wrong with gaining wisdom on earth, but we must be careful not to believe that any knowledge we've received here trumps that of God's.

Earthly wisdom is foolishness before God, because His standard differs greatly from that of men. His ways are much higher than our ways, and His thoughts are equally higher than our thoughts. The very pinnacle of the wisdom of man is the lowest point of God's wisdom. We would do well to remember that, especially when we think we know what's best for our lives.

Some women think they are very wise because they are successful and have been recognized by society for their achievements in education, or in their chosen career or business. It can be very hard for such people to submit to the wisdom of God, and it is very easy for them to lose all they have. All it takes for them to fall is just one king-size error.

This wisdom of God will give you an edge in life and will separate you from evil by guiding your thoughts and your actions in line with the Word of God. To be wise, we must turn away from evil and fear the Lord.

Prayer

Dear Lord, thank you for your wisdom at work in me. I declare that I am wise because the wisdom of God is at work in me in Jesus' name. Amen.
Further Studies: *Proverbs 3:5-6, Psalm 28:7*

Are you a Daughter of Abraham?

"Understand, then, that those who have faith are children of Abraham."
(Galatians 3:7)

If someone came up to you today and asked you if you have faith, what would your response be? What if someone asked you to describe the meaning of faith for them? Would you know how to put it into words without quoting Scripture? These are just a few important questions that we all must consider when it comes to our relationship with God and how we share it with others, specifically nonbelievers.

Faith, by definition, can mean a certain type of confidence, trust, conviction, belief, hope, certainty, dependence, dedication, or commitment. The list could go on, but essentially, faith could be described as believing without seeing. It's having an assurance that something is true even if everything around you is screaming something different.

Abraham, the spiritual father of all who believe was commended by God for his faith. God asked him to bring his one and only son Isaac up to the mountain and to sacrifice him. Abraham didn't not question God, but packed up his donkey and his son and went up the mountain to sacrifice him. He even went so far as to tie his son down and raise the knife.

Now who in their right mind would do something like that? Only someone who knew in his heart of hearts that the Lord had made him a promise about his son, and that He would keep it. Even though God was requesting something difficult of him, he knew that God's heart was never to have Abraham kill his own son, and he took that all the way to the bank... or to the altar at least.

In the midst of all that is happening around you, are you exercising your faith? I encourage you today to take faith as a shield and take it wherever you go. It will give you hope to make it through whatever you're facing. It is your faith in God that will stand the test of time when everything else falls and your faith that will be a witness to those who need to see what comes of those who live righteous lives.

Prayer

Dear Father, increase my faith where you find there is weakness in Jesus' name. Amen.
Further Studies: *Hebrews 11:1*

October

Busy Watching

"She watches over the affairs of her household and does not eat the bread of idleness."
(Proverbs 31:27)

As women, we may have a number of responsibilities outside of the home in terms of work, ministry, and relationships, but within the home alone, we are responsible for much more. You may be responsible for making sure the home is tidy, the groceries are bought, the laundry is done, the meals are cooked, carpooling is organized, and then some. The affairs of our household are never ending, so a virtuous woman must rise to the occasion every day.

Your husband and children are counting on you to take on the role of not only the heart and soul of the home, but to see to it that certain needs are met. Though there may be times that you will need to rest, beware of idleness.

Idleness can creep up on you very unexpectedly, while you're taking a break or even when you get so overwhelmed with you tasks that you just feel like quitting everything. Give yourself time limits and goals to keep from succumbing to "vegging" out and neglecting your family. Take pleasure in discharging your motherly duties, and be assured that your reward is coming. Continue to diligently perform your duties as you box away the bread of idleness. You will bring honor to your family, and one day they will rise up and say of you:

"Many women do noble things, but you surpass them all." Proverbs 31:29

Prayer

Dear Father, thank you for making me a virtuous woman. I choose to remain busy and watch my family make progress in Jesus' name. Amen.
Further Studies: *Proverbs 13:4*

Mind Control

"'Have faith in God,' Jesus answered.'"
(Mark 11:22)

One day, as Jesus and His disciples were leaving the town of Bethany, they came across a fig tree. Expecting to find some fruit on the tree, since the season and presence of leaves indicated that the tree should indeed be bearing fruit, they discovered that it was barren. So, Jesus cursed it. Sure enough, when they came across that tree the next morning, they discovered that it had shriveled up!

It would seem as though Jesus had gone through all the trouble of cursing the tree because He was angry about not getting any figs that day, but in reality, He did it to give His disciples an object lesson on what it means to have unwavering confidence and faith in the power of God.

> *"Truly I say to you, whoever says to this mountain, 'Be taken up and cast into the sea,' and does not doubt in his heart, but believes that what he says is going to happen, it will be granted him. Therefore I say to you, all things for which you pray and ask, believe that you have received them, and they will be granted you."*
> (Mark 11:23-24)

Taking a real world object (a fig tree), Jesus gave His disciples a tangible sample of what faith can do. They saw with their own eyes the way He spoke to the tree, and subsequently, the way the tree had shriveled up and died. Then Jesus took the lesson learned from the little fig tree and applied it to something as big as a mountain. If we have faith, we can move mountains, let alone the various obstacles that we face in our day to day lives.

Many people passively express some kind of faith in God, but the Greek word translated here as "have" carries a much stronger meaning than a verbal profession; it means to have control of your mind. That means that if faith has completely filled your mind, there should be no room for doubt.

Have you ever faced a situation that you took to God in prayer, but when things got worse or it took too long for the horizon to appear, you found yourself beginning to fret? The kind of faith Jesus is asking us to have is the kind of faith that remains fixed on Him and His promises, no matter what. When you come before the Father asking Him to move on your behalf in a certain area, come to Him with confidence knowing that He will respond to your request.

Prayer

Dear Father, you are bigger than any problem I could ever face. I trust you to not only answer me when I call, but to lift me up and place my feet on solid ground in Jesus' name. Amen.
Further Studies: *James 1:5-8*

Oh, to be Whole!

"For she thought, "If I just touch His garments, I will get well."
(Mark 5:28, NASB)

After twelve years, this woman with an "issue of blood" (basically a never ending menstrual cycle) had come to the end of her rope. None of the doctors could help her, and there seemed to be nothing she could do to end her misery. That is until she heard that Jesus, the Messiah everyone had been waiting for, was going to be passing by.

Gathering up her skirts, she ran into the streets and pushed her way through a tightly packed crowd. If you know anything about Jewish law, you would know that a woman in her position would be considered a social pariah. She was unclean, so she was not to touch anyone or even be found within the city limits.

What caused her to make such a risky decision? It was her faith. She had heard of Jesus and His healing power, and though she had not seen, she believed that if only she could touch even the hem of the Messiah's garments, then she would be completely healed.

To think that this woman had such confidence to believe that something as simple as a touch of Christ's garment could do what no one else had done for twelve years is pretty remarkable. It is important to note though, that her hope was not merely in His garment, as though the cloth itself were some mystically endowed relic; she was trusting in Christ.

Like many other people in the Bible that were commended for their faith in Jesus, this woman understood something about Jesus that most people didn't get. She knew that Christ was not just any other man. He was God in the form of man. The majestic, perfect and powerful nature of God was constantly manifesting itself in the body of Christ. Therefore, she likely reasoned, if the purest essence of God dwelled in Christ, coming into contact with Christ was like coming into contact with God Himself.

When you go through difficult seasons in life, especially those that seem to last much longer than you'd like, do you seek God as desperately as one who has nothing to lose? If you do seek God, do you feel as though you have grasped the weighty reality of the One you stand before? When we have a right view of God, much as this woman did with Jesus, we begin to see how big He really is in comparison to our problems. Do you have a right view of God?

Prayer

Dear Father, help me believe that you are greater than any problem that I may face in Jesus' name. Amen.
Further Studies: *Mark 5:25-34*

Shoes Prepared To Go

"and having shod your feet with the preparation of the gospel of peace;"
(Ephesians 6:15, NASB)

In Ephesians 6 Paul writes about the full armor of God, describing the purpose of each garment, how they should be used, and their implications for our engagement in spiritual battles. In this verse, shoes are used to symbolize our readiness in being prepared to take the gospel of peace into the world.

The enemy of our souls undoubtedly sets out to attack us for many reasons, but one of the biggest reasons he desires to cripple us is to keep us from spreading the gospel of Jesus. The whole time Jesus walked the earth, the enemy did everything he could to lock the Son of God down. From having the Pharisees constantly try to take Him into custody, to even the crucifixion, none of his attempts worked.

When Jesus ascended into heaven, Satan's job wasn't over. He did everything he could to keep the apostles from traveling to spread the Good News. He had them thrown in jail, tortured, and even killed. Numerous epistles of the New Testament give us great insight into what these amazing men and women of the faith endured for the sake of Christ. Even so, the Scriptures tell us that those who go into the world in the name of the Lord in spite of persecution or resistance are highly valued by God.

"How beautiful on the mountains are the feet of those who bring
good news, who proclaim peace, who bring good tidings, who
proclaim salvation, who say to Zion, 'Your God reigns!'"
(Isaiah 52:7)

When we value something, we protect it. We keep our eyeglasses in cases, we lock our fine china in a cabinet, we vacuum seal our wedding dresses to preserve them. According to God, our feet are of great value because they are the tools we need to share His Good News with the world. Therefore, we must shod our feet with the preparation of the gospel of peace. As opposed to those things we value that we lock away for safekeeping, we prepare our feet to endure the tough terrain we have to cross. We aim to protect them for the long journey ahead.

Have you prepared your feet to go and spread the Good News even if it means being called to leave the place where you have been established or feel most comfortable?

Prayer

Dear Father, what a privilege I have to be able to know the story of your son. Today, I prepare my feet to take your story into the world and to share the Good News with others in Jesus' name. Amen.
Further Studies: *Romans 10:14-15*

Come Worshipping

"A man with leprosy came and knelt before him and said,
"Lord, if you are willing, you can make me clean.""
(Matthew 8:2)

Jesus was often approached by people seeking something from Him. In most cases He used each encounter as a teachable moment for those in the crowd and for us. So what advice can we take away from the story of the leper?

The first thing we notice in this verse is that as the leper approached Jesus, he bowed down before Him. Bowing is a form of worship – something that you do in the presence of someone much greater than yourself to acknowledge that you are not only in subjection to them, but that you respect their authority.

In the same way, when we approach God in prayer, we must also come with our hearts bowed before Him. We don't just do it because it's protocol, but we do it because we understand what it means to have an appropriate fear of God.

The second thing we see in the way the leper appealed to Christ is that before he addressed his own need, he said to Christ, "If you are willing." So often we come before God just to spout off our "I want"/"I need" lists. When we handle our prayer lives in such a manner, we demonstrate a perspective that puts our desires above God's desires.

Yes, the Lord is an almighty and sovereign God, and He can do anything above and beyond what we can imagine, but He doesn't exist merely to meet our demands. He has a will, and He has a mind of His own. In fact, He has thoughts that are so supreme that they surpass our own. If we believe that He is sovereign, we should also believe that He exercises His sovereignty with wisdom. What He thinks is best is what is best. Period.

Therefore, the requests we bring before Him are subject first to His authority and secondly to His will. If He knows something that we don't know, He will likely make a decision that we won't understand, but that doesn't mean He isn't good. It means He is wise. It means that He cares for us. It means that He will do whatever it takes to look out for our best interests, even if that means temporarily disappointing us.

There is so much more to God answering our prayers than we think! Like this leper, come worshipping Christ as you bring your requests before Him and seek His will first.

Prayer

Dear Father, you are the Lord of all lords and the King of all kings. I acknowledge you today as not only a sovereign king, but as one who always has my best interest in mind in Jesus' name. Amen.
Further Studies: *Matthew 8:1-4*

Blessed Assurance

"And so, after he had patiently endured, he obtained the promise."
(Hebrews 6:15, NKJ)

Has someone ever promised you that they would do something for you or give you something, but days, weeks, and even years passed without them ever making good on their promise? Probably. We all know the disappointment of people not keeping their promises. Sometimes there are just too many external variables (i.e. lack of time, money, or support) and sometimes internal variables come into play as well (i.e. lack of motivation, willpower, or desire).

In contrast to the shortcomings of humanity, we are incredibly blessed to have a God who always keeps His word. As He says of himself, He is not a man that he should lie. When He makes a promise to us, we have no reason whatsoever to doubt that He will bring it to pass. He is faithful to keep His promises throughout space and time, and even throughout the generations. He has always been faithful and He always will be.

Even in our own lives we can all recount many ways God has displayed His faithfulness. You can surely point out specific incidents where God demonstrated His faithfulness to you or people you know, but we all have the shared commonalities of being able to wake up each morning, of receiving salvation, and of having the Holy Spirit (our Helper) available to us each day. Each morning that we wake up, we can see the faithfulness of God. Therefore, we can trust that God is and always will be faithful to keep His word as we face new, difficult situations.

Today's scripture refers to the promise that God made to Abraham. Abraham and his wife Sarah had not been able to conceive for decades. After trying and waiting to no avail, Sarah was even forced to get a concubine for her husband just to ensure that he could continue his name. Yet, as Abraham waited, he believed. He knew that no matter how old they got, God would grant them the gift of a child.

The patient endurance of trusting the promises of God is not always easy. Abraham and Sarah received a promise from God, but they did not receive this promise immediately. In fact, it was more than ten years before the promised was fulfilled in the form of their son Isaac. By the time they received the promise,

Abraham was 100 and Sarah was 90. God kept His word even though the physical circumstances made it seem like it was impossible.

If God has given you a promise, lay hold of it. It will happen, even if it seems impossible. It is His blessed assurance!

Prayer

Dear Father, thank you for the blessed assurance I have in you simply because of the nature of who you are. You are faithful, true, and you never break your promises in Jesus' name. Amen.
Further Studies: *Hebrews 11*

Knocking

"Here I am! I stand at the door and knock. If anyone hears my voice and opens the door, I will come in and eat with that person, and they with me."
(Revelation 3:20)

et's stop for a minute and get a good picture of what the first part of this Scripture means. Jesus, God incarnate on the earth, has all the authority to do whatever He wants, yet He stands at the door of our hearts and knocks. Instead of forcing us to love and respect Him, He gives us the choice of keeping the door closed or opening it and letting Him in. He is what many would call a gentleman.

For some of us He's been knocking for a very long time. Maybe you grew up in the church and you know a lot about Jesus, but haven't quite taken that step to know Him personally. Or maybe you know Jesus, but have temporarily dismissed Him from the throne of your heart so you can engage in an activity that you know He would not like.

Like a child who disappears into another room and becomes so quiet that you just know they're up to something, we too like to try and close the door on Jesus for a second so that when we do something we know He wouldn't like, we don't feel so guilty. It doesn't matter how many doors we close though, He is God and He already sees... He already knows. All He is looking for is for you to give Him the permission to come in and talk to you about it.

You MUST give him access by opening the door. To open the door means to reveal the things about yourself that you don't want anyone to see for fear of what they would think about you. Your heart is the place where you are most vulnerable, so for Christ to ask for access to it means that He is looking for you to be vulnerable with Him.

What is so great about this verse is that though we expect Jesus to enter our heart and go straight to cleaning house, we're told that He wants to dine with us. When it is all said and done, Jesus wants to have fellowship with us. This is very similar to the relationship that Jesus had with Zacchaeus. By calling Zacchaeus down from the tree, Jesus was essentially knocking at his heart's door. Zacchaeus brought the Lord into his home, and they dined together. It was during that time of fellowship that Jesus was able to speak to Zacchaeus's heart in a way that caused him to want to give up every wicked deed he was engaged in and to repent before God and man.

In the same way, Jesus seeks to fellowship with us. As we commune with Him, His kindness will lead us to repentance. Will you open the door of your heart to Him today?

Prayer

Dear Father, I choose to open the door of my heart to you today and to be vulnerable before you. I want to know the fellowship of your Spirit in a more intimate way in Jesus' name. Amen.
Further Studies: *1 John 1:5-10*

Perseverance and Faith

"Therefore, among God's churches we boast about your perseverance and faith in all the persecutions and trials you are enduring."
(2 Thessalonians 1:4)

When someone you admire expresses an admiration for you, it can feel like an incredible honor. Paul was known throughout Asia Minor as being one of the most influential apostles of Christ. Everyone knew his story of transformation, had heard of his teachings or read his epistles, and they had seen some of the miracles God had performed through him. To have this man's approval, let alone his boasting on your behalf, surely meant a lot to the members of the early Church.

In this verse Paul boasts proudly about the Thessalonians' faith. Throughout their suffering and persecution they trusted Christ unwaveringly. They could have gloried in their religious experiences, their history, their future, their possessions or their position of authority on earth, but they chose to glory in the knowledge of Christ even when they were exhausted and frustrated.

What kept them going through it all? Hope. As Hebrews 11 says of the great men and women of faith in the Bible, they knew that at the end of their lives they would receive an eternal reward, and they also knew that they would not receive the reward if they gave up the race, for the race is only given to those who endure. And so they pressed on, allowing themselves to decrease so that God could increase.

Likewise, our glory should be found in nothing but the power of God that is our strength in the midst of our weakness. It is by God's grace that we are saved, and His grace is sufficient enough to carry us from day to day, from strength to strength, and from glory to glory. When we remember this truth about our lives, we realize that we don't have to strive so much. We can cease our striving and let the Holy Spirit take control.

The Thessalonians were not able to endure persecution and affliction because of any amount of willpower or strength they had, but because the Spirit of God empowered them to be able to stand. In their own strength they would have crumbled under the weight of their afflictions, but with the Holy Spirit girding up their legs, they could stand without wavering. Without faith, we can do nothing. It is through perseverance and faith in Him that we will be able to endure our own afflictions and become an example for others to follow.

Prayer

Dear Father, help me to never give up the good fight of faith in Jesus' name. Amen.
Further Studies: *Zechariah 4:6*

The Word that is Close

"'The word is near you; it is in your mouth and in your heart,'
that is, the message concerning faith that we proclaim."
(Romans 10:8)

Have you ever felt like God was pressing your heart to speak to someone, but you had no clue as to what you were supposed to say? If so, you're not alone. Moses wondered the same thing, as did the disciples when they first got into ministry. We all sometimes feel at a loss for what to say when sharing the gospel with others.

This fear typically stems from an unhealthy focus on ourselves, our talents, and our abilities. Of course when we look at some of the tasks God assigns us, we feel like we can't do them. That's because we can't! Not without Christ, that is. If we fix our eyes on Him and remember that when He sent us the Helper (the Holy Spirit), He automatically equipped us with the supernatural power we needed to know exactly what to say.

For this reason it is important that we store the word of God in the reservoir of our hearts. That means that as we read the Bible, we ensure that we also meditate on its words. So often we can find ourselves reading the Bible simply to check it off of our to-do list for the day, but we don't let its words drip down into the reservoir of our hearts. In order for your spirit to be filled with the word, you must take the time get all that you can from it.

Filling our reservoir with the Word of God serves a twofold purpose:

First, we are able to pull from Scripture and speak to others in a way that pierces their hearts. When we share anything from the Bible, we are speaking the direct words of God, and those words are very powerful! Aside from the power of the Word itself, when Christ removed the separation between us and God, He left the Holy Spirit to dwell within us, who brings the word of God to our remembrance in just the moments that we need Him, but it is important to remember that the Holy Spirit can only draw from what we've poured into our hearts.

Secondly, a lot of times when the gospel is shared, it is at the mercy of imperfect memories and sometimes a little biased. Anyone can read the Bible and mix what they've read with a little of their own opinion. Instead of sharing the pure, unadulterated word of God, people sometimes use the Bible to simply justify what they think and feel. Hiding God's word in your heart will help keep you from becoming confused.

Have you hidden God's Word in your heart?

Prayer

Dear Father, your word is a lamp unto my feet and a light unto my path. Show me the way to go and what to say as yield myself to all its truth in Jesus name. Amen.
Further Studies: *Psalm 119:11*

Using Faith on Purpose

"In addition to all this, take up the shield of faith, with which you can extinguish all the flaming arrows of the evil one."
(Ephesians 6:16)

Earlier in this chapter we're told that we are to put on the helmet of salvation and the breastplate of righteousness as part of our protective gear. Whereas the breastplate and helmet are specific to certain areas of the body, the shield can be used to protect many parts of the body. The person wielding it just has to know how to use it.

The shield in this instance relates to our faith. Faith is ability to maintain your belief in something whether it seems plausible or not. It is the foundation of our relationship with Christ, as none of us have seen Him in person, yet we believe that He lived and died on this earth, providing us with the gift of salvation. Faith also must be used intentionally against the lies, tricks and oppression of the enemy if we want to see the victories we desire.

If the Scripture says the shield protects us against the flaming arrows of the evil one, then that means that the enemy's primary strategy of attack is to injure our faith. He wants to taint our perception of our loving Father or to get us to doubt that either God or His plans are good. Faith is the shield we use to defend ourselves.

So whenever Satan tells you that you are wasting your time spending your life chasing after God, hold up your shield of faith. Whenever he whispers that you're not a good enough wife, mother, or Christian, hold up your shield of faith. When he attacks your belief that God is the one, true God, hold up your shield of faith.

The enemy can attack us in a number of different ways, but if he can manage to get through our shield of faith, he knows that we are prone to injury and even death. Although knowledge and righteousness are important, neither of these can take the place of faith as our defense, so the enemy will always come after our faith.

After some time of being attacked again and again, your shield may be in need of reinforcement. Spend time increasing your faith by reading the Word and encouraging yourself. The more that you engage with the Spirit of God through your time in the Bible, the more steadfast your faith will become. There is no better reinforcement you can find for your faith than to read God's Word, so take up your shield of faith and press on.

Prayer

Dear Father, thank you for equipping me to fight spiritual battles daily with the shield of faith. Please increase my faith where it is weak so that I can stand against the arrows of the enemy in Jesus name. Amen.
Further Studies: *Romans 10:17*

Peace in a Godly Leader

"With him is an arm of flesh; but with us is the Lord our God to help us, and to fight our battles. And the people rested themselves upon the words of Hezekiah king of Judah."
(2 Chronicles 32:8, NASB)

It is easy for a nation to be at peace when they know that their government contains good people who hold the collective people's best interest in mind. On the other hand, in countries where dictators rule, there is a constant sense of discord among the people. The choices leaders make can effectively make or break an entire nation.

Throughout the Old Testament we can find stories of all of the kings of the nation of Israel and the way they either chose to follow the Lord or turn against Him. As a result of the leader's decisions, as we continue to read through the chapters, we discover what become of the nation as a whole. They either prospered or suffered.

National peace is a gift of God and a blessing that can be lost by disobedience. Therefore, it is of utmost importance that those we choose to be our leaders honor God as their ultimate leader. The problem with power is that is can easily convince someone that they are above the law. Then, they begin to put their trust in their manpower and their intellect. Once they do that, they begin making bad decisions. The wisdom of man is no match for the wisdom of God. We must chose people like Hezekiah whose words can be trusted and whose trust is in the Lord.

In constitutional republics, such as with the United States and similar governmental structures, women play an important role in deciding who their future leaders will be. In the most general sense, God created women to be very intuitive and wise. We utilize those skills in daily responsibilities, but we have a political responsibility that requires such skills as well.

The use of our discernment and wisdom should extend from our personal perspective and into our prayer closet or maybe even onto a platform. What God reveals to our hearts isn't merely for our own edification, but it's to edify others; to guide them down a godly path. We do it for our children, so why not for our nation?

By being politically active, our civic duty is to ensure that leaders who honor God with their whole heart come to power.

Prayer

Dear Father, I lift up my nation to you asking that you give my leaders guidance. Expose that which is wrong and raise up a standard of righteousness in Jesus' name. Amen.
Further Studies: *1 Timothy 2:1-3*

Plans for Your Good

"'For I know the plans I have for you,' declares the Lord, 'plans to prosper you and not to harm you, plans to give you hope and a future.'"
(Jeremiah 29:11)

When you were a kid, you probably didn't like it very much when your parents didn't allow you to go to certain places, do certain things, or have whatever you wanted when you wanted it. Even if they gave you a reason as to why it was forbidden, all you understood was that you really, really wanted something, and they said no. In a child's mind that usually equates to, "My parents kept me from getting what I wanted, so they're bad."

As we get older, we realize that not everything we want is good for us, and we learn to appreciate all that our parents did for us in order to protect us from ourselves and the world. We learn that the decisions our parents made didn't make them bad, but that their actions actually showed how much they truly cared for our wellbeing.

In our relationship with God, we have been given His Word, which tells us that His intentions towards us are pure and loving. Therefore, we can believe that every decision He makes regarding our lives stems from that truth. This Scripture affirms that. We can trust God to lead and guide us through this life because we know that His only desire is to give us the best. Trust in the person leading you is key.

Have you ever played that game where someone leads you blindfolded through some kind of maze (either by voice or by guiding your hand)? Imagine that someone who absolutely hated you was leading you through the maze. How willing would you be to follow her through the maze? Most of us wouldn't be very willing.

But when you trust the person leading you through the maze, even if you hit a bump or two along the way, you understand that her intentions toward you remain good. She still wants to get you to the end of the maze, it's just that the trip might be a little bumpy; there are lots of obstacles in the way, after all. It may take longer than you want or it might be rougher than you'd like, but you'll get there. Trust God and believe that His plans for you are good, even when you hit a few bumps.

Prayer

Dear Father, I trust that you love me and care for me, so I choose to follow you wherever you may lead me in Jesus' name. Amen.
Further Studies: *Proverbs 3:5-6*

Moms of Missionaries

*"Therefore, brothers and sisters, in all our distress and persecution
we were encouraged about you because of your faith."*
(1 Thessalonians 3:7)

God does not grant us anything with the aim of it only being a benefit to us. He gives us good things so that we can be a blessing to others. In the same way, we must remember that the exercise of our faith is not only meant to make us stronger, but to teach others what faith in action is supposed to look like. Our first ministry begins in the home with our children.

Our children imitate what we do, whether we realize it or not. The way you talk about your husband when he's not around is how they will talk about him; the way you engage in life with others is how they will engage with others; the way you live out your faith may also determine how your children will live out theirs.

If your children have made the decision to become followers of Christ, they are also ambassadors or missionaries. Missionaries don't have to be those who travel to other countries, but they are those who make a point to share the Good News of Jesus wherever they go. But just like many missionaries that serve God in other countries, your little missionary may endure some persecution. If they're small, they may have friends at school that make fun of them. If they're older, they may get into arguments with their co-workers or have threats posed against them.

As a mother of a missionary, you may want to protect your child, but you have to remember that if they are serving the Lord, that's His job. In the meantime, you can assist your child in their primary calling by doing two things:

1) Be ready to comfort them. When your children don't understand why people react to the gospel the way that they do or why the name of Jesus is so hated in some places, they will likely come to you with questions. Be that comforting shoulder they can lean on in their discouragement, and pray with them.

2) Share your faith and show your commitment. As mentioned before, your children are watching you, learning from you, and implementing elements of your faith into their own. Your faith may be the only

thing that keeps them going in times of discouragement, making you a partaker in their sufferings.

Prayer

Dear Father, as hard as it may be for me to give my children fully over into your hands, I commit them to you. Lead and guide them in the way they should go, and help me to be a good example in Jesus' name. Amen.
Further Studies: *2 Corinthians 5:20*

Biblical Neuroscience

"And take the helmet of salvation..."
(Ephesians 6: 17)

What is the purpose of the helmet as used in armor?

The first purpose of a helmet is to disguise the identity of the wearer. Oftentimes kings would ride out into battle with their armies. If they were to be seen on the battlefield without any covering for their head, they would be like a sitting duck. The opposing force would know exactly who they were and would undoubtedly go after them. Wearing a helmet would at least give the king or general a fighting chance to go undetected.

Likewise, salvation hides our identity in Christ, making our former self unrecognizable to the rest of the world. Those who knew you before you became a Christian would be able to recognize you in the world by your patterns, habits, and mannerisms. If you become a new creation in Christ through the power of salvation, you put off the old self and take on a new identity. You take on the nature of Christ, which acts as a cloak.

The brilliant thing about taking on the nature of Christ is that not only does it keep the enemy at bay, but it also serves to be a great support in our relationship with God. Just as the enemy can look at us and see the likeness of Christ in us, when God looks upon us, He also sees the likeness of His son.

The second purpose of a helmet was to ensure that the wearer did not sustain a brain injury during combat. Likewise, salvation should be a filter for what goes in and out of our minds. Whatever we put inside our minds usually goes into our heart and comes out of our mouth. That is why we are to guard our eyes and ears by not allowing the enemy to influence our thinking through the things we watch on television, the conversations we have with friends, and so on. The fact that we have been saved and redeemed by the blood of Christ means that our minds should be under His protection.

The purpose of the helmet of salvation is to keep us in the right frame of mind by shaping the worldview used to evaluate God and others. Are you wearing yours today?

Prayer

Dear Father, thank you for salvation and the gift of your son. Day by day help me to make the right choices to guard my mind so that I can be known as one who belongs to you in Jesus' name. Amen.
Further Studies: *Proverbs 4:23*

Another Chance

"God, my God, I yelled for help and you put me together. God, you pulled me out
of the grave, gave me another chance at life when I was down-and-out."
(Psalm 30:2-3, MSG)

On many occasions throughout the Psalms we see David crying out to the Lord in such a manner. He had many reasons to be in distress during his lifetime, but with every challenge he faced, whether dealing with a homicidal king or dealing with the consequences of his own sin, David sought the Lord.

As women, we were created to be emotional creatures. We get to experience all of the joys that come along with that, but alternatively, we also have to deal with the lows. Emotional distress is a real and present factor that we deal with on a daily basis. Dealing with the busyness and sometimes chaos of our day to day lives can prove to be emotionally draining let alone dealing with the big issues that surface from time to time.

To be victorious in this life, we like David must turn to God who created us to help, guide and direct us to emotional wholeness. The beautiful thing about the Psalms of David is that though we see the weight of David's problem and read his pleas to the Lord for help, we also read about the way that the Lord responds to His child.

"In my distress I called upon the Lord and cried to my God for help;
He heard my voice out of His temple, and my cry for help before Him came into His ears...
He sent from on high, He took me; He drew me out of many waters.
He delivered me from my strong enemy, and from those
who hated me, for they were too mighty for me.
They confronted me in the day of my calamity, but the Lord was my stay.
He brought me forth also into a broad place; He rescued me, because He delighted in me."
(Psalm 18:6, 16-19)

When we turn to the Lord in our distress, we are afforded another chance. He pulls us up from the miry clay we're sinking in, heals our afflictions, and sets us on a firm foundation. Keeping lifting your eyes up to the hills. Your help will come.

Prayer

Dear Father, you are and have always been a present help in times of trouble. I trust
you to take care of me even when I feel I'm at my worst in Jesus' name. Amen.
Further Studies: *Psalm 18*

Afraid of Giving Your All?

"The lions may grow weak and hungry, but those who seek the LORD lack no good thing."
(Psalm 34:10)

Married women have a great deal of responsibility on their shoulders. It is essentially their job to make sure that everyone in their home is clean, fed, and clothed, and on top of that, some women also maintain a job outside of the home. The amount of time spent focused on family matters alone is equal to the rigors of a full-time job. Unfortunately, not only do those things cost time, but they also cost money.

Sometimes the weight of your family's financial needs can feel insurmountable. If you have children, you have probably discovered that they always seem to be growing out of their clothes, and their stomachs tend to mimic bottomless pits. It doesn't take very long before your resources become exhausted and worry begins to settle in. A mother's worst fear is not being able to provide for her child's needs.

It is very easy in moments like these to operate in fear. The choices you make about financial preparations for the future stem from fear. The conversations/ arguments you have with your husband about money stem from fear. Even the way you spend the money that you have stems from fear. When we operate in fear, we take for granted the fact that as believers we have no reason to fear.

Our primary identity is as children of God. As children of God, we are the heirs to a kingdom that knows no end. We are the heirs to cattle on a thousand hills. We have access to whatever we need. All we have to do is ask our heavenly Father. As a good Father, God desires to give us all of these things; His ultimate aim is to take care of us.

God will not leave you hungry or lacking when you obey Him, but you must first come to an understanding of the reality of who you are in Christ and pursue a lifestyle of faith and obedience. Then you will be able to see that you indeed have no reason to fear.

"Seek ye first the Kingdom of God, and His righteousness, and all these things will be added unto you" (Matthew 6:33).

Prayer

Dear Father, thank you for taking care of me and my family. Help me to continue to look to you as my source whenever I am in need in Jesus' name. Amen.
Further Studies: *Matthew 6:25-34, Matthew 7:9-11*

Unconditional Love

"The Lord appeared to him from afar, saying, "I have loved you with an everlasting love; therefore, I have drawn you with lovingkindness."
(Jeremiah 31:3, NASB)

In every relationship, whether between family members or friends, we know we have reached the ultimate point of intimacy with that person when we can comfortably tell them that we love them. Love is not a word that most people just throw around or apply to anyone; the word love means something deep, something special. It indicates a feeling a deep affection.

As humans, our love can be... fickle. We can claim that we love someone one day, but then if they do something that we don't like, we can easily withdraw our affections. Our love comes with conditions and is mostly based on our feelings. "I'll love you today, if I *feel* like it."

Though we may use the phrase, "I love you", these words totally lose their meaning when our actions don't follow. You can't tell someone that you love them, but on the days when they're at their worst, you walk away from them. You have to show that you love them by being kind even if they're not returning the favor. Love is not an emotion, it is an action.

1 Corinthians 13 gives a list of loving actions. True love is an everlasting decision to sacrifice, forgive, and be kind. A good way to determine the strength of your love is to put your name is place of the word "love" when you read this chapter (i.e. "Pam is patient, Pam is kind..."). How does your love measure up?

As the master of this universe, God's love is never fickle. He is an everlasting God, so that attribute of His nature can be applied to every aspect of His relationship with us: His love is everlasting, His mercy is everlasting, and His faithfulness is everlasting. Were we to read 1 Corinthians 13 again and replace "love" with "God", without a doubt we could say that this Scripture describes Him, because God is love.

Just as the Lord loves you, so too, you must endeavor to love others.

Prayer

Dear Father, your love is rich and faithful, and I know that my love pales in comparison. Teach me how to love everyone I encounter the way that you do in Jesus' name. Amen.
Further Studies: *Romans 2:4*

Thinking about Thinking

"Finally, brothers and sisters, whatever is true, whatever is noble, whatever is right, whatever is pure, whatever is lovely, whatever is admirable-- if anything is excellent or praiseworthy--think about such things."
(Philippians 4:8)

If you were to take stock of the types of thoughts you think on any given day, what would the majority of them be? Positive or negative? Do you see the worst in people, situations, and life in general, or do you see the best?

Because our human nature is prone to sin, our minds can easily become congested with troubling thoughts. We may have negative thoughts as a response to various situations (i.e. your child breaks an irreplaceable family memento), or our negative thoughts may be the result of what we have been filling our mind with (i.e. "garbage in, garbage out"), or they may be related to our self-esteem or self-worth.

Generally speaking, our first inclination in any given situation is typically to default to negative thought patterns, yet God says that we are to renew our minds. We have to get rid of the old thoughts and put on the mind of Christ. To put on the mind of Christ may not always be our first response to certain situations, but it is the only way that we will be able to overcome the strategy of an enemy that specializes in mind games.

This verse in Philippians helps us to better understand how God wants our minds to function. The traits that should govern our thinking are not fear, anger, jealousy, or greed, but they are truth, honesty, justice, purity, love, virtue, and praise. All of these words are descriptors of Christ, so it goes without saying that to exhibit these traits is what it means to put on the mind of Christ.

Changing your thought life is not an easy task. It takes a daily commit. If you encounter someone with an unsavory attitude and it makes you want to think something negative, hold that thought up to this Scripture and ask yourself, "Is this thought pure, lovely, of good report, virtuous or praiseworthy?" If not, get rid of it!

Prayer

Dear Father, you have taken my old nature and replaced it with yours. Help me to rely on your thoughts to influence or replace my own in Jesus' name. Amen.
Further Studies: *Romans 12:2*

Many Bitter Troubles

*"Though you have made me see troubles, many and bitter, you will restore
my life again; from the depths of the earth you will again bring me up."*
(Psalm 71:20)

I f you take a moment to scan your body, you will probably come across a
number of scars, and it probably won't take you very long to remember where
those scars came from. It's very rare for someone to get a scar and completely
forget the events that led to its appearance.

Though scars can be reminders of painful experiences, they can also serve as
reminders of the way God used that painful experience to protect or spare your life.
Maybe a scar from an accident can remind you of the way your injury could have
been worse, or maybe a scar from a surgery can be a reminder of how God provided
an answer to a physical problem you were facing. It's all a matter of perspective.

A lot of times when we become believers we buy into the notion that life will be a
bed of roses and that we will never have to deal with sorrow again, but let's take
a look at Psalm 23:1-4:

*"The LORD is my shepherd, I lack nothing.
He makes me lie down in green pastures,
He leads me beside quiet waters...
Even though I walk through the darkest valley,
I will fear no evil, for you are with me;
Your rod and your staff, they comfort me.*

As a good shepherd, Jesus leads us through treacherous valleys and beside quiet
and peaceful streams. Troubles may leave an indelible mark in your memory and
even in your soul, but the presence of God in the midst of each trouble should
never be overlooked. There is not a single situation that He will not help us
through. So instead of counting your troubles, acknowledge the presence and
blessings of God in every situation.

Prayer

*Dear Father, thank you for being with me whether I'm going through a
valley or walking beside a peaceful stream in Jesus' name. Amen.*
Further Studies: *Psalm 23:1-4*

The Comfort He gives

"This is my comfort in my affliction, that Your word has revived me."
(Psalm 119:50, NASB)

In the midst of our seasons of suffering, our most fervent prayers tend to center on one thing: escape. We feel that we cannot experience peace unless God relieves us of our trouble, and we often tend to weigh God's goodness by how quickly He brings about that relief. But to judge God in such a way demonstrates a serious lack of understanding on our part.

God has a purpose for allowing us to pass through afflictions, so for us to look forward to the end of them is like a form of self-sabotage. If you want to learn the lesson, you have to go through the test. You can't skip ahead to the end and expect to have gleaned all that God wanted to teach you. In order to endure the test, you have to seek comfort from only one thing: the Word.

Have you ever been going through a difficult situation and upon speaking with a friend about it, they share encouragement that is exactly what you needed to hear in that moment? It works the same way when you open your Bible and read the story of someone who faced a similar situation as the one you're facing or when you find a Scripture that gives the exact answer to the questions you had been pondering. That is the power of the Bible.

God's Word is packed with promises, exhortations, and lessons we need to learn; it is the most valuable resource that Christians can have in their life. When God spoke these words to the 60 men that penned what we now use as our Bible, He knew every single situation we would ever face, and He placed every single verse in the Bible for that reason, so that when we are going through hard times, we can look to His Word and find direct encouragement from His heart to ours.

Are you cherishing and graciously receiving the comfort He gives through His word, or do you keep hoping for an escape from the situations that should bring you closer to God? Let His word revive and comfort you.

Prayer

Dear Father, your word is food to my soul – it comforts and revives me. Thank you for always providing a means of peace through the Bible in Jesus' name. Amen.
Further Studies: *Hebrews 4:12*

The Recompense of God

"Say to those with fearful hearts, 'Be strong, and do not fear, for your
God is coming to destroy your enemies. He is coming to save you.'"
(Isaiah 35:4)

Anyone who has children or has been around children can see what unbridled sinful nature looks like. When one toddler has a toy and another toddler takes that toy away, what happens? The first child will either snatch the toy away again or hit the other child. In response, the other child will probably follow suit. Children don't have to be taught retaliation, they just do it naturally.

In the same way, when people treat us wrong, we tend to feel that it is our place to retaliate. As this Scripture states, we may even become so focused on retaliation that it makes us anxious. We literally worry that if we don't pay back the wrong someone else paid to us, they'll never learn their lesson; they'll never be given the opportunity to feel bad for what they've done. Do you know what that kind of anxiety feels like?

Isaiah, also known as the Prince of Prophets, encourages us in this Scripture to take courage and fear not because God is the one who takes vengeance. He is the one who will repay the wrongs that were done to us, and He is the one who will exalt us for maintaining a righteous lifestyle. Our only job is to continue to walk blamelessly and humbly before God.

As much as we may want someone to deal with the consequences of their actions, we probably don't stop to think that if we take matters into our own hands and repay evil for evil, we disqualify ourselves from being rescued as one of God's righteous ones and instead set ourselves against God. Do you think God would overlook your sin just because you were getting back at someone? Sin is sin, and regardless of your reason for committing it, you too will have to deal with the consequences.

God is with us; He knows EVERY thing that happens, and He will deal with it all, so take courage!

Prayer

Dear Father, thank you for providing recompense for me and freeing
me from the burden of having to play judge and chief. You are a
just God and I trust your leadership in Jesus' name. Amen.
Further Studies: *Romans 12:19*

Stand Firm

*"Because of the increase of wickedness, the love of most will grow
cold, but he who stands firm to the end will be saved."*
(Matthew 24:12-13)

When you love someone, you put their needs and desires before your own. Sometimes putting others first is a conscious choice you make, like giving your husband the last slice of pie even though you really want it for yourself, and sometimes it just comes naturally, like cleaning up after your child when she gets sick. The basic point is that when you care for someone, you put action behind it.

As wickedness increases and becomes more commonplace in our culture, and even in our churches, people will become more self-centered and selfish. In order to engage in sin, one truly has to be focused on indulging themselves in something that they feel benefits them, whether to bring pleasure to themselves (i.e. stealing) or to temporarily protect themselves (i.e. lying). It is impossible to care for someone else's needs as you sin.

The more people engage in sin, the more their love for Christ will grow cold, as will their desire to put His will before their own. As the Bible says, people will become lovers of themselves, and they will call what is evil good and what is good, evil. In such an environment, believers can easily be persuaded to forsake their first love to pursue what makes themselves happy, but this is antithetical to the first and greatest commandment that God has given us to follow:

*"You shall love the Lord your God with all your heart, and with all your soul,
and with all your mind. This is the great and foremost commandment. The
second is like it, You shall love your neighbor as yourself. On these
two commandments depend the whole Law and the Prophets."*
(Matthew 22:37-40, NASB)

If you truly love God, you will obey His commands because you know that that is what He desires; it's what makes Him happy. As we focus on Christ, His strength and grace will enable us to make it to the end.

Prayer

*Dear Father, as the culture around me changes, help me to remain
steadfast in my love and obedience to you in Jesus' name. Amen.*
Further Studies: *1 Corinthians 1:9*

Light and Salvation

"The LORD is my light and my salvation— whom shall I fear? The LORD is the stronghold of my life— of whom shall I be afraid?"
(Psalm 27:1)

A lot of children, mostly toddlers, spend their early years absolutely terrified of the dark. In fact, the night light industry will probably never go out of business, because there will always be children to keep their business in production. Around the age of 2 or 3 is when the imagination becomes active, therefore the dark becomes the hiding place for all sorts of creatures, as far as children are concerned.

It's not only children that struggle with fear of the dark though, even some adults carry that fear well into adulthood. Many women are afraid to walk down dark alleys or to even walk their own neighborhood streets alone, if it means they have to walk in the dark. We fear the unknown. We fear the dark.

There is a good reason for that. The darkness is and has always been a dwelling place and even a stronghold for the enemy. He typically operates under the cover of darkness. There's a reason why when even children do things they know they're not supposed to do, they try to hide it in the dark. That is why many of the biblical prophets and even Jesus compared Christianity to light, as an opposing force to the power of darkness.

Light illuminates darkness, and that is what the Lord does for us. Jesus Christ is our light and salvation, and not only does His light shine, but He also saves so that we need not be afraid of people or to be fearful in general. Whatever schemes the enemy plots under the cover of darkness, when they're exposed to the light, they fall flat. Actually, when the enemy himself is exposed to the light of Christ, he has to flee!

What are you afraid of? What terrifies you? Allow the Lord to be a lamp unto your feet and a light unto your path and let Him lead you out of the darkness and into His marvelous light.

Prayer

Dear Father, thank you for shedding your light on my life and revealing that when you're with me I have nothing to fear in Jesus' name. Amen.
Further Studies: Acts 26:18

The Rock

*"My soul finds rest in God alone; my salvation comes from him. He alone is
my rock and my salvation; he is my fortress, I will never be shaken."*
(Psalm 62:1-2)

As a woman, I find that I often bite off more than I can chew, so it's very easy for me to become extremely exhausted. So many people approach me on a daily basis with so many needs that it's difficult for me to say no. It's in our DNA as women to "mother" everything and everyone, and before we know it, we are in overload mode.

Yes, there is something to be said for knowing when to say no and how to manage your time, but the reality of the matter is, sooner or later we all will become overwhelmed by situations that occur in our lives – many of which will be out of our control. But regardless of the situations we face or the decisions we need to make, this Scripture assures us that God is our rock and our fortress, and we will never be shaken!

If you've ever visited the Grand Canyon or any other mountainous region, you have probably been amazed at the size and strength of the massive rocks. They are basically impenetrable, and can serve as a mighty fortress to anyone seeking shelter. It is nearly impossible to stand at the base of a mountain without realizing how small and insignificant you are in comparison.

God is our mighty fortress and refuge. When we are afraid or overwhelmed, we can rest in the fact that when we hide within His walls, nothing can harm us. It is through His protection that we are saved. When you get a good visual of God as a mighty fortress that we can run into, you understand how it's so easy to find rest in Him. Anyone who knows they're in a safe place can manage to breathe a little easier.

There are many other things in our lives that may offer to be a refuge for us, but they end up only being a temporary fix or they may even become a distraction from God, our true refuge. Lift your eyes to the mountains and know where your help comes from.

Prayer

*Dear Father, you are the safest hiding place and refuge for my soul. I choose to run
to you to be my salvation instead of anything or anyone else in Jesus' name. Amen.*
Further Studies: *Psalm 91:2*

Encourager

"We faced conflict from every direction, with battles on the outside and fear on the inside. But God, who encourages those who are discouraged, encouraged us by the arrival of Titus. His presence was a joy."
(2 Corinthians 7:5b-6, NLT)

Many action-adventure movies end up playing out the same way at one point or another: the hero is surrounded by the enemy and has to fight one against one hundred. Do you know what that feels like? Of course you probably haven't had to demonstrate your Taekwondo skills against one hundred highly trained ninjas, but you do know what it's like to have trouble on every side.

Life can be a battle; many problems can come at us from several different angles, and sometimes all at once. You can face conflict between friends and family members, in the workplace, in your church, within yourself, and even with God. As King David described numerous times throughout the Psalms, the weight of it all can make you feel like you're being suffocated.

God can send relief and encouragement in a number of ways, but one particular way He encourages us is through other believers, as in the case of Titus. Paul and some friends had arrived in Macedonia and encountered spiritual opposition. When Titus arrived, he brought good news to encourage them, thereby restoring their joy.

Women often have the natural gift of discernment. You may be able tell when something is going on with someone long before they even open their mouth. Use that gift to see into situations where people need to hear an encouraging word from you. Share the good news of Jesus or a Scripture or your personal testimony. Listen to the Spirit and speak as He directs.

Whether the person is a friend or a stranger, she needs to hear that she will still make it despite her failures. She needs to know that whatever she has done in the name of Christ is worth the work she put in. She needs to know that she is not alone. We are benefactors of encouragement, so please, encourage the ones that God puts in your life.

Prayer

Dear Father, you have always been a great source of encouragement to me. Help me to be an encouragement to others as well in Jesus' name. Amen.
Further Studies: *1 Thessalonians 5:11*

I Am

"Jesus said to them, 'Truly, truly, I say to you, before Abraham was born, I AM.' "
(John 8:58, ESV)

A mother's love is constant. Before her child is even born, she loves him. As she watches her child grow, she loves him, and even if her child were to leave this earth before her, she would go on loving him. There's a unique bond between the heart of a child and mother that occurs during the nine months the child resides in his mother's womb, and it lasts the entirety of her life.

Though a mother is one of the most dedicated beings on earth, her dedication can fall short due to the frailty of humanness. Her child can do something to shatter her emotionally and force her to withdraw, and because she is also subject to the laws of mortality, it is also impossible for her love to endure forever. Only the love of God can manage that.

Abraham was the father of the nation of Israel. The origin of the Israelites is often described as having come from Abraham's bosom, therefore depicting him like a mother. Here Jesus declares His sovereign omnipresence to His people and compares it to the most mother-like figure the Israelites could imagine: the progenitor of their entire race.

On top of that, Jesus describes Himself using the forbidden words that were only to be used to describe God: I AM.

"I AM" is present tense; happening now, yet its meaning spans many facets of the nature of God. He is the beginning and the end, the alpha and omega, the first and the last; He is the one true God and no one can compare to Him.

This statement also speaks of His presence. In the time that God shared this descriptor of Himself, He was appearing as pillars of clouds and fire as He led His people through the wilderness. When Jesus shared the same descriptor of Himself, He was sharing that He is Emmanuel, God with us. He was walking the earth with the very same people He created, living life with them and loving them. In our own lives we can trace evidence of God's presence being with us every step of the way.

You can rest in the ever-present power of I AM. Nothing or no one else is like Him; He changes not – guaranteed!

Prayer

Dear Father, you are the everlasting God from whom all things were created. I praise you, my King Eternal, in Jesus' name. Amen.
Further Studies: *Psalm 27:10*

No More

"Do not be afraid; you will not be put to shame. Do not fear disgrace;
you will not be humiliated. You will forget the shame of your youth
and remember no more the reproach of your widowhood."
(Isaiah 54:4)

Alicia hung her head in shame. She knew the disgrace her pregnancy had brought to her family, and she felt their shame hanging over her head when she had the abortion. Years later, even after she had married, she still carried that shame.

The season of youth is one of the hardest seasons we face as humans, let alone women, because we make a lot of unwise decisions. These decisions not only cause serious problems for us and the ones we love most, but they also create a garment of shame for us. This garment is a one size fits all, so many people continue to wear it into adulthood and even to the grave.

As Christians, we often believe that our sins are so bad that even Jesus cannot bear to look at us, but that is not the case. Take, for instance, the story of Gomer (a representation of Israel). God told the prophet Hosea to marry Gomer, knowing full well that she was a harlot. Even during their marriage she continued to be unfaithful. But even after all her unfaithfulness, this is the response of our loving God.

> *"Therefore, behold, I will allure her,*
> *Bring her into the wilderness*
> *And speak kindly to her.*
> *"Then I will give her vineyards from there,*
> *And the valley of Achor as a door of hope.*
> *And she will sing there as in the days of her youth,*
> *As in the day when she came up from the land of Egypt."*
> Hosea 2:14-15

God redeemed the youth of Gomer/Israel, and He desires to redeem your youth as well. You don't have to carry the shame of your youth anymore. Just lay it at Jesus' feet and experience His grace.

Prayer

Dear Father, you are a merciful and loving God. Thank you for extending kindness to me and exchanging my garment of heaviness for one of joy in Jesus' name. Amen.
Further Studies: *Romans 8:1*

Father

*"As a father has compassion on his children, so the LORD
has compassion on those who fear him."*
(Psalm 103:13)

Dad
Daddy
Papa
Baba
Abba

These are just a few of the many terms we typically use to address our fathers. We may not always use them in our prayer life, but they are also terms that we can use to address our heavenly father when we approach His throne of grace. Because He is the King of all kings and the creator of the universe, we sometimes may feel like we should address Him as royalty. Yes, this is true of who He is, but He is also our Daddy.

There's an intimacy that comes in a relationship between a father and his child and that cannot be compared to any other relationship, especially that of a dad and his little girl. Not everyone can come into the throne room of the king informally, but you are able to come right up to His throne and sit in His lap.

Part of a father's responsibility is also to deal with the spiritual, mental, and emotional upbringing of his children. When children make mistakes, the father is the one to get them back in line. When they need help, he's there to be their support.

I had a dad who was negative, and maybe some of you did as well. But when I came in contact with God the Father there was a remarkable difference. He showed me what a tender and compassionate father looks like, now I no longer cower in fear or cover my ears to block out the negativity. This Father loves me! He loves me in spite of myself and guess what? He LOVES YOU TOO!

Regardless of the type of relationship you had or didn't have with your earthly Father, our Father God is different. Give Him a chance to show you what a good Father is supposed to look like. Let Him melt away the pain of any past experiences you had and restore your hope. He will not let you down!

Prayer

Dear Abba, I could not ask for a better father than you.
I love you, Daddy in Jesus' name. Amen.
Further Studies: *Matthew 7:9-11*

Great Faith

*"Then Jesus said to her, 'Woman, you have great faith! Your request
is granted.' And her daughter was healed at that moment."*
(Matthew 15:28)

I f you're a mother, you know very well how horrible you feel when your child is
ill. Normally, you're used to taking care of every need your child has – you are a
nurturer after all. But when he gets sick, there's nothing you can do to make him feel
better. He just has to let it run its course until the sickness relinquishes its control over
his body. Still, the waiting game can be maddening, especially if the illness is serious.

Imagine then this mother whose child was demon possessed. She had to stand by
and watch her child unwillingly hurt herself and possibly others day after day,
and there was nothing that she could do about it. No imagine the kind of faith it
took for her, a Canaanite woman to approach a Jew (something that was totally
forbidden in those days) and ask him for help. She had to have been desperate.

It requires great faith to believe God for your children at any stage of their lives. This
doesn't only apply to when they're sick. Even when they are infants, without faith, a lot
of mothers would constantly be by their baby's side, checking to see if he's breathing.
When he becomes a toddler and easily get into things and hurts himself (often), it's
almost enough to make a mother want to duct tape her child in bubble wrap.

Once your child gets older, the faith journey doesn't stop. They make new friends
who introduce them to new ways to get into trouble, and once again... it's out of
your jurisdiction. You have to trust that God has the power to oversee the process
and bring your child into the plan that He had for him from the beginning.

Whatever your child is doing or not doing, have faith that God will see him through,
whether he has lived up to what you have taught him or not. Like this woman,
exercise your faith and trust God to heal your children, bless them and set them free.

Prayer

*Dear Father, you are and have always been a good father to me. Now I
entrust my children into your hands as well in Jesus' name. Amen.*
Further Studies: *Matthew 15:21-28*

A Friend

*"A man of many companions may come to ruin, but there
is a friend who sticks closer than a brother."*
(Proverbs 18:24)

Proverbs gives a word or two about friendship. When God created man, He decided that man needed a companion, a helpmeet, a friend, an ally, a confidant, someone to talk to, and someone that man could trust and rely on (Genesis 2:18, 23). God brought Eve into the garden to be Adam's friend.

Even God had a friend in the person of Abraham (James 2:23). Our father and creator knows the importance of friendship, and He went as far as developing a friendship relationship with Abraham. It was that relationship between God and Abraham that saved Lot from destruction. (Genesis 18:18-23)

It's sad to say, but there are many types of "friends." A true friend, however, will love and stay with you even when things are bad. Sometimes having too many friends causes chaos in your life. However, when you meet that special friend, a best friend, it adds value to each of your lives so much so, that even if relatives are not there for you, you can count on them.

In life, it is important to be a good friend and to receive good friends in order to maintain a balanced lifestyle. God created us in such a way that we have need for good company and association. I have also come to discover that marriage works best when you and your husband become the best of friends. It will definitely pay off.

Prayer

*Dear Father, I thank you for the gift of a good friend. Teach me to
value my relationships and to be the very friend that can stand by
my friends when they need me most, in Jesus' name. Amen.*
Further Studies: *Proverbs 17:17*

Do You Believe?

"If you believe, you will receive whatever you ask for in prayer."
(Matthew 21:22)

Alison looked suspiciously at the women as they prayed in earnest. She had tried praying about something once before, but nothing seemed to happen, so she had resigned herself to view prayer through a very skeptical lens. *"If prayer really works, then why hasn't God answered my prayer?"* she wondered.

This was Alison's first time with this particular group of women, and she was very wary. She wasn't sure why she had accepted her friend's invitation to come to the prayer meeting, but she was pretty sure that she had seen all they had to offer. As the prayer meeting progressed, each woman came forward and spoke from her heart about what God had done, what He was doing, and what she anticipated He would do. The question each testimony left tugging at her heart was, "Do I really believe?"

Most of our prayer life is spent asking God for things. We may ask for something seemingly trivial, like a good day or for a task to be completed successfully, or we may ask for something serious, like healing from a life-threatening illness. Regardless of how serious we believe the request to be, the one factor that must always be present is our belief that God can do what we ask.

Think about it for a minute. When you pray for healing, how confident are you that God can/will actually heal? According to the first chapter of James, the lack of confidence that God is able or willing to respond to our prayers is what we call doubt, and as James says, "The one who doubts is like the surf of the sea, driven and tossed by the wind. For that man ought not to expect that he will receive anything from the Lord, *being* a double-minded man, unstable in all his ways." (James 1:6-8)

God is always available and willing to do His part, and our only job is to have faith. You'll notice throughout many of Christ's encounters with people that approached Him with requests, He commented on the strength of their faith. If you find yourself in a similar headspace as Alison, it's time to ask the Lord to help you with your unbelief and allow him to work in his sovereign way.

Prayer

Dear Father, I believe, but help me with my unbelief in Jesus' name. Amen.
Further Studies: *James 1:5-8*

November

Blessed

"Her children arise and call her blessed; her husband also, and he praises her."
(Proverbs 31:28)

One of the simplest ways that we can show appreciation to those who have done so much for us is to say thank you. There's something about those two little words that can move a heart to tears.

They can especially move the heart of a hardworking mother to tears when she hears them from her husband and children. Now imagine the honor that comes with being called blessed among all other women by your family members.

That is just one of the rewards of being a Proverbs 31 woman. When you go about your daily routines with your husband and children in a way that is excellent and praiseworthy, they won't be able to keep from praising you and declaring blessing upon you.

Just as it is your joy and honor to serve your family, it will be their joy and honor to tell the world how much of a blessing you have been to them over the years. So don't become weary in well doing. One day you will receive your reward.

Prayer

Dear Father, I thank you for the opportunities I have to show love to my family. Help me to be worthy of their praises in Jesus' name. Amen.
Further Studies: *Proverbs 31:28-31*

I Am Here

*"They had rowed three or four miles when suddenly they saw
Jesus walking on the water toward the boat. They were terrified,
but he called out to them, 'Don't be afraid. I am here!'"*
(John 6:19-20, NLT)

As women, we go through many different seasons in life. Some are welcome and enjoyable, like those times when you're surrounded by loved ones and everything is going your way, but other seasons can be devastating, like the loss of loved ones or a financial crisis. Sometimes we would rather go into hibernation until a particular season passes, instead of facing the season head on, but it doesn't work like that.

In this particular instance, the disciples had left Jesus on one side of the sea and had begun crossing over to the other side. As they journeyed, it became dark and the sea began to stir. Imagine being trapped in the middle of the sea in the dark with violent wind and waves all around. You might then understand why the disciples were totally terrified.

Now imagine the relief that came when they spotted Jesus – the man that they knew could cast out demons and heal the sick and raise the dead – walking on the water to come and meet them. Imagine the relief that washed over their anxious hearts when he uttered the words: "I am here."

It's very much like a child who is afraid of the dark or the deep rumblings of a thunderstorm. When they are alone in their bedroom, fear can control them, but if they run into their mom and dad's room and snuggle in between the two people they know will protect them from anything, suddenly they can rest easy and sleep. It typically works like a charm.

The same goes for us. Whenever we face the storms of life, if we look up, we will find Jesus saying, "I am here." No matter the season of your soul, He will be with you.

Prayer

*Dear Father, thank you for never leaving me alone and for bringing
me comfort when I need it most in Jesus' name. Amen.*
Further Studies: *Psalm 73:28*

Be Still, He IS God

"Be still, and know that I am God".
(Psalm 46:10a)

Kids are quite funny to watch when they're somewhere where they're required to be still. Have you ever tried taking your small child to an important meeting and asked him to sit still until you were done? How'd that go for you?

I don't know about you, but being still has never been one of my finer traits either. Whenever it comes time to be still, I find myself fidgeting, complaining, and anxious for it to be over. Though I know that it's not exactly appropriate behavior for a child of God, it still seems to be something I struggle with.

Have you been there? Maybe sometimes we wonder why it's so important for us to be still. What does it matter to God if we're moving while He works or if we're still? He's not human, so it's not like when our parents used to tell us to be still for the sake of their own sanity or concentration. So why?

Well, it's for our own good. As women, we know what it means to be busy. We are natural fixers and DIYers. Oftentimes we can pray and ask God to take over something, but then mere minutes later we find ourselves trying to fix the problem ourselves because brilliant idea popped into our heads just after we got off our knees.

But God is asking that when we pray, we leave our request at His feet and wait quietly in expectation for Him to do what He does best: respond in the way that only He can. We aren't just to be still for the sake of being still though. As we are quiet, we are to reflect on the fact that He is the almighty God whose plans can never be thwarted.

It is enough to literally take Him at His word. He does not lie; what He says is true. He is God who sits on the throne, rules supremely, and has EVERYTHING under control. So be still, He IS GOD!

Prayer

Dear Father, I trust you, and I choose to show you how much I trust
you by remaining still and watching you work. You are God alone,
so help me to let my words be few in Jesus' name. Amen.
Further Studies: *Ecclesiastes 5:2*

Hiding Place

"You are my hiding place; you will protect me from trouble
and surround me with songs of deliverance."
(Psalm 32:7-8)

The phrase "hiding place" reminds me of the stirring story of Corrie Ten Boom's life. She was a Dutch Christian who, alongside her father and other family members, helped many Jews escape the Nazi Holocaust during World War II by giving them a safe place to hide. She and her family were eventually imprisoned for what they did.

The thing with hiding places is that there is always a nagging fear in the back of your mind that you will be caught or found. Even though Corrie Ten Boom's family provided refuge for people, with every negative report they heard on the radio or every loud noise that erupted outside of their home, they couldn't help but to continue to fear for their lives. They could never totally be at peace.

But Corrie's story doesn't end there. Even though she was placed in a concentration camp where she watched all of her family members die, she found another place to hide. She hid under the wings of her almighty God. Yes, she was at the mercy of ruthless people, but her heart was protected by her merciful God, so she no longer had to be afraid of those who sought to bring her harm.

God is our hiding place. With Him we don't have to be afraid of the enemy, no matter how loud or close he gets. We are safe. We can NEVER be caught or imprisoned. We can take refuge in this hiding place, depending solely on God's grace and mercy as we trust Him unswervingly.

One of the most beautiful things about this verse is that as the Lord protects us, He surrounds us with songs of deliverance. If you can imagine being imprisoned, you can also imagine how sweet these songs must sound to the soul. The sweetest gift one in prison could ever receive is their freedom, so in His kindness, God sings songs of deliverance to remind us that we won't always need to hide. There is freedom when we hide beneath the shadow of His wings.

Prayer

Dear Father, I have found the safest place beneath your wings. Open my ears to
hear your songs of deliverance in every season of my soul in Jesus' name. Amen.
Further Studies: *Psalm 32:7-11*

Lamplighter

"It is you who light my lamp; the Lord, my God, lights up my darkness."
(Psalm 18:28, ESV)

Leaving aside the fact that dark streets can be quite scary, a street without light can also be pretty hazardous. One can easily injure themselves or be injured by someone else who may be lurking in the shadows. That's why it's so important that every street be lit. Historically, a lamplighter was a town employee who walked the streets near dusk carrying a long wick on a pole and manually lighting each of the <u>street lights</u>.

Light is metaphor that is commonly used in the Bible for various reasons, but generally speaking, light refers to revelation and guidance. It's like that symbolic light bulb that flashes over our head when we have a great idea. Without the light of God illuminating our lives, we would be walking in darkness – without revelation and utterly lost.

But we thank God that He is our Lamplighter. We thank Him for His beautiful and faithful light that guides our every step and removes all fear. From the moment we receive His salvation until the day we finally walk into the glorious light of His presence, we can rest in the fact that God will always provide a light for us to follow, even if we're walking through the Valley of the Shadow of Death.

What particular situation do you have that needs a little or a lot of light today? It doesn't matter how much light it needs or how long it has been in darkness, the Lamplighter will light it. Open up the hidden places of your mind and heart to the Lord and receive the revelation He desires to give you.

Take every dark situation to the lamplighter; He is waiting with open arms with the light that each situation needs. Then you will be able to walk away lit and light.

Prayer

Dear Father, thank you for leading and guiding me every day of my life. I continue to seek your light as you reveal yourself daily to me in your word in Jesus' name. Amen.
Further Studies: *Isaiah 9:2*

According To His Purpose

"And we know that in all things God works for the good of those who love him, who have been called according to his purpose."
(Romans 8:28)

The little girl sat and labored tirelessly over the pieces of the large puzzle before her. She had put nearly half of the puzzle together, but that was not good enough. She would not sleep a wink until she had put all of the pieces into place, because she was oh so curious to see the finished picture.

Life is a puzzle. It takes the union of many pieces to make sense, to make something beautiful. A lot of times, when we're in the midst of living our lives, we frantically search and to fix the piece that we think will fit, but how many times have you been putting a puzzle together and discovered the piece you needed was the last place you looked or it was a piece that you didn't think would work at first glance?

God has a bird's eye view of our past, present, and future (the picture on the box, so to speak). He knows exactly what we need to encounter each day of our lives if we're going to be mature and holy in our faith and love, so for that reason He'll hand us pieces that we think wouldn't be a great fit. Yet, He's the one holding the finished picture, not us, so it's safe to say that we can trust Him when He says, "Try this piece."

Paul records that even difficult situations can be used in God's overall plan for good. As we know in our heads (not always in our hearts), God tends to use negative situations, such as crucibles, to bring forth gold that is rooted deep within us. That's one of the beauties of puzzles – when a few pieces come together, you begin to the see the beautiful picture the pieces have formed, and the excitement of seeing those pieces in place urges you to keep putting the rest together.

Meanwhile, the master of the puzzle looks on smiling because He knows that in spite of everything it took to get to that point, all the pieces will fit together according to His purpose.

Prayer

Dear Father, I trust you with all the pieces of my life. Put them together as you see fit in Jesus' name. Amen.
Further Studies: *Jeremiah 29:11*

Intricately Made

"Are not five sparrows sold for two pennies? Yet not one of them is forgotten in God's sight. But even the hairs of your head are all counted. Do not be afraid; you are of more value than many sparrows."
(Luke 12:6-7)

If you had a doll when you were growing up, it's likely that one of your favorite things to do was to comb and style her hair. Did you ever try counting the strands of hair on the doll's head? It's pretty impossible, right? Even if you had tried, you would have probably been overwhelmed and either gotten frustrated or miscounted at some point in your pursuit. And yet, here Jesus tells us that the hairs on our head have been counted. Imagine! Now that is something!

This verse compares us to even the most seemingly insignificant creatures. Sparrows were essentially of no value, yet they were precious in the Lord's sight. He still kept record of their lives and provided for them on a day by day basis. If He felt that way about the sparrows, how much more does He keep an account of our lives (though we number over 7 billion)!

No two persons are alike, each of us are intricately made and very precious and valuable to God. Situations in life, people, and even the enemy of our souls will often try to convince us otherwise. The sad thing is, we can easily be tricked into believing those lies. And we end up living our lives as women without any special worth or purpose on this earth.

This should not be so, my friend!

When God knitted you together in your mother's womb, He knew who you would be. He breathed that destiny into your life when He breathed life into your body. It is deep rooted, and only He can bring it about. If you haven't discovered it yet, you will in due time, but in the meantime just keep in mind that no one keeps tabs on anyone or anything that they don't care about. If God's keeping track of you, it means He's got some expectations for your life, so be on the lookout!

Prayer

Dear Father, thank you for caring for me enough to know even the number of hairs on my head in Jesus' name. Amen.
Further Studies: *Matthew 6:25-34*

The Sovereign God

"I am the LORD, the God of all mankind. Is anything too hard for me?"
(Jeremiah 32:27)

I am intrigued and comforted by the lyrics to Maurette Brown's "The Sovereign God". They truly serve to illuminate the message behind this Scripture.

> *"A wave of your hand can command the seas to hold their peace*
> *If you can handle the seas*
> *Then I know that you can deal with all my needs*
> *So I put every situation into your capable hands*
> *He is able to do exceedingly abundantly*
> *Above all we ask or think*
> *So take all your burdens*
> *And lay them at His feet and watch Him meet the need."*

Sometimes we have to remind ourselves of who God actually is if we want to be able to fully hand over our problems or our needs. When we forget who He is and how powerful He is, we easily begin to lose sight of why we should trust Him; we easily begin to lose our sense of fear and wonder.

But there is no one in heaven above, or on the earth below, that can compare to God. He is God alone and everything – and I mean EVERYTHING – is under His control, even the enemy of our souls. We all remember the story Job and all that he endured, but do you remember the way the Lord responded to Job towards the end of the story? He reminded Job who He was. He reminded him of the way He commanded all things to exist and how He continually maintains the order of the universe.

When the enemy tries to get you to believe that your situation is hopeless, remind yourself of who God really is. Let that embolden you to believe the truth about your situation: there is NOTHING too hard for God!

Prayer

Dear Father, I believe that there is nothing too difficult for you, and I trust you with all of my cares and my life in Jesus' name. Amen.
Further Studies: *Job 38*

Undivided Heart

"You must always act in the fear of the Lord, with faithfulness and an undivided heart."
(2 Chronicles 19:9, NLT)

When someone travels from a third world country into a first world country, one of the first things they'll notice is how much variety can be found. Take restaurants, for instance. In third world countries most of the restaurants only serve local food, which means they all pretty much serve the same thing. In first world countries there are dining options from all over the world. And don't even get me started on the variety of options in the menu!

It's difficult in our fast paced world to cultivate an undivided heart. There are always options that seek to capture our attention, so before we know it, we can find ourselves in multitask mode. Most women know this phase very well, it's probably the story of their lives. In multitask mode, you've got a million things going on at once, yet you try to give each task as much attention as possible. We can put our spiritual lives on multitask mode as well.

Spiritually speaking, we can have divided hearts when we focus on what's going on in our lives and put those things before our relationship with God. Whether it's our daily responsibilities, hopes and dreams we're pursuing, or even ourselves (what we want), when we put those things before God, our heart is divided. We're supposed to give God our all, but you and I know very well that multitask mode requires compartmentalizing your energy.

A heart that is undivided is powerful because it allows you to focus all of your energy and strength on one purpose. Therefore you're able to effect change more swiftly and efficiently. With such a conviction, perseverance will prevail no matter the difficulty faced. An undivided heart provides that sense of loyalty that will let you attempt and do the impossible for God.

It does not matter the state of your heart now; pray for the cultivation of an undivided heart that will transform your life, circumstances and the world in singleness of purpose. Move past the trivialities of life, and reverence the Lord with fear as you exercise faithfulness.

Prayer

Dear Father, you are first and foremost in my life. Help me to honor you as such and to remain single-minded and wholehearted unto you in Jesus' name. Amen.
Further Studies: *Psalm 27:4*

Throw It Away

"If your right eye causes you to sin, gouge it out and throw it away. It is better for you to lose one part of your body than for your whole body to be thrown into hell."
(Matthew 5:29)

I read a book recently that had a chapter entitled "Kill What Kills You." Pretty intense, right? When it comes to sin, this is the mentality that we need to have. It's very radical, but it's the only thing that will ultimately work. Although Jesus was addressing adultery in this particular passage, this principle most certainly relates to any type of bad habit that needs to be broken in our lives.

This is the problem with sin: when it gets attached to you, it rapidly festers and grows. Think of sin as a malignant tumor. When it is small, doctors can easily remove it and keep it from doing too much damage, but if you allow the tumor to grow, it can intermingle itself with vital organs and make it very difficult to remove. In some cases, removing the tumor might mean causing an untimely death.

In the same way, when we allow habitual sins to gain a foothold in our lives, we have the same option: cut it off early on or allow it to fester and spread until your spiritual death is the only option available. Sin is like a fatal disease. If you don't remove it from your body soon enough, it will take over.

Many times we can make excuses for our sin, "Oh, I'm not gossiping. I'm just filling my friend in on how so-and-so is doing" or "I know I said I wouldn't read these kind of novels anymore, but it's just one time." But the more excuses we make, the stronger the grip sin gets on our lives.

Whatever causes you to stumble needs to be cut off. Period. Ask yourself today: What is causing me to stumble? Once you've identified it, throw it away! Don't allow everything else that God has given you to be lost because of this one habit. It truly is a matter of life and death.

Prayer

Dear Father, please reveal to me today by your Holy Spirit what I need to remove from my life, and then I ask that you would give me the strength I need to not only cut it off, but to keep it off in Jesus' name. Amen.
Further Studies: *Colossians 3:5-6*

From Generation to Generation

"His mercy extends to those who fear him, from generation to generation."
(Luke 1:50)

Mary, the mother of Jesus, was a remarkable woman in the Bible, yet she was just as ordinary as you and I. Had God not selected her to be the means through which He would bring the Messiah into the world, I'm sure that no one else in her community would have seen anything *that* great about her. I may even go as far as to say that she might not have even thought there was anything too special about herself.

But Mary had an encounter with God that changed her life forever and with gratitude she sang this song to the Lord:

"My soul exalts the Lord,
And my spirit has rejoiced in God my Savior.
For He has had regard for the humble state of His bond slave;
For behold, from this time on all generations will count me blessed.
For the Mighty One has done great things for me;
And holy is His name.
And His mercy is upon generation after generation
Toward those who fear Him."
(Luke 1:46-50)

Mary recognized that it was only by the grace of God that she was chosen, but she also knew that the Lord has chosen her because she had been humble, faithful, and because she held a deep reverence for Him in her heart. Her joy came from that realization as well as the fact that she would have a great legacy to pass to her future descendants.

Like Mary, we all have legacies to leave for our children. It is my prayer that we all leave legacies of truth, holiness, righteousness, faith, commitment, grace, and fortitude. It will make all the difference in who our children become.

Prayer

Dear Father, help me to leave a great legacy of faith and spiritual fruit
for my children and generations to come in Jesus' name. Amen.
Further Studies: *Proverbs 13:22*

The Feast

"People will come from east and west and north and south, and
will take their places at the feast in the kingdom of God."
(Luke 13:29)

St. Louis, Missouri, is considered one of the biggest melting pots of the United States. Many refugees and immigrants come through the St. Louis port and ended up settling. Because of that mix of nationalities, there are a number of churches in the city that give a glimpse into what this scripture will look like one day. On any given Sunday, congregates can spend the worship service singing in five different languages, and the pastor himself can be from one of many countries.

It's amazing how salvation has the power to draw people from different cultures, counties, ethnicities, and colors together to stand beneath the banner of Jesus Christ as one. No matter how much we progress as a people, we always seem to have issues with racism, but under the leadership of Jesus, there is no discrimination, and all are welcome.

This is the beauty of salvation. It is no respecter of persons; it is a free gift available to anyone and everyone who chooses to believe. When Jesus stretched His arms out on the cross and died for the world, He extended the gift of salvation to anyone in the world that would receive Him. And it is my joy to declare that all over the world, many have received that gift.

Have you ever thought about what that day will be like when we're all united on the sea of glass or at the table of the wedding feast? In our imaginations we probably hear everyone crying "Holy, holy, holy is the Lord God Almighty" in English, but there will be thousands upon thousands of people declaring the same thing in various languages. Though we are different in many ways, the bond of the Spirit will make us one.

It's going to be absolutely incredible. Make sure that you are there.

Prayer

Dear Father, thank you for my brothers and sisters around the world
who stand with me as one of your children in Jesus' name. Amen.
Further Studies: *Ephesians 4:4-6*

Living Water

"Whoever believes in me, as Scripture has said, rivers of
living water will flow from within them."
(John 7:38)

Water has numerous benefits for the human body. Some of them include the following:

- Water aids in the relief of digestion and constipation.
- Water flushes out toxins.
- Water promotes healthy skin.
- Water helps regulate body temperature.
- Water aids in proper blood circulation.

Aside from the benefits we experience by increasing our water intake, there is one factor that trumps them all: life. Water can hold the power of life and death. We can only last three days without water (some people have made it to 8-10). That makes water pretty powerful stuff, if you ask me.

Now imagine "living" water flowing from our bodies. If intake of water has such benefits, how much more beneficial will be that which flows out of us! According to other Scriptures, living water not only quenches our thirst, but it also satisfies our soul eternally. We first drink of it when we receive salvation.

Once we've taken of the living water, we never thirst again and that living water begins to flow throughout our spiritual body. Almost 60% of our human bodies are made of water, so it goes without saying that water has a very big effect on our health and wellbeing. The same goes for us in the spiritual sense. When the living water is flowing through our veins, it's enough to bring about serious renewal in our lives as well.

Our belief in Jesus qualifies us to be purifying and survival agents to those around us. Let the word of God and His love flow as living water to everyone we meet.

Prayer

Dear Father, thank you for the living water you've placed inside of me. Continue filling me up to overflowing, so that I may pour it out on others in Jesus' name. Amen.
Further Studies: *John 4:14*

The Son Who Saves

*"She will give birth to a son, and you are to give him the name
Jesus, because he will save his people from their sins."*
(Matthew 1:21)

Have you ever known someone that seems to have one bad thing after another happen to them or to their family? Some people constantly deal with physical ailments while others can never seem to get a break in any sphere of their life. We might feel tempted to look at such people and feel that they are in need of a savior, but the truth is that we all need a Savior.

As far as God is concerned, sin is sin. It doesn't matter how we judge, and we tend to put sin on some sort of hierarchical list, anything we do that is outside of His will is sin. Period. So if you lied about anything, looked at someone with lust in your eyes, mistreated someone less fortunate than you, or called someone an "idiot," according to Jesus Himself (Matthew 5), you have sinned.

The announcement of the arrival of Jesus came with a promise: "He will save His people from their sins." This statement gives us the assurance that we have a fighting chance because there is someone who will do the fighting for us; someone who conquered death so that we wouldn't have to be a slave to it.

The arrival of Jesus had been long awaited by the Jews, and once He came, the world as they knew it would never be the same. Jesus broke off the yoke of religious responsibility that had come as a result of the law and the standards that people felt they could never reach. With His sacrifice came the opportunity for us to take on His righteousness as our own so that we can live eternally with Him one day.

Let us therefore embrace Jesus the savior and be sure to introduce Him to others who are in need of a savior.

Prayer

Dear Father, I would be so lost if you had not sent your son Jesus to come and save me from my sin. Thank you for Jesus and thank you for salvation, in His name I pray. Amen.
Further Studies: *John 3:16*

The Healer

"This was to fulfill what was spoken through the prophet Isaiah:
"He took up our infirmities and bore our diseases."
(Matthew 8:17)

The list of infirmities and diseases that plague humanity are inexhaustible. If you were to research the various types of diseases that have existed in years past alongside those that exist today, you would undoubtedly become quite overwhelmed. Some diseases are minor, but there are others that can completely ravage the body or even cause death.

You may know people affected by these types of diseases, or you may have issues with them yourself. This is one of the painful realities of our fallen nature as humans. We are prone not only to all manners of sin, but also all manners of disease.

But Jesus Christ came to set us free from sickness the same way He came to set us free from sin. He is the healer, and for EVERY sickness that has ever been named and for EVERY sickness that is yet to be named, He has taken them all upon Himself so that we don't have to be bound by them.

So why do we continue to live as though sickness and disease has any right to be in our lives?

Many Christians believe wholeheartedly that Jesus came to save us from our sins, but they struggle believing that Jesus also wants to heal our sickness. If a very large portion of Jesus's ministry on earth was to heal people from sickness, why would His motives have changed with us? He desires to heal just as much as He did 2,000 years ago when He made the blind to see and the lame to walk.

What ails you today? Are your emotions in turmoil or is your body aching with pain? Is your mind unstable? Come to the healer. He is waiting.

Prayer

Dear Father, thank you for healing me 2,000 years ago when
your son died on the cross in Jesus' name. Amen.
Further Studies: *Isaiah 53:5*

Come and Drink

"On the last and greatest day of the festival, Jesus stood and said in a loud voice, "Let anyone who is thirsty come to me and drink."
(John 7:37)

What happens to your body when you feel thirsty? Your mouth might get dry, you may pant a little, and you probably have this overwhelming *feeling* of needing something to drink. Thirst is an entirely different beast than hunger, because you can ignore a grumbling stomach and even learn to silence it, but thirst is a longing that is much harder to satisfy.

I sat and watched the kids scramble to the cooler after their game on the field had ended. Each and every child was anxious to get water to quench their thirst. It reminded me of long distance races and the way there are various water stops along the way to help the runners rehydrate. The more energy we exert, the more we sweat, and the more our body craves water to replenish our systems.

The same could be said for us as we run the race of life. This race is long and hard, and some of us have been running it for a very long time. As physically exhausting as a long distance race is on the body, so can our spirit man become weary. In order to refresh, rehydrate, and refuel our spirit, we must search for a spiritual form of water. That comes in the form of none other than Jesus Christ.

We're told of Jesus in John 1 that "the Word became flesh and dwelt among us." Jesus is the Word in the form of flesh, so when He tells us to drink of Him, we do that best by digging into His Word. Some of the psalmists and prophets even compared the Word to food for the soul or a fountain that never runs dry.

The invitation is clear: come and drink. Jesus will quench every thirst and strengthen you throughout your journey of life.

Prayer

Dear Father, I want to taste of you and not only see that you are good, but to be refreshed by the washing of your Word. Thank you for renewing me in body, soul, and spirit in Jesus' name. Amen.
Further Studies: *Isaiah 12:3-6*

In the Last Days

"In the last days, God says, 'I will pour out my Spirit on all people. Your sons and daughters will prophesy, your young men will see visions, your old men will dream dreams.'"
(Acts 2:17)

When God speaks a word, it goes into the earth, accomplishes what He sent it to do, and then it returns to the Father. Because God exists outside of time, from our perspective, His words can be spoken and hang in the air for hundreds of years before they're "activated." Sounds a little Sci-Fi, right? Well, there's a lot about the nature of God that is incomprehensible.

Hundreds of years before Jesus came to the earth, God spoke through the prophet Joel about things that were yet to come – an awesome outpouring and empowerment of the Holy Spirit. Essentially speaking, the same Spirit that searches the deep things of God (the same Spirit that was on Jesus during His ministry on the earth) would be poured out on the earth, and people would be able to operate in the very same anointing that Jesus had.

The prophecy of this Scripture has been fulfilled in part through previous generations, specifically in the book of Acts on the Day of Pentecost, but right now, at this very moment, this Scripture continues to hang above us in our atmosphere, waiting to be fulfilled. The fulfillment might come in our day or it might come in our children's day or it may even come for the children of our children. It doesn't matter when it will come to pass; just that *it will*. If God said it, it will happen.

We know what it was like for the disciples on the Day of Pentecost, but can you imagine what it will be like in those days before Jesus comes? At that point in time the earth will be filled with all manners of wickedness and chaos, YET the Spirit of the Lord will also be poured out in a powerful way. No power on earth will be able to compare!

In the last days the Spirit of God will reign supremely on all. Wait expectantly for it.

Prayer

Dear Father, your Spirit enables me to do more than I could ever think or imagine. I look forward to the day when I will be able to see the fullness of your Spirit poured out on mankind in Jesus' name. Amen.
Further Studies: *Joel 2:28-32*

Refreshing Comes

"Repent, then, and turn to God, so that your sins may be wiped out, that times of refreshing may come from the Lord."
(Acts 3:19)

We all understand the importance of repentance. God is holy, and He makes it very clear that the only people that can approach Him are those who have clean hands and a pure heart. As long as we have sin clinging to us, we cannot approach the One who dwells in unapproachable light. We must get rid of our sin, and the only way to do that is through confession and repentance.

Though we all struggle with different sins, there is one particular culprit behind our sin that most of us women have in common: our emotions. Women are very emotional beings, and if we're not careful, those emotions can govern the decisions we make, our actions, and even the state of our heart.

Did you realize that sin has to be preceded by a particular emotion? Anger usually precedes arguments and negative speech. Fear usually precedes lying and mistrust. Jealousy usually precedes gossip and slander, and pride usually precedes greed and poor treatment of others. You get the picture. If you don't have a good handle on your emotions, you cannot get a good handle on your sin.

Because we're human and the Lord knows we're prone to sin, we are going to fall short – no matter how diligently we try to keep our emotions in check. You know that feeling... You've committed to being kind to your husband, but one day he does something that rubs you the wrong way, and suddenly your resolve to be kind flies out the window. It happens to the best of us.

But thank God for His grace and mercy! Though we stumble, we can repent, get our slate wiped clean, and get back into the race. In His mercy, the Lord takes our sins and throws them as far away as the east is from the west, and He remembers them no more. So the next time you stumble, don't be too hard on yourself. Bring it to the Lord with a humble and contrite heart, and let Him take care of the rest.

Prayer

Dear Father, thank you for forgiving me when I come to you in repentance. It's only by your grace that I'm able to keep fighting the good fight in Jesus' name. Amen.
Further Studies: *Psalm 24:1-6*

Greatest in the Kingdom

"Therefore, whoever takes the lowly position of this child
is the greatest in the kingdom of heaven."
(Matthew 18:4)

Isn't it ironic that the world teaches that to be successful we have to "act like an adult" or to even "man up." yet Kingdom principles teach quite the opposite? In this world we value logic, climbing whatever ladders we can (social, career, etc.), and becoming the boss, but in the Kingdom of God, success is determined by faith, humility, and honesty – all characteristics of a child.

Children can sometimes be looked upon as a nuisance. The disciples certainly thought so when a group of children approached Jesus one day. They tried to shoo the kids away, yet Jesus rebuked the disciples and said, "Let the little children come to me." Why would Jesus do that? Because He could see past the noise and energy exuding from the children; He saw a teachable moment.

First, children are entirely dependent on their parents to take care of them. In the same way, we are to be entirely dependent on the Lord. Instead of believing that we can take care of ourselves or do things on our own, we should realize that all things come from our Father's hand.

Secondly, children speak freely. Whatever they're thinking usually comes right out of the mouths. As we get older, we learn to guard our thoughts and mouths (sometimes for better and sometimes for worse), but we generally replace transparency with skepticism. We never know who we can trust with our secrets. But God wants us to be completely open with Him, to come to Him with our burdens and concerns and share without inhibition.

Finally, children have very strong faith. When they're told something, they believe it. God wants us to take Him at His word and to believe that He is who He says He is and that He'll do what He said He would do. The greatest in the Kingdom is the lowly position of a child. They may not be invited to the table of our important meetings here on earth, but they will surely have a seat of honor at the table of the Lord for the marriage supper of the Lamb. It would therefore seem that you and I need to follow suit and take up our positions.

Prayer

Dear Father, help me to be more like a child in my dependency, transparency, and faith in Jesus' name. Amen.
Further Studies: *Matthew 9:13-15*

Which Measure?

"With the measure you use, it will be measured to you and even more."
(Mark 4:24b)

This concept of measurement comes up a lot in the Bible. It is often referred to as the law of retribution. You know, an "eye for an eye," "forgive as you want to be forgiven," "deny Jesus and He will deny you." Basically, regardless of the situation, whether positive or negative, you will reap what you sow, so you should be sure to sow only that which you want returned to you.

In this particular instance, the law of retribution comes into play in a positive sense. The measure with which you utilize the knowledge you have gleaned from the Word and the more you labor to understand it and share it with others, the larger measure of spiritual knowledge will be given back to you.

It's similar to the parable of the three men that were given varying amounts of talents. The master gave five talents to one, two to another, and one to yet another. The two men with five and two talents worked hard to double the amount they had been given, while the third man buried his talent in fear of his master. The third man's talent was taken from him and given to the man with ten talents, and he lost his position, while the other two received great reward and blessing from their master.

In the same way, we have a responsibility to take the Word and not only be hearers, but to become doers. We are to put our knowledge into action, and when we lack knowledge, we should search for it as for hidden treasure. God loves to honor people who pursue Him and His Word. Remember the Bereans?

Today let's look at which measure we utilize because assuredly that's what we will get in return. Ensure that it is the best measure.

Prayer

Dear Father, your word is food to my soul. I choose today to take the knowledge you have given me and use it to the best of my ability in Jesus' name. Amen.
Further Studies: *Matthew 25:14-30*

Yea and Amen

*"For all the promises of God find their 'Yes' in him. That is why it is
through him that we utter our 'Amen' to God for his glory."*
(2 Corinthians 1:20)

A judge's gavel is the ultimate symbol of authority in a court room. It has the power to bring an entire room of rowdy people to a hushed silence, and it can establish whatever verdict the judge has declared. It may just be a small carved block of wood, but with one bang of this gavel, a matter is established.

Judges are very powerful people in their own right. They uphold the standards of the law, control the proceedings of the court, and make decisions impartially all in the name of justice. They can set people free or send them away for the rest of their lives. If you ever have to appear before a judge, you'd better hope you are standing before one that is merciful.

But there is no judge more powerful or merciful than the Almighty God.

When God makes a promise, I envision Him lifting His gavel and hitting it. As He does so, He does not only firmly establish the words He has declared, but He also interrupts all the rules and proclamations of the enemy that would forfeit it from being fulfilled. Whatever word He speaks becomes law, and there isn't anyone or anything that can overturn the laws of God.

Therefore, if God has made a promise, there is no reason to question its validity; the answer is "Yes." No matter what the situation looks like, the answer is "Yes." He will be faithful to do what He said He would do. So the only appropriate response on our part should be, "Amen," which means "so be it." Whatever He has promised, we agree with and declare that it shall be done on earth as it is in heaven.

Prayer

*Dear Father, your word stands forever. Thank you for being
a kind and merciful judge in Jesus' name. Amen.*
Further Studies: *Psalm 106:3*

What wages are you working for?

"For the wages of sin is death, but the gift of God is eternal life in Christ Jesus our Lord."
(Romans 6:23)

No matter what kind of job you work – whether you're deck attendant at the local swimming pool, a manager of a grocery store, or a high level executive – you expect to be compensated for the work you've done. How much you receive is dependent upon the contract you signed, your scope, and the amount of time you've worked. This is a basic principle of society and economy.

Things don't work any differently in the economy of sin and salvation. The payment we receive for sin is death: both physical and spiritual. Before sin entered the picture, Adam had what could have been an eternal life with eternal relationship with God, but the stain of sin meant that he lost out on all of that. All that was due him was death and separation from God.

Because of the sin of Adam, the father of humanity, we were also condemned to die, so Jesus had to come and take on that penalty for us and die in our place so that He could renew that eternal relationship with God. He had to bridge the gap between us and God that sin had built.

Therefore, salvation's wages are eternal life in Christ Jesus. When we receive the gift of salvation that Jesus paid for with His blood, we not only receive the gift of eternal life, but we also get to spend that eternity in the presence of God. Who could ask for anything better?

Every day of your life you have a choice about what kind of wages you will receive. Either you engage in sin and reap the wages of death, or you engage in your salvation and reap eternal life. What wages are you working for?

The choice is yours to make; weigh the options choose life. It will be worth it!

Prayer

Dear Father, thank you for the gift of being able to spend eternity with you in Jesus' name. Amen.
Further Studies: *Romans 5:12*

Not Forgotten

*"They will ask for the way to Zion, turning their faces in its
direction; they will come that they may join themselves to the Lord
in an everlasting covenant that will not be forgotten."*
(Jeremiah 50:5)

Have you ever run into someone who claims that they know you from some point in your past, yet you do not recognize them at all, nor do you remember the nature of your relationship to them? Moments like that can prove to be quite awkward for both parties involved. No one likes to feel like the impression they left on someone wasn't one worth remembering.

Imagine then how someone would feel if they had made a promise with someone and then that person totally went back on the promise or flat out forgot that the promise had been made. That would surely feel worse, maybe even like a betrayal of sorts.

As believers, we have a covenant with God. We are His people, and He is our God. When we choose to live under His leadership, we vow to live in obedience to Him, and He vows to care for us and to love us with an everlasting love. This covenant was signed in blood, the blood that Jesus shed for us. It is binding and eternal.

Though God never forgets His promise to us, we sometimes slip back into old habits or discover other "loves" that force us to break our covenant with God. Essentially, we forget the promise we made with Him. Thankfully for us, God in His mercy knows that we are weak, so He forgives us and upholds the covenant on our behalf.

One day we will set our faces to seek Him and we will pursue Him and the covenant that we've made between ourselves will not be forgotten on either side. The covenant has always been eternal, but on this day our love and faithfulness will also be eternal, and we will never forget. Let's make that day today.

Prayer

*Dear Father, I choose today to recommit myself to you and to never
forget the covenant that we have. Thank you for never breaking your
end. Help me to be as faithful as you are in Jesus' name. Amen.*
Further Studies: *2 Timothy 2:11-13*

Cast Your Anxiety on Him

"Cast all your anxiety on him because he cares for you."
(1 Peter 5:7)

Your mind is racing and so is your heart. As sweat pours from your brow, you try to hold on to what you know is true, but the truth seems to be eluding you. Fear has taken over. Your body is tense, your stomach is in your throat, and you are certain that danger is nearby. This is a description of what it feels like for someone to have an anxiety attack. For those of us who have had them, they can be terribly frightening and debilitating.

Anxiety can creep up on us in many ways, it doesn't have to be in the form of a full out anxiety attack, but we all know what it feels like to be fearful and worried about situations. Anxiety often comes as the result of focusing on problems and allowing ourselves to become overwhelmed by them.

For women who lean towards being more introverted, they are also more prone to issues with anxiety because they have a habit of mulling over things. When you mull over a problem again and again, every time you recycle the thought in your brain, it becomes bigger and harder to deal with.

The recommendation is to cast your anxiety on Jesus Christ. The weight of the problems we face in life is too much for us to bear. We weren't meant to carry them, but Jesus is. He was sent to this earth for that very purpose, to take our burdens upon Himself. When we fall prey to anxiety, we choose to hold onto the burden and forsake the open arms of Jesus. Friend, this should not be so.

Whenever you feel like a particular problem is causing you to have anxious thoughts, worry, or fear – take a deep breath, fix your thoughts on Jesus, and mentally give that problem over to Him. You will be able to breathe freely, experience peace and find solutions.

Go ahead and do it today!

Prayer

Dear Father, I cast all of my anxieties on you today, knowing that you are more than able to bear the weight of them in Jesus' name. Amen.
Further Studies: *Proverbs 3:5-6*

Planted by the Father

"He replied, "Every plant that my heavenly Father has
not planted will be pulled up by the roots."
(Matthew 15:13)

n this passage of Scripture, the word "plant" can be used as symbolism for the physical person and for particular habits, doctrines, and beliefs. You may be familiar with the parable of the sower that represents God as the sower, the seed as His word, and the various types of soil as the state of our hearts, but it is important that we realize that God isn't the only one who can sow into our lives.

As for the first point of symbolism, plants representing people, this verse can refer to people that do not belong to the Lord as compared to those who do. Jesus was addressing the Pharisees here, people who clearly were not messengers of God, but messengers of religious law. He wanted them to know that those who were established in the Jewish community that had not been put there by God would be removed.

The Pharisees were wicked leaders, but as far as the rest of the Jewish community knew, they were representatives of what God expected of them. They were themselves, bad seeds. We also have leaders that appear to be good, but have ulterior motives or bad intentions. Just as the Pharisees were, those people will also be uprooted when the time comes.

The second point of symbolism is more applicable to our lives. It refers to false teachings and doctrines. Again, this is what the Pharisees in that day and age were teaching, and it was abominable to Christ. In this wise they were planting bad seeds in others. By speaking this statement, Jesus was declaring that the plant of the Pharisees would one day be uprooted, and the only thing that would remain is the Word of God.

God, the good sower, only plants what is true, noble, of good report, and lovely. Those are the things that we should be meditating on. Let's endeavor to stay planted by reading His Word, praying, fasting and meeting together.

Prayer

Dear Father, I ask that if there is any plant rooted in my heart that was
not planted by you, that you would remove it. I prepare my heart to
be good soil, ready to receive your word in Jesus' name. Amen.
Further Studies: *Matthew 13:1-30*

Stand Firm

"Therefore, my dear brothers and sisters, stand firm. Let nothing move you. Always give yourselves fully to the work of the Lord, because you know that your labor in the Lord is not in vain."
(1 Corinthians 15:58)

Beth has experienced her fair share of storms, promotions, setbacks, illnesses, births and marriages, deaths of loved ones, weddings, birthdays, grandchildren, and anniversaries – among other things. As she reflects on her life in her old age, she remembers the intermingling of pain and joy that accompanied each and every moment. Oh, what a tangled web life wove for her.

Regardless, Beth has learned not to allow any of these things to move her. Instead of dwelling on the negatives and allowing despair or depression to overtake her, she chose to celebrate each trial she faced, because she knew that one day she would see the fulfillment of a promise the Lord gave her: one day she'll enter His rest where there would be no more pain, tears, or suffering, and she would see her loved ones again. She will receive her great reward.

When you have a hope like Beth's to look forward, it makes it much easier to do as this Scripture says, and give yourself fully to the work of the Lord. Sometimes God calls us to make very hard decisions, to leave people we love, and to give until we feel like we have nothing left to give. In those moments we can question God or complain, but that would only serve to demonstrate a lack of vision and trust in His plan.

What we have to remind ourselves is that no one whose hope is in the Lord will ever be put to shame. We don't have to be scared that one day we're going to find out that all of our efforts for the Lord were in vain. Everything done in the name of Jesus will stand the test of time and even if you don't see the reason or the reward from your service in this lifetime, you will see it when you stand face to face with the Lord in eternity.

It really is a matter of perspective, so stand firm and don't be moved.

Prayer

Dear Father, I trust and believe that one day it's all going to be worth it, every struggle, every tear, and every question. Help me to align my perspective to yours more and more in Jesus' name. Amen.
Further Studies: Psalm 25:3

Forgiveness

"For if you forgive other people when they sin against you,
your heavenly Father will also forgive you."
(Matthew 6:14)

Many people are familiar with the Lord's Prayer or even know it by heart, but not many people know the verse that directly follows the Lord's Prayer. It's the one listed above. Did you know that the effectiveness of the Lord's Prayer is contingent upon whether or not we forgive? Leave alone the Lord's Prayer for a minute, did you know that your prayer life is greatly affected by the relationship that you maintain (or don't maintain) with people?

Just one chapter before this one, Jesus begins His Sermon on the Mount by telling His disciples that if they are preparing to bring an offering before the Lord but have issues with their brother, they are to leave their offering there, go and make amends, and then return. That's how much God values us having a clean slate before we approach Him in prayer.

Though forgiveness comes highly commanded by God, our obedience to this command does more than keep us in line with His Word; it liberates us. To live in unforgiveness can literally wear you down emotionally, physically, mentally, and spiritually. Many people have discovered that the root cause of illnesses they're facing is unforgiveness. It's a very powerful tool that the enemy loves to use to keep us in bondage.

To forgive is to release negative thoughts such as resentment, bitterness, and the desire for revenge. As much as we were hurt by someone or as much as we feel they need to pay for what they did to us, the longer we harbor unforgiveness in our hearts, the quicker it turns to bitterness, and as it turns out, you are the only one being hurt by your bitterness. It clogs up *your* soul and dampens *your* relationship with God, but does nothing to anyone else.

Regardless of the offence that was committed against you, you have to choose to give up the desire to execute judgment. Judgment belongs to the Lord, not to you, and as a good judge, God measures the way He'll forgive you against the way you forgive others. Make the choice today to forgive so that you can be set free and continue to enjoy your open line of communication with the Lord.

Prayer

Dear Father, you have forgiven me of so much. Help me to forgive others in the same way in Jesus' name. Amen.
Further Studies: *1 Corinthian 13:4-7*

Legacy

"Only be careful, and watch yourselves closely, so that you do not forget the things your eyes have seen or let them fade from your heart as long as you live. Teach them to your children and to their children after them."
(Deuteronomy 4:9)

Before the process of turning papyrus into paper came about, stories were shared orally. A grandfather would sit down and share stories of his past and the valuable lessons he learned therein, while his children, grandchildren, and great grandchildren gathered around and listened.

Sharing stories in this way was vital to keeping memories alive, because unless a memory was passed from one person to the next, it would be lost forever when the person carrying that story left this world.

When God delivered the Israelites from Egypt, He reminded them constantly to share the story of how He delivered them from slavery with their children and their children's children. That story was pivotal in the relationship between God and Israel, and God wanted every generation thereafter to know what He had done for the sake of His people. For the sake of love.

We also have a mandate to share the story of how we were delivered by the blood of Jesus with our children. We are to share our testimonies with them so that one day, when they're in the midst of trouble, they can say, "The same God who was faithful to my mother and father will surely be faithful to me."

Prayer

Lord, empower me to tell of your miracles every day in Jesus' name. Amen.
Further Studies: *Psalms 105*

Training

"Train a child in the way he should go, and when he is old he will not turn from it."
(Proverbs 22:6)

You must understand that we, as parents, have a God-given responsibility to train our children and bring them up in the right way. Though both parents are responsible for training their children, much of the training is typically done by mothers, because mothers are usually the ones that spend more time raising the kids.

This isn't by accident. No, it is a very great opportunity God has given you to pour into the lives of your children. Therefore, you should view every minute you get to spend with your children as time that God has ordained for you to provide teachable moments and to live the kind of lifestyle you would want your children to live.

Our opening scripture is not just wise counsel, but it is a command which you must obey; not only because God said so, but because it's the only way to ensure that when your children walk out of your home as young adults, they do so with a good head on their shoulders.

We have all been trained in one way or another (i.e. sports, fitness, academics, etc.) and can identify with the benefits that training gives. It's never an easy process, and sometimes it isn't even fun, but it's worth it. Therefore, be diligent with training your children. God will work out the rest.

Prayer

Dear Lord, I thank you for the responsibility of training the children in my care. I thank you because I have the grace and the understanding to do so diligently in Jesus' name. Amen.
Further Studies: *Proverbs 29:15*

Like Sarah

"...like Sarah, who obeyed Abraham and called him her lord. You are her daughters if you do what is right and do not give way to fear."
(1 Peter 3:6)

n this scripture, the act of Sarah calling Abraham lord was an act of submission and obedience, as "lord" means *a person who has authority, control, or power over others; a master, chief or ruler.*

Submission is a word that makes many of us women cringe because it has been overly misused. Most often it has been used as a way for men to do what they want with little to no input from their wives. Considering the gift of intuition the Lord has given women, it goes without saying that to be forced to follow someone that believes contrary to yourself isn't easy.

Still, when the Lord told Sarah that she would have a child at the ripe old age of 90, as laughable as the notion was, she showed her husband respect by calling him "lord" instead of "fool," or any other name she could have used. She may not have agreed entirely with what Abraham believed, but she still honored him by submitting to him and trusting that as the head of their household, he had heard from the Lord.

Like Sarah, be submissive and obedient and see how God will work things out for your good. If you want to enjoy your marriage, you must operate by the Word of God. You don't need to be married to practice submission though. We should submit to those in authority. Godly submission is faith that God will work through your authority to accomplish what is best for you.

Prayer

Dear Lord, I choose to live in line with your Word by submitting to the relevant authorities in Jesus' name. Amen.
Further Studies: *Ephesians 5:21-24*

December

Praise at the City Gate

"Charm is deceptive, and beauty is fleeting; but a woman
who fears the LORD is to be praised.
Give her the reward she has earned, and let her works bring her praise at the city gate."
(Proverbs 31:30-31)

Fashion, beauty, and body shapes seem to be the most important things to women of this generation. There are many women out there who will do anything humanly possible to maintain their youthful looks after having kids. There is nothing wrong with having and maintaining a good shape. The problem comes when that is all you care about.

Our opening scripture teaches that charm is deceptive because it will fade; beauty is fleeting because with time wrinkles will set in. The character and quality of your spirit is what makes you a woman worth being praised. The word of God is the material for us to build a good character, so if you fear the Lord, you will live and pattern your life by His word.

You've seen and admired women who have stood the test of time and wondered, "Can I be like her? Do I have the courage?" Women such as Abigail in I Samuel 25, Eleanor Roosevelt, and Rosa Parks. You have got it in you, you love God, and you keep His commands and strive to become more like Jesus. By doing these things, you will not only be praise worthy on this part of eternity, but you will also be praised in heaven as well.

It's not about how you look, nor does it has nothing to do with your charisma. It is the fact that you fear God and live your life to please Him ensures that you will be rewarded with praise at your city gate.

Prayer

Dear Father, thank you for placing beauty deep inside of me when you created me. Help me to live by that standard of beauty instead of the world's in Jesus' name. Amen.
Further Studies: *1 Peter 3:1-6*

You will be Blessed

"When you give a reception, invite the poor, the crippled, the lame, the blind, and you will be blessed, since they do not have the means to repay you; for you will be repaid at the resurrection of the righteous."
(Luke 14:13-14, NASB)

Jesus used the parable of the great supper to illustrate a very important spiritual lesson for us. In this parable, a man was planning to host a big dinner. He had invited many people of noble status throughout the country, but all that he got in return for his invitation was a bunch of excuses from everyone.

His response: replace the ones who ungratefully rejected his invitation with those who would have nothing but gratitude for receiving something they knew they either did not deserve or could not afford.

Through this parable, Jesus encourages us to follow suit. Whether we realize it or not, we have a tendency to do good things for people that we know can do good things for us in return. It's kind of a "you scratch my back, and I'll scratch yours" mentality. But as natural as it may seem, this frame of mind is certainly not a kingdom perspective.

The kingdom perspective says that we should go the extra mile to serve others; to be kind to those that we know are not able to repay us. Think about your relationship with Jesus for a second. Spiritually, before you met Him, you were poor, crippled, lame, and blind. Just as this group of people were outcasts within their society, you were an outcast. You did not deserve, nor did you have the means to repay, all that Jesus did for you, but He did it anyway. All that He is asking is that you extend the same courtesy to others.

True kindness or generosity gives in spite of what you expect to receive in return – and that includes a "thank you". Sometimes people will receive your gift without even acknowledging how grateful they are, but even if you are never thanked for the kind deeds you do for others here on earth, you must believe that you are storing up a reward for yourself in heaven, and you will receive that reward in due time.

God sees what is done in secret, and He rewards you for it. Truthfully, He actually prefers it that way because He views those secret acts of kindness as worship unto Him. When we do things for the praise of men, unfortunately, that is all the reward we get, so endeavor to serve others. It is the way to live and honor God.

Prayer

Dear Father, thank you for being so kind and merciful towards me when I was rejected and an outcast. Help me to do the same for others in Jesus' name. Amen.
Further Studies: *Matthew 6:1-4*

Fishers of Men

"'Come, follow me,' Jesus said, 'and I will make you fishers of men.'"
(Matthew 4:19, BSB)

Long before Jesus had shown up on the scene, some of His disciples had become well acquainted with the lifestyle of a fisherman. They knew how to make proper nets for the size of fish they needed to catch, they knew where to fish, when to fish, and the best rates for their product. They may have known a lot about catching fish, but little did they know, the Son of God was coming to teach them to become fishers of men.

So what exactly is a fisher of men? Well, let's assume that in this metaphor the ocean represents the world with all its sin and pollution, and we are the fish in the sea. The boat represents the kingdom of God, and the fishermen in the boat are ambassadors of that kingdom. Their job is to catch our attention with the Word of God (the net) and bring us into the kingdom. Sounds simple enough, right?

Well, if you know anything about the kind of fishing these men did, you would know that it wasn't that easy. These men normally caught a ton of fish at once, and as the fish were being lifted out of the water, they would all writhe and struggle at once. If the fisherman was trying to pull the lot in by himself or if he was not properly prepared, he could easily lose his grip on the net and drop the fish (his meal ticket) back into the water.

In the same way, fishing for men isn't always simple. We may not cast our net as wide as the disciples back did then and lead hundreds of people to the Lord at once, but even on our single fishing line, with that one person on the other end, we may encounter some "pull-back." Have you ever tried witnessing to someone only to have them fight their need for Jesus or to even try to fight you? Fishing for men takes a lot of patience and endurance.

One thing that helps us to become better in this fishing business is to remember what it was like when you first came to the Lord. You undoubtedly had questions and concerns, and maybe you even pulled back against the line as the Holy Spirit used people to draw you in. Ask yourself what you needed most in that moment of your life. What most people need is someone to gently lead them in the way that they should go; someone to be empathetic to their situation and lovingly introduce them to their new life after receiving the salvation of Jesus Christ. Will you be that person for someone today?

Prayer

Dear Father, you have made me a fisher of men, and I want to excel at this task. Teach me to be kind and empathetic to those you want me to bring into the fold, in Jesus' name. Amen.
Further Studies: *Matthew 4:18-22*

Repentance

"And Jesus answered and said to them, 'It is not those who are well who need a physician, but those who are sick. I have not come to call the righteous but sinners to repentance.'"
(Luke 5:31-32)

At the time that Jesus spoke these words, He had been dining with Levi, a tax collector (the type of person that was known for being a notorious thief). Jesus had just called Levi to become his disciple, so Levi invited Jesus into his home for a feast. Some of the teachers of the law sat around grumbling and complaining about the way Jesus (the King of the Jews, no less) was spending so much time with sinners.

What the Pharisees were really asking were, "Why would you spend time with *them*, when we're so much more righteous?" The Pharisees took great pride in how "close to God" they were, and they took every opportunity to let other people know about it. Whether it was in their loud and proud prayers, their announcements of their good deeds, or even in the type of clothing they wore, everyone believed that the Pharisees were untouchable. Everyone that is, except for Jesus. When He said this statement, He said it directly to the Pharisees.

Likewise, the perspective that most people, both Christians and non-Christian alike, maintain about the church is that the people in it are supposed to be perfect. Yes, God will one day give us a sin-free life in eternity with Him, but there is no reason for us to live in pretense and act as though everything is perfect now.

Much like the Pharisees, we may announce our good deeds and tidbits about our relationship with God on social media, use the most eloquent language we can muster up when we pray, and we make sure that we wear our "Sunday best," but that's not what Jesus came for. Now none of these things are bad in and of themselves, but they can pose a problem when we begin to exclude others because they don't meet our standards.

The only standard that we should be aspiring to reach is that of daily repentance and contrition. We all have sinned and fallen short of the glory of God. We all are in need of forgiveness. As David Alan Campbell said, "Avoiding God because you've made mistakes is like avoiding a doctor because you got sick... You're running from the exact person you need." So when we gather together, instead of pretending we have it all together, let's try confessing our sins and being real with one another. That's what Jesus wants to see, and it's what we really need.

Prayer

Dear Father, your word says that no one is righteous, not even one. Help me to never rely on my own righteousness and to continually come to you in repentance in Jesus' name. Amen.
Further Studies: *James 5:16*

Teacher and Lord

"You call me 'Teacher' and 'Lord,' and rightly so, for that is what I am."
(John 13:13)

With her face tilted up towards the rising sun, Maya smiled as the light gently washed over her, illuminating her entire frame. There was something about the sunlight that always managed to fill her heart with an abundance of radiant joy. Its rays had a way of soaking through her skin and bringing a sweet warmth into her heart.

If you've ever basked in the sun, you know how good the sunlight can feel on your skin. But have you ever thought about the way Jesus, the Great Teacher and the Light of the World uses the Word to illuminate our hearts and minds? The process is equally beautiful.

Back in the days of Jesus, young Jewish boys would find a rabbi or teacher that they could "yoke" themselves to, and they would follow him around and learn whatever he had to teach – much in the same manner that the disciples did with Jesus. The rabbi had a responsibility to share with his students everything that he knew.

These two words, "Teacher" and "Lord" refer to Jesus' position as the rabbi of His twelve disciples. They understood their relationship to Him within the confines of the Jewish context, but as far as Jesus was concerned, their relationship went much deeper than that.

Jesus was doing more with his disciples than simply teaching them the intricate nuances of the sacred text. When Jesus was teaching the disciples, He was revealing deep mysteries of God, illuminating revelation in their hearts about the reality of who He really was, and equipping the disciples to become "mini-Christs" and followers of the Way so they could carry on His work after He left.

There were kingdom principles that had not yet been unlocked in Scripture and details about the nature of God that not even the Psalmists had glimpsed into, yet the Rabbi Christ was freely sharing this information with His disciples. They were so privileged!

We have that same privilege. The Lord wants to illuminate our hearts and minds and fill them with the knowledge of Himself, His Word, and His plan for mankind. If we're willing to listen and receive His light, we can go very far. Will you make Him teacher and Lord of your life too?

Prayer

Dear Father, I want to feel the illumination of your word
in my heart today in Jesus's name. Amen.
Further Studies: *Psalm 119:105*

The Will of the Father

"Not everyone who says to me, 'Lord, Lord,' will enter the kingdom of heaven, but only he who does the will of my Father who is in heaven."
(Matthew 7:21)

Do you look back on your early days of your relationship with Jesus and feel as though you are currently nowhere near how intimate you used to be with Him? Maybe you used to spend hours in the secret place with Him or you felt like you were easily able to engage with His Spirit. How does that compare to your relationship with Him now?

A woman's mind is complex and typically spends most of the day working in overdrive. This only becomes more of an issue when you add the responsibilities of being a wife and mother. Everyone needs you for this and that, and you can easily get sidetracked from whatever you intended to do that day – including spending time with God. This may be the reality of your life, but it doesn't have to be. It just means that we have to challenge ourselves to make a concerted effort to keep our relationship with God on track.

Entrance into the kingdom of God is all about relationship. Think about it. The Church is called the Bride of Christ, and when this world ends, it will end with a celebration – a marriage celebration between the Church and Christ. If our lives are supposed to end in a marriage, then shouldn't we be living our lives as one who is betrothed to be married? Shouldn't we be developing our relationship with Christ in anticipation for our wedding day?

Part of our preparation as a spiritual bride is to not only be hearers, but also doers of the word. It's to have a relationship so close with the Lord that you can hear His voice when He speaks and because your trust is so firm, you don't have to second guess Him. It's to be a friend of God.

So we must be diligent to stay focused on doing God's will. There may be a million other things vying for your attention, but you have to make a choice to prioritize your relationship with God. Ask the Holy Spirit to give you spiritual insight on how to organize your life around Him instead of trying to fit Him in otherwise. He'll know what to do.

Prayer

Dear Father, what a privilege it is to be called your Bride. Help me by your Spirit to be one who walks worthy of that calling so that I can be pure and spotless when you come for me in Jesus' name. Amen.

Further Studies: *James 1:22*

Call on the Name of the Lord

"And everyone who calls on the name of the Lord will be saved."
(Acts 2:21)

You may recall back when you were a kid the way you responded whenever you were in distress. If you hurt yourself on the slide, who did you call? Mom. If you got sick to your stomach and needed someone to take care of you, who did you call? Mom. If you were afraid of things that go *bump* in the night, who did you call? Mom. Kids know that they can call their mothers because they know that once Mom shows up, everything will be okay.

In times of deep distress and sorrow, sometimes it's only the whisper of the name of the Lord that can get one through turmoil. Take for instance one of the powerful accounts of King David:

"In my distress I called upon the Lord, and cried to my God for help;
He heard my voice out of His temple, and my cry for help before Him came into His ears.
Then the earth shook and quaked;
And the foundations of the mountains were trembling
and were shaken, because He was angry.
Smoke went up out of His nostrils, and fire from His
mouth devoured; coals were kindled by it.
He bowed the heavens also, and came down with thick darkness under His feet.
He rode upon a cherub and flew; and He sped upon the wings of the wind.
He made darkness His hiding place, His canopy around Him,
darkness of waters, thick clouds of the skies.
From the brightness before Him passed His thick clouds, hailstones and coals of fire.
The Lord also thundered in the heavens, and the Most High
uttered His voice, hailstones and coals of fire.
He sent out His arrows, and scattered them, and lightning
flashes in abundance, and routed them.
Then the channels of water appeared, and the foundations of the world were laid bare
At Your rebuke, O Lord, at the blast of the breath of Your nostrils.

He sent from on high, He took me; He drew me out of many waters.
He delivered me from my strong enemy, and from those
who hated me, for they were too mighty for me.
They confronted me in the day of my calamity, but the Lord was my stay.
He brought me forth also into a broad place; He rescued me, because He delighted in me.
(Psalm 18:6-19)

Whatever the situation you are facing, remember the Lord delights in you. Call on His name, and you will be saved.

Prayer

Dear Father, I trust that as You did for David, You will
come through for me in Jesus' name. Amen.
Further Studies: *Psalm 145:18*

Poor but Rich

*"Listen, my dear brothers and sisters: Has not God chosen those
who are poor in the eyes of the world to be rich in faith and to
inherit the kingdom he promised those who love him?"*
(James 2:5)

There are numerous beauties to behold when visiting a third world country: the breathtaking natural scenery, the simplicity of daily life, and even the people. But there is something even more beautiful that is typically a commonality in third world countries and among the poor in first world countries. It's their faith.

When you meet people who would be considered poor in the eyes of the world, you'll discover that they don't hold onto their possessions very tightly. In fact, they don't derive much pleasure from their "things" at all. What they do value, is their belief that God is watching out for them and providing for every single need that they have.

I remember hearing the story of a missionary who had visited South Africa with a large team of missionaries who were canvassing a slum and developing relationships with the people in order to get them connected with a local church. There was one particular woman in her early twenties that this missionary encountered one day.

This woman had given birth to a child, but the father of the child had not only left her, he had also recently died of AIDS, which he had given to her. The woman was forced to live with her mother as she awaited the fate of her own mortality, as well as that of her child's. When the missionary came to visit this woman, the woman poured out her heart and shared her story, so the missionary prayed with her and shared some words of encouragement.

As the missionary and her team were preparing to leave, she asked the woman if she wanted a Bible. The young woman's eyes lit up her entire face, and she yelped, "Yes!" When the Bible was revealed, the woman hungrily grabbed it and began flipping through the pages and jumping up and down. You would think the Bible was some kind of treasure the way she lovingly held it to her chest.

Even though the young woman's world was crumbling around her, the one thing that brought her joy was her faith – God's Word was literally food to her soul. The world may not think much of her now, but one day she will be exalted to a high place in the kingdom of God for her strong and continual faith. Let's be challenged by the faith of this woman and those around us who maintain their love for Jesus in spite of their poverty.

Prayer

Dear Father, please help me to remember my spiritual poverty in Jesus' name. Amen.
Further Studies: *Matthew 19:30*

Led by the Spirit

"For those who are led by the Spirit of God are the children of God."
(Romans 8:14)

I often wonder how people survive without God in their lives. How do they make decisions for themselves or for their family? How do they trust that their needs will be met from day to day? If you ask me, life without God is pretty scary.

Back in the Old Testament, everyone knew that the Israelites were God's children because there was an obvious pillar of cloud that led them through the wilderness during the day, and a pillar of fire during the night. They would follow each respective pillar to a location, set up camp, and when the pillar moved again, they knew it was time to pick up and move as well. It was hard for the world not to notice who they belonged to! I believe God used this as a symbolic example of what He would do for future generations.

Today, the Holy Spirit's guidance is what helps us as believers make it through each day. He whispers directions into our hearts and keeps us from going down the wrong path or from making bad decisions. Many times it is that still small voice that keeps us out of danger and gives us the solutions we need.

The Holy Spirit's job is to help us navigate the many pathways of life and to bring us to full maturity in Christ. As talented or as smart as we think we are, we would be nothing without His guidance. There's no better source for us to get our directions from than the very spirit of the Living and Almighty God!

Just as all the people in surrounding areas could see the pillars of cloud and fire and know that the people following those pillars belonged to the Lord, so does the evidence of the Holy Spirit within us show people that we are children of God. People who follow the guidance of the Holy Spirit embody His fruit: love, joy, peace, patience, kindness, goodness, faithfulness, gentleness, and self-control. They serve others above themselves; they share the Good News of Jesus. In all we do and say, we show the world that the Holy Spirit lives in us, and those in the world will know that we are Christians by our love.

Thank God for the precious Holy Spirit who counsels us. Allow the Holy Spirit to help you today.

Prayer

Dear Father, thank you for sending your Holy Spirit to counsel me. I will incline my ear and listen to what He has to say in Jesus' name. Amen.
Further Studies: *Isaiah 30:21*

Secret Giving

"...so that your giving may be in secret. Then your Father,
who sees what is done in secret, will reward you."
(Matthew 6:4)

Frida had a friend that was going through a difficult financial season. The friend had shared how hard life was at that point in time, and how much she had been praying for help. Frida knew she needed to help her friend, but instead of writing a check right there on the spot, she decided to do something different.

She took some cash and placed it in an envelope and wrote "Love, Jesus" on it. Then she went to her friend's apartment and slid the envelope under the door, making sure to quickly leave the building without her friend knowing. A few days later the two friends were in the car together when the woman who had received the gift began sharing about the "miracle" that had happened earlier that week. The other woman quietly sat and listened without saying a single word. Guess who got all of the glory from that story when it was all said and done? Jesus.

God often uses people to answer prayers, both large and small, throughout the world. There are times that He uses us and there's no way for us to hide our part in it, but God loves it when we can be used by Him and then get out of the way so that the praise isn't misdirected in our direction. A lot of times we give because we like the way that it makes us feel. We like having people show gratitude to us, but our goal should always to do everything unto the glory of God.

You can imagine that for Frida, listening to how much her gift blessed her friend made her want to blurt out that she was the one that had done it, but the longer she was silent, the more she heard her friend thank God for looking out for her needs. The longer she was silent, the more she realized that God wanted her to see how He allowed her to partner with Him to be a blessing to someone else.

When we give in view of others, it can be hard for the recipients of the gift and even ourselves to see who the real gift-giver is. We are to be the hands and feet of Jesus, not the face. Let's give as generously as we can and let the face of God be the only face that people see.

Prayer

Dear Father, I want you to receive all of the glory from any good deeds that I do. Let me never boast in myself, but always in you in Jesus' name. Amen.
Further Studies: *Matthew 6:1-4*

Above and Beyond

*"If you greet only your brothers, what are you doing more
than others? Do not even pagans do that?"*
(Matthew 5:47, NASB)

One of the most watched genres of television shows for women is reality-based TV. For some reason we love to watch all the drama, the romance, and general hi-jinx unfold. A major theme in most reality shows, especially the ones that are dating based, is jealousy and revenge. If a bunch of women are all competing for one guy, it won't be long before you see the claws come out!

On most of the shows, the women make alliances with each other and gang up on whichever woman they want to be kicked off of the show. Once an alliance is made, all of the girls within the alliance will publicly snub or ignore the targeted contestant and sometimes even treat them very poorly to embarrass them. Although this is a description of the behavior of women on reality television, it isn't too different from the way we can behave in our own lives – and that even includes our behavior at church!

Let's say you had a falling out with someone from your church one week. The following Sunday, when it's time to greet everyone, you see that person, but make a point not to greet her. Is this Scripture not for you?

Little do we realize when we exhibit such behavior, we are not only demonstrating a lack of the fruit of the Spirit in our lives, but we are also demonstrating a possible root of bitterness in our hearts. Bitterness occurs when we allow unforgiveness or anger to fester in our hearts. There are some people that have not spoken to people at church for years over some incident that happened eons ago. It's really quite sad.

To greet someone is probably the simplest kind action that we can use with others. That's why Jesus used it as an example. It's really saying a lot if you can't perform an action as simple as smiling as saying "Hello." That is a very clear indicator that something is not right.

If you know that this verse is speaking to you and your relationship with someone, go and repent to that person right away. Let's remember that we are the light and the salt of the earth, therefore we go above and beyond.

Prayer

Dear Father, if there is any bitterness in my heart that causes me to be unkind to others, especially my brothers and sisters in Christ, please forgive me and help me to do better in Jesus' name. Amen.
Further Studies: *Luke 6:31*

He has the Authority to Forgive

"But I want you to know that the Son of Man has authority on earth to forgive sins."
So he said to the paralyzed man, "I tell you, get up, take your mat and go home."
(Luke 5:24)

There's a story about two kids named Johnny and Sally. One summer the two kids went to visit their grandparents. Their grandmother had a pet duck that she loved very much. The duck was practically part of the family!

One day Johnny was playing with his slingshot outside, and he accidentally shot his grandmother's pet duck and killed it. In shock and in fear of what his grandmother would say, he hurriedly buried it in the woods. What he didn't know though, was that his sister saw everything.

That evening Sally approached Johnny and demanded that he do her evening chores. Johnny tried to get out of it, since it wasn't his turn, but then Sally blackmailed him. "I saw what you did to Grandma's duck, and I'll tell if you don't do it." Fear crept into Johnny's heart once again and he lowered his head and obliged.

For weeks Sally tormented Johnny by forcing him to do her bidding and threatening to tell if he didn't do exactly as she said. It didn't take long before Johnny got so frustrated that he felt anything his grandmother would do to punish him would be better than what his sister was doing to him.

So one evening he mustered up the courage to tell his grandmother what happened. With tears in her eyes, she listened before reaching out to grab his shoulders. "Johnny," she said. "I saw you shoot the duck. I knew from the beginning. I was wondering how long you were going to let Sally torture you before you came to me."

So often we find ourselves in the same position as Johnny. When we sin, instead of bringing it to the one who is able to forgive us and totally wash us clean of our wrongdoing, we allow the enemy to torment and condemn us into believing otherwise. This should not be true of a follower of Christ.

Jesus has the authority to forgive. He is the righteous judge, so there is no one better to pardon us from our sins than Him. And that is His heart. He desires to forgive us so that we can continue the race. We just have to allow Him to do so. Choose this day to submit to the authority of Jesus, the righteous judge, and allow Him to forgive you.

Prayer

Dear Father, I believe that you are able to forgive me of my sins. Now I submit to you today and allow you to do so in Jesus' name. Amen.
Further Studies: *Luke 7:48*

Agree with Another

"Again, truly I tell you that if two of you on earth agree about anything they ask for, it will be done for them by my Father in heaven."
(Matthew 18:19)

Women throughout the history of mankind can attest to the fact that their bond with other women has been a tremendous source of support in their journey to become better people, mothers, and wives. Many of us have an uncanny ability to nurture, which comes in handy for our children, but we also have the ability to empathize and encourage, which is a great contributor to the camaraderie we feel with friends.

No matter how close you are with your husband, your relationship with him cannot replace your relationship with your girlfriends. Men typically like to fix problems while women like to talk about them. Though it may be difficult to vent as much as you'd like with your husband, when you talk with your girlfriends, you know that you can talk as much as you want and they'll not only listen, but they'll do their best to see things from your perspective, share similar stories they've heard or experienced themselves, and give any bits of applicable wisdom.

One of the most powerful things women can do when they gather together is to pray. If your church has weekly prayer meetings, you'll probably notice a trend that actually occurs worldwide: prayer meetings are usually populated nearly entirely by women. Though the ideal is for men to be more involved in such areas, there's something to be said about that fact. When women gather together in prayer, we get things done.

According to this Scripture, the bare minimum qualification for prayer gatherings is for two people to come together in agreement. If that's the case, imagine what's happening in the spiritual realm when you have a room full of discerning women who are sensitive to the Spirit praying together in one accord! Things start shaking!

Even on a small scale, if it's you and one friend, be sure to always add prayer into your conversations. If you meet for lunch and share about some problems that you've been facing, pray and agree together for the solution. Your prayers are powerful because of the one who is in your midst.

That's the way to get things done, no matter how small or how great the problem may be that you face; you and another can and will get it done! Agree, and let the Father act.

Prayer

Dear Father, thank you for my sisters in Christ and the support that they are for me emotionally and spiritually. Thank you for hearing us when we call out to you in Jesus' name. Amen.
Further Studies: *James 5:14-15*

Attentive to Your Prayer

"For the eyes of the Lord are on the righteous and his ears are attentive to their prayer, but the face of the Lord is against those who do evil."
(1 Peter 3:12)

As I think about prayer, the latest movie by the Kendrick brothers entitled "War Room" comes to mind. It tells the story of a woman whose marriage is in shambles, and it follows her as she attempts to regain control her life. One day she comes across an elderly woman who encourages her to fight for her marriage through prayer, and relinquish control into God's hand. Then her whole life changed.

The movie is a powerful representation of what perseverance in the prayer closet can really do. A lot of times, as women, we feel like the best way to handle problems is through talking. God gave us "the gift of gab" as some would call it, so we want to talk the problem through to process and to find a solution.

Well, men weren't created the same way, and talking isn't their strongest suit. That's why the more we try to pressure them to talk about the problem, the more they feel like we're nagging. It is good to communicate with your spouse about problems that are occurring, but sometimes we can waste our words on the wrong person.

Instead of hounding our husbands or even complaining to friends, we should be using our words in the place of prayer. We should be taking our requests, concerns, fears, and doubts to God and asking Him to do with them what he does best.

In the movie the husband made some bad decisions, and his wife could have turned around and made some equally bad decisions. As the world would tell us, she had every right to get him back for what he did, but as this scripture says, God is attentive to the cries of the righteous. If we want Him to hear our prayers, we must repent and seek out his forgiveness for our sin.

As a mother with adult children, I know the value of prayer. There are some days where the only way you feel you can get by is with supernatural strength. God doesn't give us things like that unless we ask for it, so we really have to press in and ask for His help. Thankfully, God is attentive to every word you pray, so keep on praying!

Prayer

Dear Father, teach me how to pray. I don't want to keep facing these problems alone. I need your help. Thank you for hearing me in Jesus' name. Amen.
Further Studies: *Matthew 6:6*

Acknowledge Jesus

"I tell you, whoever publicly acknowledges me before others, the Son of Man will also acknowledge before the angels of God."
(Luke 12:8)

t's that time of year again. Advent season has begun. Throughout the years there have been numerous attempts to remove our focus from Jesus during this season, but without Christ, there would be no reason to celebrate. After all, without Him, where would you and I be? We certainly would have no joy and no hope. It's only because of the arrival of Jesus that we have a hope for our future.

This is a truth that we should acknowledge every day of our lives, but this season is one that has been set aside to remind us of Christ's humble beginning, His birth on this earth. He was a king who sat at the right hand of the God who created all things, both seen and unseen. He had all power and authority to do whatever He wanted, and yet He lowered himself to our status, and allowed himself to become what one poet described as "a mewling, puking infant." How humble is our King!

From the time Jesus entered the earth until the time He left the earth, there were people who hated Him so much that they wanted to kill Him. This was the story of His life. Jesus was just a toddler and Pilate was after Him. When He turned 30 and began His ministry, the Pharisees were after Him. He was despised and rejected, as the prophecies foretold He would be.

Now even though Jesus has ascended into heaven and no longer walks on the earth, we find that His name is still hated among many. As those who bear His name and image as a banner over our lives, the world in turn hates us. For some, that can be enough to make them turn away from Christ or at least reject Him publicly.

The sad thing about people who choose to deny Christ is that one day when they're standing before His throne awaiting their judgment, He will also declare that He doesn't know them. That will be one of the most dreadful days for many people.

It is worthwhile then, for us to use our time on earth to be about His business. To declare His name and His goodness for all the world to hear so that they can learn of this God who clothed himself in flesh to save their souls.

Prayer

Dear Father, I want to boldly declare that I not only know
you, but that I love you in Jesus' name. Amen.
Further Studies: *John 15:18*

Keys of the Kingdom

"Jesus wept."
(John 11:35)

And there you have it. The shortest scripture in the entire Bible: "Jesus wept." A scripture with only two words, that typically had the pleasure of being the punch line to corny Christian jokes when I was a kid, hardly seems substantial enough to warrant an entire devotional. But these two words hold a great amount of insight into the heart of Jesus.

From these two words we can clearly understand the *"who"* and the *"what"* of the story, but what remains to be discovered is the *"why."* Why did Jesus weep? Well, if you read the rest of John 11, you'll discover that a very dear friend to Jesus named Lazarus had just died, and this verse is the result of Jesus being informed of Lazarus's passing. He was grieving the loss of a friend.

Oftentimes, when we go through difficult seasons in our lives (the loss of loved ones, personal pain and suffering, rejection, etc.), we feel as though God is distant. Many people have uttered the words, "God, where are you?" in the midst of their sorrow. It can be hard to recognize His presence in the middle of our pain. Sometimes we may even blame Him for the wrong that has happened in our lives.

But if there's anything to be gleaned from this scripture, it's that God *feels*. When we cry, He cries with us. The same way that Jesus was emotionally stirred when He watched His friends grieve over the loss of their brother is the same way He grieves with us in the midst of our sorrow. We're not able to see it as they did, but we should feel it.

We should feel the presence of a God who comes near to the brokenhearted (Psalm 34:18). We should feel the nearness of a God who comforts all who mourn (Matthew 5:4). We should be comforted by the knowledge that our God is so close to us in our grief that He collects all of our tears in a bottle (Psalm 56:8).

We are not alone when we grieve. Jesus is there with us and He grieves with us. Allow that truth to comfort you as you rest in the knowledge that He truly does care about what is important to your heart.

Prayer

*Dear Father, thank you for caring enough for me to grieve
with me when I grieve in Jesus' name. Amen.*
Further Studies: *John 11*

Perseverance

"As you know, we count as blessed those who have persevered. You have heard of Job's perseverance and have seen what the Lord finally brought about. The Lord is full of compassion and mercy."
(James 5:11)

Perseverance is persistence in doing something despite difficulty, or a delay in achieving success. As we know from the Bible, perseverance is a trait that God desires all believers to develop. It is an essential part of becoming the fullness of who He envisioned when He spoke us into existence. Without perseverance, we cannot finish the race.

One of the biggest tactics of the enemy is to get us to give up on our race. The best way he knows how to accomplish that is to feed us lies about the nature of God. If he can get us to believe that God is not good or that once we finish the race we'll discover it wasn't worth it, he knows that he's won. Who would want to keep running a race to reach a God that they didn't believe cared about them?

This is why the Apostle James reminds us in this Scripture of the true nature of God: "full of compassion and mercy." If we continue to remind ourselves of these truths, and all of the other truths about God that we can glean from His Word, then we can be emboldened to keep persevering. The best way we can fight the lies of the devil with the sword of the Spirit, the Word of God.

Another point of encouragement when it comes to perseverance is to remember those who have gone before us who demonstrated what it means to persevere. James mentions Job as an example, but you can find countless testimonies of others throughout the Bible and even within your own spheres of influence to encourage you. Take a moment to read the following quotes about perseverance from people who have been where you are, and be encouraged:

"Great works are performed not by strength but by perseverance." -Samuel Johnson

"Perseverance is failing 19 times and succeeding the 20th." -Julie Andrews

"Perseverance is the hard work you do after you get tired of doing the hard work you already did." -Newt Gingrich

Keep doing what you are doing; put your nose to the grindstone, get help if you must, rest when you need to, and you will reach your goal.

Prayer

Dear Father, I want to finish this race and finish it well. Help me by your Spirit to persevere in Jesus' name. Amen.
Further Studies: *James 1:2-4*

Rejoice

"Rejoice in the Lord always. I will say it again: Rejoice!"
(Philippians 4:4)

There are only seven days left until Christmas! We are in the midst of the most joyous season of the year, or as some would say, "The most wonderful time of the year." What do you have to rejoice about?

As believers, we have much to rejoice about. Of course we all share the commonality of being able to rejoice in the Lord of our salvation. That's what this season is all about, after all, but each of us also has our own specific and personal reasons to bless the Lord. We have our own testimonies of how God has pulled through for us time and time again. When is the last time that you counted your blessings?

It is good to count our blessings from time to time, because it keeps us grateful and humble. When we think upon the goodness and faithfulness of the Lord, it should be enough to make our hearts burst at the seams with joy. He has been so good to us, it's the least that we can do!

Though it takes time and maturity to get to this point, it is also important that we learn to rejoice in the midst of those situations that don't always seem to be the most ripe for rejoicing (i.e. physical pain, the loss of loved ones or a job, or the general disappointments that life brings). Rejoicing in the midst of such situations is an art that we need to cultivate with the help of the Holy Spirit.

Our natural inclination is to throw a pity party for ourselves when things aren't going the way we'd like, but the scripture here says not once, but twice, that we are to rejoice in the Lord ALWAYS. That means we need to ask the Holy Spirit to show us the hidden reasons for why we should thank God even when the car breaks down in the middle of nowhere. It's easy to see the negative, so sometimes we need help to spot the positive.

Regardless of whether you see the positive in the situation or not, the fact still remains that God is good and He is worthy of our praise and adoration. So no matter what, we can choose to rejoice in that. Besides, if we think about it long enough, we will realize there are more things going right than wrong. So let's REJOICE!

Prayer

Dear Father, I want to rejoice when I'm happy and when I'm sad
simply because you're worth it. In Jesus' name, amen.
Further Studies: *Philippians 4:4-8*

Taught by the Holy Spirit

"...for the Holy Spirit will teach you at that time what you should say."
(Luke 12:12)

As a teenager, Lisa was short tempered and had a very sassy mouth. If her friends back then were to see her today, they would be shocked to find her a quiet and sweet tempered woman. What caused the change, you wonder? Lisa has learned to be sensitive the Holy Spirit; she has learned to let her words be few.

The disciples had followed Jesus around for three years before He ascended into heaven. The entire time He was here, they watched Him closely, noting the way He responded to the people He encountered each and every day. If Jesus were to ask the disciples to do something, He would typically instruct them on what to say. "Go to this man and tell him I sent you"... He also made sure that they were equipped with knowledge and words to speak before He sent them anywhere.

Now imagine how bewildered the disciples must have felt when Jesus had first left them on their own and they had to share the gospel by themselves. They were probably terribly afraid. This is why Jesus had to send them, and us, a helper. We desperately need someone to tell us what to say and when to say it, especially when we're speaking on the Lord's behalf.

Sometimes, when we share God's Word, we feel like we have to say everything perfectly, but it's not a matter of saying anything perfectly by our standards; it's a matter of saying what He wants us to say when He wants us to say it. And if we have His Holy Spirit living inside of us, that shouldn't be a problem – even for someone like the person that Lisa used to be.

Nowadays, one of the messages Lisa likes to share with younger women is centered on humility. In order to listen to the Holy Spirit without trusting your own wisdom to say the "right thing," you must be able to exhibit humility. You must be able to listen.

When we get emotional we can say a lot of things that either we don't really mean or that are seriously out of line with the heart of God. Therefore, we must be careful how we engage with others. Be taught by the Holy Spirit. He will not let you down, and you'll be safe as long as you follow His instructions. Every situation has a right response, and if you listen carefully before you speak, you'll know how to respond every time.

Prayer

Dear Father, thank you for guiding not only me, but also my speech, by Your Holy Spirit. I will quiet my mind and heart to listen in Jesus' name. Amen.
Further Studies: *Ecclesiastes 5:2*

He has Overcome

"I have told you these things so that in me you may have peace. In this world you will have trouble. But take heart! I have overcome the world."
(John 16:33)

When Jesus spoke these words, it was after He had just informed the disciples that one day they would all betray Him and leave Him alone, essentially foretelling what would happen during the crucifixion. The disciples were surely baffled by Christ's comment. They had been following Him for three years and devoted their lives to Him! Knowing their hearts, He reassured them with this statement.

As earth-shattering as the former news had probably been to the disciples, Jesus wanted them to know that regardless of what was about to happen, He was still sovereign. Not only did He know that everything would happen as He said it would, but He had already taken care of it all. He had overcome.

There are many times in our lives that we need the same reassurance that Jesus gave His disciples. Trouble can come in many forms: misunderstandings or divisions in relationships, physical illness and pain, persecution, the loss of loved ones, abuse, betrayal by someone close to you, and so on. The list could go on and on.

It helps us to be able to face such difficult moments when we know that Jesus sees us in the midst of it all. There is a particular perspective of God as this toymaker who created the earth as some kind of wind-up toy and wound its dial only to sit back and passively watch it go. People who maintain this perspective believe that God is not involved in their lives, but only a silent spectator.

But this is not so! God is actively engaged in our lives, even directing the way it unfolds on a day by day basis, and as Jesus comforted His disciples, so can we be comforted by the fact that He sees, He knows, and He's doing something about it. Jesus has overcome the troubles of this world, and because we have been purchased by His blood and made one with Him, we are able to overcome the troubles of this world as well.

So no matter what comes our way, we can take heart. He has overcome. Don't allow the troubles of this world to overtake you. Stand on the promise Christ has given you. You are more than a conqueror. You are an overcomer.

Prayer

Dear Father, I believe that by the blood Jesus shed, I have been given the power to overcome anything this world may throw at me. Help me to stand on that promise in Jesus' name. Amen.
Further Studies: *Romans 8:31-39*

Power and Authority

"I have given you authority to trample on snakes and scorpions and to overcome all the power of the enemy; nothing will harm you."
(Luke 10:19)

One of the best parts of the movie "The Passion of the Christ" happens at the very beginning when Satan is speaking to Jesus in the Garden of Gethsemane. Jesus is anguishing over the decision He has to make of whether or not to go through with His voluntary self-sacrifice. We know from Scripture how difficult that moment in the garden was for Christ, and yet in this part of the movie, Satan appears and begins taunting Him.

One of the forms of torment Satan used came in the shape of a snake. He releases the snake, and it ominously slithers towards Christ. Finally, when Jesus makes the decision to do the Father's will, He gets up from the place where He is praying, and His foot crashes heavily on top of the snake. It's such a powerful image of the authority of Jesus and the power that He has over Satan and of the fulfillment of the prophecy,

"And I will put enmity between you and the woman, and between your offspring and hers; he will crush your head, and you will strike his heel."
(Genesis 3:15)

The most wonderful thing about such authority, is that Jesus has given the same authority to us. We can also crush the enemy's head. You and I have been equipped with power and authority to demolish every form of evil set against us with the assurance that we will not be harmed.

The enemy would very much like us to believe that we are weak and powerless against him, but "greater is He that is in us than he that is in the world." The enemy would very much like us to think that he has us right where he wants us, but "the seed of the woman shall bruise the serpent's head." His power pales in comparison to that which God has given us through His Son Jesus.

We have been given power to reject and even overturn any plans the enemy sets against us, so why not use it? Why believe the enemy's lies anymore? It's time that we walk in the authority of Jesus and show the enemy exactly where the

Scriptures tell him he belongs: under the foot of Jesus. Let's use the tools we've been given to live victorious lives in Christ today.

Prayer

Dear Father, help me to walk in the authority of your Son; to crush the enemy as well as anything he tries to throw at me or my family in Jesus' name. Amen.
Further Studies: *Romans 16:20*

Good News

"But the angel said to them, "Do not be afraid; for behold, I bring you good news of great joy which will be for all the people; for today in the city of David there has been born for you a Savior, who is Christ the Lord."
(Luke 2:10-11)

Good news is like a breath of fresh air that gives us hope and fills us with joy. We experience this joy when we hear of the safe arrival of a newborn, when our children are performing well in academics or extracurricular activities, or even when we get a promotion of some sort. We have all had our fair share of good news and can recall how happy we were when we received it.

But there is no good news better in all the world than the news the shepherds received the night that Christ was born. We understand how good this news was for us, because it meant that the source of our eternal salvation had come, but imagine how good the news was for the Israelite community.

For hundreds and hundreds of years before that night, they had been waiting in anticipation for the arrival of their king. Having faced years of slavery, a rough exodus in which thousands of their people died, war on every side, and having been conquered by stronger surrounding territories, the Jews were desperate for their Messiah to come and save them.

At the time of Jesus' arrival, they were under the rule of the Roman Empire, and as we know from history, the Romans were not the kindest in their treatment of the Jews. Yet, the Jewish community had this hope:

> *"He will stand and shepherd his flock in the strength of the Lord, in the majesty of the name of the Lord his God. And [Israel] will live securely, for then his greatness will reach to the ends of the earth. And he will be their peace."*
> (Micah 5:4-5)

This is the good news that the angels brought to the shepherds that day. With the blasts of their trumpets, they infused hope into a very weary people. We are so blessed to be able to share in this hope with them, as the angel announced that these good tidings were for *all people* of all time. What a blessing! Take the good news of the Messiah's coming and tell it to the world.

Prayer

Dear Father, thank you for sending your son to save your people from their bonds of slavery to sin, and thank you for extending that grace to me in Jesus' name. Amen.
Further Studies: *Isaiah 52:7*

Joy and Gladness

*"And you will have joy and gladness, and many will rejoice at
his birth, for he will be great in the sight of the Lord."*
(Luke 1:14-15a)

As a mother, I quite understand the joys that come with having a child – after
the pains of labor subside, of course. Some mothers vow never to give birth
to another child again, only to be found a number of months or years later
giving birth yet again. There's something quite beautiful and captivating about
bringing a new life into the world.

Friends and family come to greet the arrival of the newborn, and everyone is full
of joy and anticipation at seeing one of the most magnificent wonders of God's
creation in the form of a child. Their little hands and feet, and their eyes full of
wonder. The smell of a newborn alone is enough to bring gladness to any heart.

So if this is true of all children, imagine how Elizabeth felt when she gave birth
to John the Baptist after having been barren and well into her old age. She must
have been absolutely exhilarated. When we are denied something for so long,
finally receiving that thing makes the heart not only glad, but full of gratitude.
No heart could have been more grateful for a child than Elizabeth's.

But there was an added bonus. This child would not only make his parents glad,
but God had purposed for him to make the hearts of many glad as he prepared
the way for the arrival of Christ. When your children perform well in school,
arts, or sports, you probably know the sense of delight you feel in your child.
Elizabeth's son was meant to be the forerunner to the Messiah! How could she
not be glad?

Jesus could have easily come without John the Baptist, but after years of waiting
for their Messiah, the Israelites had allowed their hearts to become cold. A lot
of them probably believed the Messiah would never come. Likening them to the
parable of the soil, the soil of these people's hearts had to be extremely hard. So
God needed to send someone to till the soil before Jesus came to plant the seed.

With every word that John the Baptist spoke during his ministry, he infused hope
into the people of God. He made hearts that once felt like there was no hope,

remember the promises of God, and by doing so, he restored their joy. Although John had a specific calling from the Lord, it doesn't differ too much from what God is calling us to do. We also are to prepare the way of the Lord and to make sad hearts glad. Go, therefore, and do likewise.

Prayer

Dear Father, I rejoice in knowing that you sent someone to prepare the way for me to come to you, and now I seek to prepare the way for others in Jesus' name. Amen.
Further Studies: *Psalm 92:4*

The Gift

"Thanks be to God for His indescribable gift!"
(2 Corinthians 9:15)

It's that time of year when gift giving is at its optimal peak. From the end of Thanksgiving until Christmas, we are bombarded with advertisements for all of the gadgets and gizmos we can purchase for our loved ones, and we enjoy the process of engaging in the search to find the "perfect gift."

Most women are especially skilled a choosing or creating the most thoughtful gifts. Because we listen well and are in tune to others' needs and desires, gift giving can come quite naturally. We can easily recall past conversations or what we know about the person and find something that we know would mean something to them. Meaningful gifts are usually the best, and you can usually tell by the response of the recipient how "on point" your gift is.

The gift spoken of here, however, is so good that the only word to describe it is *indescribable.* Words clearly fail to describe how precious this gift is and how much it is worth to the recipient. Have you ever received a gift that left you absolutely speechless? That's when you know that you hit the jackpot of all gifts!

We thank God for His gift of Jesus, because we know that we would be dead in our sins without Him and the sacrifice that He made, and at first glance, we would think this verse is speaking about Jesus, but this particular verse actually speaks of an indescribable gift that comes through our hands.

Prior to this verse, Paul is describing the actions of the Corinthians and their generosity. In fact, he even boasts about them and their eagerness to help others. Paul continues to commend the Corinthians for a promise they made to give support to needs of God's people and rejoices in their generosity.

We think about gift giving a lot in this particular season, but generosity should be a major component of the lifestyle of believers. The indescribable gift is the Church. It's a body of believers with the potential to give in ways that confound the world. It's a body of believers with the potential to change the world through their giving.

This gift is immeasurable and keeps on giving as long as we maintain the heart to give. In the same way that God gave us a gift that outweighed our expectations and desires, let us endeavor to give our best gift *all the time* to others.

Prayer

Dear Father, thank you once again for the gift of Jesus. I want to be just as generous in my giving as you have been with me in Jesus' name. Amen.
Further Studies: *2 Corinthians 9*

Immanuel

"'Behold, the virgin shall be with child and shall bear a Son, and they shall call His name Immanuel, which translated means, 'God with us.'"
(Matthew 1:23, NASB)

Merry Christmas! God is with us! On this day we commemorate the birth of our Lord and Savior – the moment when the fullness of God was fully manifested within the tiny body of an infant, Jesus. It was truly the most miraculous moment in all of the history of mankind. God Himself became a man.

Before the birth of Christ, the presence of God was confined to the Most Holy Place, where no one but the high priest was able to enter. The people of God had no contact with God, as in those days God spoke with people audibly, and the religious leaders of the day were corrupt, so it was difficult for the people to get a direct word for the Lord from them. Then Jesus came.

Whereas the people of the Old Testament trembled in fear of the Almighty God who thundered from the mountains, we received God in the form of the least harmful of creatures: a human baby boy. God clothed Himself in the human form so that He could once again be among His people to live with them and restore life to them.

And praise be to God, even though the physical form of Jesus is no longer here, we have the assurance that He will be with us every day of our lives. He left His Spirit to dwell inside of us, and His Spirit also carries the full essence of His divine nature. Our Immanuel is still here with us!

Let us celebrate the fact that Immanuel has come and that He is here to stay. As His Word says, He will never leave us nor forsake. We belong to Him and He belongs to us. He has made a vow to see the sanctifying work He began in us completed, and He will keep that vow until the end.

Regardless of what the year has been like, whether you faced many disappointments or many moments of celebration, it is time to embrace the truth herein and be glad. Rest assured that He is with you, He is with me, He is with us all.

Prayer

Dear Father, what a privilege it is to know that you cared for us so much that you chose to remove the distance between us. May I live every day of my life pressing in to get even closer to you in Jesus' name, Amen.

Further Studies: *2 Corinthians 8:9*

Worship Him

"When they saw the star, they were overjoyed. On coming to the house, they saw the child with his mother Mary, and they bowed down and worshiped him. Then they opened their treasures and presented him with gifts of gold and of incense and of myrrh."
(Matthew 2:10-11)

Christmas day may be over, but the season of rejoicing in the Lord is not over; it has just begun.

After having spent yesterday remembering the day of Christ's birth and thanking God for the gift of His son, our hearts should be re-energized to worship Him. Who could think upon the goodness of God and the wonderful gift that He has given us without feeling the joy of worship bubbling up in their soul? This should be an everyday occurrence, friends. Let's take our cue from the wise men.

The night that Jesus was born, the Star of Bethlehem appeared in the sky. Because the wise men spent their lives reading and tracking the stars, they immediately noticed the presence of this anomaly and understood its significance. So from that moment forward, they did the only thing they knew to do: they set out to find the one whose birth announcement was written in the stars, so that they could worship him.

For two years these men traveled the earth looking for Jesus. For two years they embarked on a holy pilgrimage of worship. It didn't matter that they had not arrived in Bethlehem on the night that Jesus was born; the point was that He had been born. He was on the earth and would be there until He accomplished what the Father had sent Him to do.

I imagine that the excitement of all that Christ's arrival meant for these men drove them on to keep searching. The wise men knew of the significance of Christ's birth, and they knew that He was the designated King; therefore, they sought after Him until they found Him.

The same should be true of us. Just because Christmas is over doesn't mean that we stop worshipping or that we stop seeking the presence of the Lord. Jesus is still the Messiah today, just like He was back then, and He will always be the

Messiah. If He never changes, we should never stop searching. So let us draw near to adore Christ the Lord.

Prayer

Dear Father, you are worthy of worship every day of my life. Let me never lose my will to worship you in Jesus' name. Amen.
Further Studies: *Matthew 2:1-12*

Bow Down

"May all kings bow down before him and all nations serve him."
(Psalm 72:11)

There was a particular moment in time that the disciples were able to get a glimpse into what this day would look like. Can you guess when it happened? No, it wasn't when Jesus was surrounded by thousands of people when He taught, or even during the triumphal entry when everyone waved palm branches and shouted "Hosanna!"

This moment came the day that the centurion, the commander of a Roman legion (around 6,000 soldiers), had an encounter with Jesus. In Matthew 8:5-10 we're told that the centurion appeals to Jesus to heal his servant. Jesus agrees, but the centurion tells him that he believes that Christ is so powerful that He doesn't need to go, but He only needs to speak the word and His will would be done. Jesus admonishes the centurion for his faith and heals the servant.

As far as the Jewish community was concerned to the Roman population, they were no better off than dogs. If a Roman was carrying a load along the road and crossed paths with a Jew, they had a legal right to demand that the Jew carry their load for them for at least a mile. So in such a context, you can imagine how shocking it was for the disciples to see an official of the Roman Army coming before Jesus in such a manner. It was unthinkable! If the centurion had wanted anything from Jesus, he could have easily just demanded it.

What was different about this man though, is that he recognized the power that Jesus possessed. He knew that despite what his law told him about Jews, the God of the Jews had given Jesus a power that the centurion could not find anywhere else. Therefore, he humbled himself and bowed before him.

One day everyone in the world – including kings, chiefs, and presidents – will see exactly what the centurion saw that day. They will see the King of all Kings standing at His throne with the scepter of righteousness in His hand. On that day every knee will bow and every tongue confess that Jesus Christ is the Lord of all.

Prayer

Dear Father, you are the living God enduring forever, and your kingdom will never be destroyed. I long for the day when the whole world will see you as such in Jesus' name. Amen.
Further Studies: *Jeremiah 10:10*

He's with us!

"The LORD is near to all who call on him, to all who call on him in truth."
(Matthew 18:20)

This holiday season and our study together throughout the advent season has served to be a great reminder of the blessed assurance we have in Jesus. It is my prayer that it helps us to remember that Jesus Christ is with us every day of our lives; through good and bad days and circumstances.

Part of that assurance is realizing that when we gather together in prayer, there isn't necessarily power in any of the words that we speak or even how long we meet together, but that our power comes from the presence of God in our midst. He is what makes our prayer powerful and effectual, and only Him.

Have you ever been to a prayer meeting and felt the presence of God in a mighty way? That is the fulfillment of this passage. When everyone in the room is focused on the same thing, the spirit of unity is attractive to God. Our great Intercessor joins in on the prayers and actively sends angels to go into the very situations that are being prayed for.

God places a very high value on unity. If you look in the Old Testament, especially in 2 Chronicles 5, you will find that when all of the people were on one accord, the glory of God would fall. Again, in the New Testament, specifically on the Day of Pentecost, when everyone in the room was on one accord, the Holy Spirit descended upon them like flaming tongues of fire.

The same is true of our relationship with each other today. If we can gather together and be of one heart and mind and seek the Lord as one, He meets us in the middle and works with us in the spiritual realm to bring about change in the earth.

If you want to be an agent of change, the best way to get it done is to get on your knees. But don't think that you can go it alone. The scripture tells us the one person can put 1,000 enemies to flight, but two people can put 10,000 (Deuteronomy 32:30). Again, I don't believe it has to do with us and the power that we possess, but because God loves unity so much that when He sees us working together

He releases a special anointing. Therefore be bold and confident in prayer when gathered together in His name.

Prayer

Dear Father, I want to surround myself with people that I can agree with in prayer. We looking forward to meeting with you in Jesus' name. Amen.
Further Studies: *Zephaniah 3:17*

Saved by Grace

"My grace is sufficient for you, for my power is made perfect in weakness."
(2 Corinthians 12:9)

Rick Warren says the following about grace: *"What gives me the most hope every day is God's grace; knowing that his grace is going to give me the strength for whatever I face, knowing that nothing is a surprise to God."*

If we were to rely on our own doing; our mind, heart and emotions, we would surely crash and burn. How many times have you believed that you had the answer to a problem, but it didn't work out? No matter how hard we try to understand the world we live in and the people in it, including ourselves, the more confused we become.

It is impossible then, with our limited understanding and abilities, to save ourselves from ourselves, let alone all of the attacks of the enemy. Our flesh is weak and rotten through and through. We cannot trust it to do anything but to bring us down. That is why we need the grace of God.

Thankfully for us, grace (unmerited favor) is a gift that God gives us freely. God knows very well that we cannot be holy as He is without some major help from Him. What kind of God would He be to command us to live holy lives yet refuse to equip us with the supernatural tools we need to make that happen?

This scripture tell us that God's grace is sufficient for all of our needs. So often we believe that this Scripture means that grace is a day by day realization or something we have to ask God for whenever we feel our grace has run out, but I believe that this means when we receive the gift of salvation, we also receive the gift of grace to live the Christian life, and the amount of grace God gives is sufficient to cover our needs.

It's not like a tap that runs out. His grace is like a fountain that never runs dry. From the moment of our salvation to the day that we die, we can dip into the fountain of grace. It covers all; it is sufficient. The only thing that needs to change is our mindset.

We have to stop coming to God like we're paupers and simply acknowledge the gift He already gave us. We must ask the Holy Spirit to help us shift our thinking. It's already there, we just have to access it and thank Him for it.

Prayer

Dear Father, thank you for your gift of grace. I believe that it is and has always been sufficient to cover every single one of my needs in Jesus' name. Amen.
Further Studies: *Romans 3:20-24*

Sun and Shield

"For the Lord God is a sun and shield; the Lord bestows favor and honor.
No good thing does he withhold from those who walk uprightly."
(Psalms 84:11)

love the comparison the psalmist makes of God to a sun and shield. At first glance it might not make sense why these two items would be placed together in a sentence. Wouldn't the shield nullify the sun if it protects us from the sun's rays? But if you dig a little deeper, you'll find a pretty interesting reason for this comparison.

Let's begin with the description of God as a sun. Many times throughout the Bible we find that each member of the Trinity is often compared to light in one form or another. Jesus is the light of the world, God is the Father of lights, and the Holy Spirit is the giver of light and knowledge. This is actually one of the more common descriptors of the nature of God.

Now, to specify the sun as opposed to means that we have to narrow our focus on light to the function of the sun. The distance of the earth from the sun ensures that life is made possible on the earth; therefore the sun = life. Without the sun shining throughout the day, we would not be able to see where we are going or what is around us; therefore, the sun = guidance and revelation. So from this first part of the verse, we get that God gives life and guidance.

Let's take a look at the shield aspect of this comparison now. As we all know, a shield provides protection. Spiritually speaking, it keeps the fiery darts of the enemy from penetrating our hearts. In relationship to God, this verse is saying that God Himself is a shield of protection for our lives.

So how do the two work together? Let's put it this way... God is a light to show us the way to eternal life and a shield to ward off the perils we may face as we follow His path. With His light come favor and honor, so our journey is bound to be filled with plenty of blessings along the way. Don't you just love how God works? He know only provides and protects, but He blesses!

What a mighty God is He! He is a sun and shield who gives favor and honor and gives good things to those who walk uprightly.

Prayer

Dear Father, thank you for being my sun and leading me on the path to eternal life in Jesus' name. Amen.
Further Studies: *Psalm 28:7*

Thanksgiving and Praise!

"Oh give thanks to the Lord; call upon his name; make known his deeds among the peoples! Sing to him, sing praises to him; tell of all his wondrous works!"
(Psalms 105:1-2, NASB)

It's New Year's Eve, the perfect time for thanksgiving and praise! As we reflect on our lives this past year, we have much to thank God for.

You are probably very familiar with the notion of creating resolutions for the New Year, essentially outlining what you hope to do better than you did this year, and maybe that's something that you want to challenge yourself to do this coming year, but before you look forward to what changes you want to make, why not take a moment to look back?

Ask yourself the following questions, and take a moment to remember all that God has done for you:

1. How has God shown Himself as faithful to me this year?
2. What problems did God deliver me from?
3. What reasons do I have to rejoice today?

Even if this year brought a lot of negative events your way, you still have a reason to praise God. You're still here, are you not? He brought you through it, did He not? And if you're still going through it, you can thank God that He will bring you through at the right time.

If God's mercies are new every morning, you can't help but have a great year if you choose to accept His mercy for your life and walk in His grace daily. Let us give resounding thanks to God and call upon His name. Why don't you close this year by letting others know what He has done in your life? Sing your song of adoration as one year ends and another begins.

God is good all the time, and all the time God is good.

Prayer

Dear Father, thank you for all that you have done in, through, and for me this year in Jesus' name. Amen.
Further Studies: *Philippians 4:4-8*